WITHDRAWN

Structures of Power

SUNY series in Latin American and Iberian Thought and Culture
Jorge J. E. Gracia, editor

Structures of Power

Essays on Twentieth-Century Spanish-American Fiction

Edited by
Terry J. Peavler
and
Peter Standish

State University of New York Press

Published by
State University of New York Press, Albany

© 1996 State University of New York

For information, address State University of New York Press,
State University Plaza, Albany, NY 12246

Production by Cynthia Tenace Lassonde
Marketing by Bernadette LaManna

Library of Congress Cataloging-in-Publication Data

Structures of power : essays on twentieth-century Spanish-American
    fiction / edited by Terry J. Peavler and Peter Standish.
        p.   cm. — (SUNY series in Latin American and Iberian thought
    and culture)
    Includes bibliographical references and index.
    ISBN 0-7914-2839-7 (alk. paper). — ISBN 0-7914-2840-0 (pbk. :
alk. paper)
    1. Spanish American fiction—20th century—History and criticism.
    2. Spanish American literature—Political aspects.   3. Spanish
    American literature—Social aspects.   4. Authors, Spanish
    American—20th century—Political and social views.   5. Power
    (Social sciences) in literature.   6. Literature and society—Latin
    America.   I. Peavler, Terry J., 1942–   .   II. Standish, Peter, 1942–
III. Series.
PQ7082.N7S87   1996
863—dc20   95-20009
                                                                CIP

10 9 8 7 6 5 4 3 2 1

Contents

Notes on Contributors

Sara Castro-Klarén is Professor of Latin American literature at Johns Hopkins University, Homewood Campus. She writes on contemporary and colonial prose. She has published books and articles on the works of José María Arguedas, Julio Cortázar, Guaman Poma, Mario Vargas Llosa, Jean de Léry, and Diamela Eltit. Her current research falls within the theoretical scope of feminist criticism and cultural studies.

Rosalía Cornejo-Parriego is Assistant Professor of Spanish at Penn State University. She writes on contemporary prose fiction from Spain and Spanish America. In addition to her book, *La escritura posmoderna del poder*, she has written several articles on novels of dictatorship.

David William Foster is Regents' Professor of Spanish at Arizona State University. Among his many books are *Gay and Lesbian Issues in Latin American Literature* (1991), *Contemporary Argentine Cinema* (1992), *The Argentine Generation of 1880: Literature, Ideology and the Social Text* (1990), the second edition of the *Handbook of Latin American Literature* (1992), and the English translation of Miguel Méndez-M.'s *Peregrinos de Aztlán* (1993).

Todd S. Garth is completing his doctoral studies in Spanish at the Johns Hopkins University. His dissertation focuses on the post-Romantic challenge to the concept of the individual and its role in the formation of the avant-garde at the beginning of the twentieth century.

Rosemary Geisdorfer Feal is Associate Professor of Spanish at the University of Rochester, where she also teaches courses in women's studies, African and African-American studies, and comparative literature. She is the author of *Novel Lives: The Fictional Autbiographies of Guillermo Cabrera Infante and Mario Vargas Llosa*, as well as numerous articles on Spanish American literature.

José Carlos González Boixo is Catedrático de Literatura Hispano-americana at the University of León in Spain. He has written on colonial literature, including critical editions of Bernardo de Balbuena, Sor Juana Inés de la Cruz and Juan de Espinosa Medrano. He is an authority on Juan Rulfo and author of *Claves narrativas de Juan Rulfo* and a critical edition of *Pedro Páramo*, as well as several articles.

Sharon Magnarelli, Professor of Spanish at Quinnipiac College, is the author of *The Lost Rib: Female Characters in the Spanish American Novel* (1985), *Reflections / Refractions: Reading Luisa Valenzuela* (1988), and *Understanding José Donoso* (1992). She has published numerous articles on contemporary Spanish American theatre and prose.

Terry J. Peavler is Professor of Spanish at Penn State University. His books include *Individuations: The Novel as Dissent* (1987), *El texto en llamas: El arte narrativo de Juan Rulfo* (1988), and *Julio Cortázar* (1990). He has published numerous articles on Spanish American literature.

Peter Standish taught for many years in British universities before becoming Head of the Department of Foreign Languages and Literatures at East Carolina University. His publications range over linguistic and literary topics, with much on the authors of the Boom. His books include *Variedades del español actual, Mario Vargas Llosa: La ciudad y los perros*, and the forthcoming *Color y línea*.

INTRODUCTION

Art is impotent.
—W. H. Auden in "The Real World"

El poder se funda en el texto.
—Carlos Fuentes in *Terra nostra*

Any volume on literature that bears the title *Structures of Power*, particularly in the context of Spanish America, is obliged to establish its parameters from the outset: this book is not about "literatura de compromiso" (only); neither does it seek to be geographically nor historically representative, as a glance at the list of contributions will confirm. Moreover, it does not seek to add another to the many volumes that find it perfectly acceptable to write about politics and literature, or literature and revolution, rather than restrict oneself to a discussion of literature on the purely aesthetic level.[1] What it does offer is a collection of essays devoted to issues of hegemony as manifested in modern Spanish American fiction. The themes of political, social, military, religious, economic, and familial power have been mainstays of Spanish American literature since the discovery, while gender, gay, and even genre issues have risen to prominence in recent years, not only in creative writing, but in critical discourse as well. Generally, critical and theoretical volumes that have been concerned with hegemony in Spanish American literature have been restricted to carefully defined perspectives, offering, for example, Marxist, feminist, or gay readings of a number of texts, or tracing the history of a particular type of socially committed literature; or they have focused on a narrow region or historical period; or they have done both.[2] What is sometimes lost in such discussions is an awareness of just how complex the issue of power in Spanish American society is, and more to the point, how complex it can become in its literature. The issue of power ranges from the traditionally notorious (the conquest, slavery, caciquismo), through the nouveau notorious (misogyny, homophobia, "dirty little wars," death squads), down to quite significant, but often overlooked issues of how a fictional father treats his children, or an author struggles to create literature by "exorcising" his demons, temporarily gaining the upper hand over language, or replacing the real world with a new fictional creation.[3]

Structures of Power is open to all such issues, and its contributors have made the most of this freedom. We do not assume that power in literature is necessarily ideological, but allow also that hegemony may depend on relationships of control or complicity between fictional characters, between author and reader, or even between author and text. Whether interpersonal or strictly personal, as one of our essayists points out, power is always relative, never absolute. Or, as Foucault would have it:

> Power in the substantive sense, *'le' pouvoir*, doesn't exist . . . . The idea that there is either located at—or emanating from—a given point something which is a 'power' seems to me to be based on a misguided analysis, one which at all events fails to account for a considerable number of phenomena. In reality power means relations, a more-or-less organised, hierarchical, co-ordinated cluster of relations (*Power/ Knowledge*, 198)

Some of our essays offer original insights into traditional questions of the relations that exist between author and country, art and politics. Some are equally concerned with the wielding of social and economic power as reflected thematically in fiction. Others explore the often subtle, yet enormous power of the struggle between the sexes, and still others the subversive nature of literary creativity itself. The essays thus range from rather traditional studies of institutional or personal ideologies, through matters of technique and literary vision, into questions of gender, into pressures brought about by institutionalized artistic expectations, into the power struggles that inevitably arise between the artist, the created work, and the reader. Their common purpose is to investigate, through the close analysis of specific fictional texts, ways in which Spanish American authors have addressed issues of hegemony, how these treatments and these issues have affected literary works for better or worse, and how, in some cases, the creative struggle entailed has itself effected literary works of the highest order.

The questions that seem to arise from the apparently contradictory quotations with which we began are these: of quite what can literature be said to be impotent?; of what does the power Fuentes sees as vested in the text consist? We see these comments as posing theoretical questions at a high level of generality, as much as culturally specific ones. Thus, while the essays that follow deal in depth with texts by Spanish American writers of our century, and the analyses evidently reflect and depend upon certain local cultural realities, they explore issues that go beyond the geographical confines of Spanish America; collectively, the essays attempt to provide a sense of the complex notion of the powers of fiction.

In "La palabra enemiga" ("The Enemy: Words"), the final chapter of his *La nueva novela hispanoamericana*, Carlos Fuentes tells how a shipment of copies of a novel was sequestered by the Argentine authorities on the grounds that it was subversive Marxist propaganda. The novel in question was Stendahl's *Le rouge et le noir*; the mere mention of red in the title had sufficed to have it banned. There is a certain irony in the fact that it was none other than Stendahl who asserted that politics in literature was as welcome as a gunshot during a concert, and perhaps, too, there is irony in the fact that Marx himself (though not all his followers) saw that many periods of great artistic development had no direct link with the general development of society. However, recognizing that words speak as loudly as actions, authoritarian régimes, whether of the right or the left, have often sought to limit free speech, suppress or control the printed word, and, more recently, the mass media. The list of hounded or silenced writers, even in the present century, is a long one.

The tradition of suppression is also long. The Spain of Columbus, a country monolithic enough in its thinking to have forced its minorities to convert to Catholicism or go into exile, plundered a new continent with crusading fervor, backed by the Inquisition: books were banned, burned, bowdlerized. The emerging countries of Latin America shook off the Spanish yoke, often only to fall prey to the north; and where revolution occurred it turned sour, became institutionalized and authoritarian, imitating the excesses of the many military dictators. Small wonder, then, that writers in Latin America have often been persecuted, forced into exile, or made to capitulate like a new generation of *conversos*. Even those writers who are treated more gently tend to see their role in much more social terms than do their counterparts to the north or in Europe; for most of them it is simply inconceivable to write exclusively for self-satisfaction, for purely literary ends. Faced with daily evidence of political

and economic abuse, with the awareness that poor masses subsist surrounding the privileged few, with the marginalization of the indigenous
non-Latin Americans, peoples whose roots run deepest and who might be
thought to be most deserving of the benefits their lands have to offer,
many intellectuals demand that writers explicitly make propaganda for
reform. Claribel Alegría, writing in reference to the role of literature in
her native Nicaragua and in El Salvador, and "fully aware of the pitfalls
of attempting to defend a transient political cause in what presumes to be
a literary work," nevertheless concludes that "if there be no place for
'pure art' and 'pure literature' today, then . . . so much for pure art and
pure literature . . . . It matters little whether our efforts are admitted into
the sacrosanct precincts of literature" (Meyer, 309, 311).

Yet, in its most unpalatable form, this attitude often smacks of the
same authoritarian intolerance that those who express such views seek to
undermine. Thus literary activists are able to dismiss a writer like Borges,
who, with his bookish universalism, is dubbed disloyal or even an "anti-
Latin Americanist": "almost ingenuously Eurocentric, ethnocentric,
phallocentric, a vicarious militarist and imperialist contemptuous of tribal
cultures and native peoples everywhere: in short, an anti-Latin Americanist ashamed, like a significant stratum of Argentinian and Uruguayan
society, to share the continent with Bolivians and Paraguayans, an idealist,
an ideological perpetuator of the civilization-barbarism dichotomy (your
barbarism confirms my civilization), and thus a brilliant player of the
double game, duplicitous as well as dualist" (Martin, 161–162). In a
similar way, the voluntarily exiled writer can become outlawed by the
Latin American intellectual community, despite the fact that some of the
most deeply felt and powerful indictments of Latin American societies
have been written by Spanish American writers living as refugees. Such
was the fate that awaited virtually all of the major Cuban writers who
sought refuge in Europe and the United States. Even Mario Vargas Llosa,
once he began to drift noticeably to the right, was roundly condemned by
the literati.

As André Gide pointed out, good sentiments tend to make for bad
literature. Julio Cortázar argued that good artists do not need to fly the
colors of their political commitment in their creative writings, and that, in
fact, emphasis on political "correctness" may be used to try to compensate for inferior talent: "Sólo los débiles tienden a enfatizar el compromiso personal de su obra, a exaltarse compensatoriamente en el
terreno donde su aptitud literaria los vuelve por un rato fuertes y sólidos

y del buen lado." [Only the weak use their literary aptitude as compensation to make them seem strong and solid and on the right side. (Cortázar, *Vuelta*, 2, 192)]. For his part, Octavio Paz asserted that his duty as a writer was to keep his distance from the State, from political parties, from all ideologies and even from society itself (Paz, 306). No one, however, can claim immunity from the historical process: isolation is, in itself, a posture, as Manuel Maldonado Denis points out (Zavala and Rodríguez, 290). In 1964, with Franco very much in power in Spain, Juan Goytisolo spelled out the position rather uncompromisingly:

> When there is no political freedom, everything is politics, and the split between writer and citizen vanishes. In this case, literature agrees to be a political weapon, or ceases to be literature and becomes an inauthentic echo of the literature of other societies situated at different levels (the proliferation of Spanish, Mexican, Portuguese or Argentine Robbe-Grillets, following upon hosts of Faulkners and Kafkas, is a good example of what I mean) (Goytisolo, 36).[4]

For those writers who enjoyed a certain degree of freedom, however, including all of the major figures of the "Boom," foreign authors provided badly needed inspiration. José Donoso's *Historia personal del boom* provides a compelling insider's account of the transition from parochial literature to the "Boom," one of the most important literary phenomena of the twentieth century. Early successes in experimental narratives gave the Spanish Americans the confidence they needed to carry out even more radical experiments, to the point of questioning the very authority and identity of the author (one thinks of *Terra nostra*, *El obsceno pájaro de la noche*, *Yo el Supremo*, and, on another scale, of *Crónica de una muerte anunciada*). The dictatorial omniscience of traditional writers (an authoritarianism that in some cases may have served to mask a sense of cultural inferiority vis-à-vis the European masters) gives way to fictions that willfully undermine their own authority, shifting narrative perspective, giving conflicting versions of the "truth," obliging the reader to be part of the creative process. Ultimately, the writer may enjoy a Godlike status, but he or she spends much time suggesting otherwise. Thus, the notion of power in literature takes on a different guise: such texts, which can at first appear to be self-servingly literary, may in fact be read as analogies addressing questions of power in a broader sense: the desire of El Señor in *Terra nostra* to become master over certain manuscripts is in fact a desire to confirm his absolute authority: "knowledge, power and authority become inseparable" (Kerr, 80).[5]

How, then, is a writer concerned with aesthetic quality to confront the fact of historicity or to deal with the pressures exerted by the advocates of literature as a means towards sociopolitical reform? What of the pressures of commercial interests? Can a way be found to marry literary aims with sociopolitical ones? Can a successful writer resist the temptation to write to formula or to the demands of the marketplace? These problems are, to a greater or lesser degree, faced by all Latin American writers; few, however, have been able to reconcile their sensitivity to the need for change with the potential conflict between that need and aesthetics, most eloquently demonstrated by Julio Cortázar in his open letter to Roberto Fernández Retamar (*Ultimo Round*, 2, 265–280).

Along with many intellectuals and successful writers of the "Boom," Cortázar supported the Cuban Revolution until it became clear that it was beginning to curtail the freedom of the citizens it claimed to represent. The limits of tolerance of artistic freedom were officially defined in 1971;[6] in particular, the spectacle of the poet Heberto Padilla being forced publicly to recant and denounce even his wife led many intellectuals to part company with a revolution they had once enthusiastically backed. In the case of some writers, it is not altogether clear to what extent this withdrawal was independent of the undeniable fact that they were becoming very successful personally and leaving the ranks of the have-nots. In a case such as that of Vargas Llosa, at one time a Marxist and one of the most insistent advocates of the notion of the writer as rebel, the disaffection with Cuba must be seen in the context of his personal evolution towards his current stance as hero of the Peruvian haves, and a surprisingly conservative presidential candidate.[7] But many continued to be of the left, although recognizing the Cuban oppression. García Márquez maintained his support for Cuba, if only on the grounds that it was the lesser of two evils. Cortázar, for all his reservations over Cuba, became active in support of the Sandinistas and gave the royalties of some of his books to them. Yet, though Cortázar the polyglot wrote in a very *porteño* Spanish, his literature is in many ways amongst the least obviously Latin American of all, second only to that of Borges, who, as we have noted, was much criticized because of his "Eurocentrism." On the other hand, Vargas Llosa invariably writes of things that are palpably Peruvian. The early Vargas Llosa advanced the theory that great literature could only come about in societies in crisis. In the relative comfort of stable and developed countries, he claimed, literature would decline into sterile formal experimentation and self-contemplation ("En torno a la nueva novela en Latinoamérica," 122–123). If that were true, one could expect wonders from a continent characterized by political upheavals and economic uncertainty. The more urbane and never uncomfortable Carlos Fuentes expressed a similar view: the historical circumstances that generated the admixture of cultures in Latin America, coupled with the inescapable horrors of everyday life there, should, at very least, make for interesting literature ("En torno a la nueva novela," *passim*). Alejo Carpentier's *real maravilloso* recognized that reality is larger than life, and that the extraordinary is somehow less so in the literature of Latin America. It becomes axiomatic that anyone who writes about Latin America, or who writes as a Latin American, whether exiled or not, cannot claim immunity from the sociopolitical realities of the continent. Some writers openly embrace this fact, others reflect it in a more subtle manner.

These realities notwithstanding, the present book goes beyond biography and the manner in which writers have used the pen to strike out against traditional institutions (social, economic, political, religious, familial) that, by their very nature, seek to curtail individual freedom, exacting a price of conformity in exchange for belonging—"Isn't disloyalty as much a writer's virtue as loyalty is the soldier's?," asks Eduardo Mallea quoting Graham Greene (97). Nor is our only concern with the Gramscian idea of the "organic" intellectual engaged with ideological change, with political movements or parties, with literature "as an active force invoking [revolutionary currents]" (Beverley and Zimmerman, 49).[8] Our topics thus range from examining the literature of dictatorship to the dictatorship of literature. As far as the former is concerned, García Márquez shows us in *El otoño del Patriarca*, and Roa Bastos in *Yo el Supremo*, that part of the power of an authoritarian régime is that it controls information and spreads favorable myths (stories) about itself. The antidote is literary: "Hoy . . . la palabra posible del escritor demuestra que las palabras del poder son imposibles" (Fuentes, *La nueva novela,* 88); ["Today . . . the writer's valid words prove that the words of Power are invalid" (*Literature in Revolution*, 114)]. As to what we have dubbed here the dictatorship of literature, the quasi-divine authority of the writer is the result of creating empowering literary structures; the reader, who, upon opening the book, tacitly declares his willingness to be dictated to, is somewhat like the ordinary person at the pleasure of the powerful.

In some instances, authorial ideologies are of primary concern, as, for example, when José Carlos González Boixo delves into Rulfo's critical portrayal of the abuses of "caciquismo" in rural Mexico, or when Terry J. Peavler explores the entanglement of sociopolitical, personal, and creative obsessions in the work of one of Cuba's most renowned refugees, Guillermo Cabrera Infante. On the other hand, the essays by Rosemary Geisdorfer Feal and David William Foster deal with issues of feminism, gender, and sexuality. Geisdorfer Feal demonstrates "how Valenzuela's presentation of the politics of 'wargasm' posits strategies for feminine subversion of dominant sexual, social, and political orders," while Foster's central concern in his study of Alejandra Pizarnik's *La condesa sangrienta* is her "meditation on the horror of absolute power . . . expressed in sexual terms."

Many of the essays deal with authors and works that are central to the "Boom." In "Monuments and Scribes: *El hablador* Addresses Ethnography," Sara Castro-Klarén traces what she calls the "inextricable web of the poetic and the political." Rosalía Cornejo-Parriego examines García Márquez's undermining of authority in "The Delegitimizing Carnival of *El otoño del patriarca*," and Peter Standish explores the ramifications of "the managed, staged performance and the extent to which it can be read as a metaphor of a number of strata of authority" in "Magus, Masque, and the Machinations of Authority: Cortázar at Play." This last essay and several others examine the manner in which major authors have undermined or at least questioned their own authority. In "Politicizing Myth and Absence: From Macedonio Fernández to Augusto Roa Bastos," Todd S. Garth concludes that for the Paraguayan, "privileging the social dynamics—the political *presence*—of cultural creation . . . is the only viable way to protect the space of absence, of mythmaking, of cultural creation, from the presence of individual identity and the self-ish structures imposed by it." Sharon Magnarelli, in "See(k)ing Power/Framing Power in Selected Works of José Donoso," argues that "each time we think we have relocated power, found it where it did not seem to be, we discover that it is situated still elsewhere, for that power is contextual, transactional, and always unstable."

Thus, a central concern with the internal and external dimensions of literary power unifies a collection of studies which range from traditional treatments of socio-political concerns to innovative discussions of the powers of literary discourse and its ramifications in Spanish American fiction, from the mainstream to the offbeat, from Macedonio Fernández, who died before the "Boom" even began, to some of the most prolific and important authors of the "new" novel, and on to figures who are only now gaining recognition for the significance of their contributions. Even so, we have been less concerned with coverage than with quality, and make no apology for the omission of the many writers whose works could equally well have claimed a place in a volume such as this. What brings our contributors together here is their shared passion for the subject, the keenness of their thought, and their possession of what may well be the greatest power of all, that of persuasion.

This collaboration was helped by a grant from the British Council and the Fulbright Commission. We should also like to acknowledge our debt to the Kentucky Foreign Language Conference, where we first met, and where, some time later, we were able to organize some sessions from which two of the contributions grew.

TJP
PS

Notes

1. Internationally, the political turmoil of the 1960s produced many worthwhile studies, including a lengthy double issue of *TriQuarterly* in 1972, in which Noam Chomsky, Frederick Crews, Carlos Fuentes, Harry Levin, Raymond Williams, and other luminaries debated "to what extent does the study and practice of literature in a particular time relate to contingent current social and political upheaval, and, conversely, to what extent do such events (or, in fact, their absence) influence the way we *do* literature?" (4). Closer to the point, at least geographically, the famous debate involving Oscar Collazos, Julio Cortázar, and Mario Vargas Llosa, *Literatura en la revolución y revolución en la literatura*, appeared in 1970. The topic continues to be a heated one, having recently yielded, among many other works, a special issue of *Critical Inquiry* devoted to "Politics and Poetic Value" (Spring 1987) in which the editors proclaim that, "The Arnoldian notion that criticism, or even poetry, is ever disinterested is now fully discredited in American academic circles" (416), and a book entitled *Nation and Narration* (1990), which "explore[s] the Janus-faced ambivalence of language itself in the construction of the Janus-faced discourse of the nation."

2. Obviously, studies need not limit themselves to only one or two of these concerns, as a fine new entry into the discussion, Cynthia Steele's *Politics, Gender, and the Mexican Novel, 1968–1988: Beyond the Pyramid*, illustrates.

3. Peruvian novelist Mario Vargas Llosa has made this phrase famous. He sees the art of the novelist as a process of "exorcism" in which the author replaces the real world with one he or she creates. See especially *García Márquez: Historia de un deicidio*.

4. For a recent account of attitudes among Spanish American writers, see Enrico Mario Santí: "Politics, Literature and the Intellectual in Latin America," *Salmagundi*, 82–83, 1989, 92–110.

5. Lucille Kerr bases her lengthy disussion of Fuentes' novel on Foucault's view of power "not as property but as a strategy . . . its effects of domination [being] attributed not to 'appropriation' but to dispositions, manoeuvres, tactics, techniques, functionings" (Foucault, 94).

6. Regarding the attitudes of the Sandinista government in Nicaragua, of which he was a member, Sergio Ramírez writes:

> I always feel like a writer on loan to the revolution. And I think that its a much more serious road than that of the politician on loan to literature; they've never made very good writers . . . . We're going to have a new culture here . . .with lots of creative freedom, without dogmatism, without sectarianism, encouraging freedom which is the very dynamic of the revolution. This is something that seems very important to me, that no one sits down to write recipes about what literature should be, what sculpture should be, what painting should be. Here we simply try to provide the possibilities for creativity (Randall, 39–40).

7. The subsequent dismissal by Vargas Llosa of many of his fellow Latin American writers ("la mayoría baila aún obedeciendo a reflejos condicionados") as corrupt, citing García Márquez, Cortázar and Benedetti among them, provoked an indignant yet generous reply from the latter in "Ni corruptos ni contentos" (*El desexilio y otras conjeturas*, 153–156.)

8. Their argument that "literature has been in Central America not only a means of politics but also a model for it" (xiii) may well be valid for all of Latin America.

Works Cited

Auden, W. H. "The Real World." *The New Republic* 47 (1967).

Benedetti, Mario. *El desexilio y otras conjeturas*. Mexico: Nueva Imagen, 1985.

Beverley, John and Marc Zimmerman. *Literature and Politics in the Central American Revolutions*. Austin: U of Texas P, 1990.

Collazos, Oscar, Julio Cortázar and Mario Vargas Llosa, *Literatura en la revolución y revolución en la literatura*. Mexico, D.F.: Siglo Veintiuno, 1970.

Cortázar, Julio. *Último round*. 9th ed. 2 vols. Mexico: Siglo Veintiuno, 1985.

Cortázar, Julio. *La vuelta al día en ochenta mundos*. 21st ed. 2 vols. Mexico: Siglo Veintiuno, 1986.

Donoso, José. *Historia personal del boom*. Barcelona: Anagrama, 1972.

Foucault, Michel. *A History of Sexuality*. New York: Pantheon, 1978.

Foucault, Michel. *Power/Knowledge: Selected Interviews and Other Writings, 1972–1977*. Trans. Colin Gordon, Leo Marshall, John Mepham, Kate Soper. Ed. Colin Gordon. New York: Pantheon, 1980.

Fuentes, Carlos. *La nueva novela hispanoamericana*. Mexico City: Joaquín Mortiz, 1969.

Fuentes, Carlos. "The Enemy: Words." Trans. Suzanne Jill Levine. In Newman and White, eds., *Literature in Revolution* 111–122.

Fuentes, Carlos. *Terra nostra*. Mexico City: Joaquín Mortiz, 1975.

Goytisolo, Juan. "Literature Pursued by Politics." *The Review of Contemporary Fiction* 4,2 (1984): 34-38.

Kerr, Lucille. *Reclaiming the Author*. Durham: Duke U P, 1992.

Mallea, Eduardo. *Poderío de la novela*. Buenos Aires: Aguilar, 1965.

Martin, Gerald. *Journeys Through the Labyrinth: Latin American Fiction in the Twentieth Century*. London and New York: Verso, 1989.

Meyer, Doris. *Lives on the Line*. Berkeley: U of California P, 1988.

Newman, Charles, and George A. White, eds. *Literature in Revolution*. Spec. Issue of *TriQuarterly*, 23–24 (1972): 1–640. Evanston: Northwestern U P, 1972.

Paz, Octavio. *El ogro filantrópico*. Barcelona: Seix Barral, 1979.

Randall, Margaret. *Risking a Somersault in the Air*. San Francisco: Solidarity Publications, 1984.

Steele, Cynthia. *Politics, Gender, and the Mexican Novel, 1968-1988: Beyond the Pyramid*. Austin: UT Press, 1992.

Vargas Llosa, Mario. "En torno a la nueva novela en Latinoamérica." *Teoría de la novela*. Ed. Germán and Agnes Gullón. Madrid: Taurus, 1974, 113–25.

Vargas Llosa, Mario. *García Márquez: Historia de un decidio*. Barcelona: Barral, 1971.

von Hallberg, Robert, ed. *Politics and Poetic Value*. Spec. Issue of *Critical Inquiry* 13.3 (1987): 415–676. Chicago: U of Chicago P, 1987.

Zavala, Iris M. and Rafael Rodríguez. *The Intellectual Roots of Independence*. New York: Monthly Review, 1980.

Sharon Magnarelli

SEE(K)ING POWER/FRAMING POWER IN SELECTED WORKS OF JOSÉ DONOSO

There can be little doubt that all of José Donoso's works, but especially those since his masterpiece, *El obsceno pájaro de la noche* (1970), encompass struggles for power. Revealingly, that quest for power is articulated in overtly political terms in only two of his works: *Casa de campo* (1978) and *La desesperanza* (1986). In the other works, as we shall see, power struggles most often unfold on the interpersonal level and revolve around possession, hierarchism, and the desire to centralize the self. But as Donoso repeatedly demonstrates, the personal is political and the political is rooted in the personal. Furthermore, whether political or interpersonal, the search for power in Donoso is related, both thematically and technically, to how and what one sees, hence the parentheses of my title—see(k)ing; to seek power is to seek to influence how someone sees or is seen.

The discussion that follows consists of three parts. The greater part of my analysis will focus on two works, *El jardín de al lado* (1981) and *Naturaleza muerta con cachimba* (1990). But before examining those two texts in depth, we will need to consider power in general and then take a quick incursion into some of Donoso's better known fiction to see how power is articulated (in both technique and theme) in relation to possession, hierarchism, and vision. Then, using that cluster of observations as a starting point, I propose to examine *Jardín* and *Naturaleza* in detail. As we shall see, each novel perpetuates the tendencies found in earlier Donoso texts, yet each revolves around a complex inversion of power on the level of both theme and technique, story and narrative. Furthermore, each undermines traditional perceptions of power by foregrounding both perspective (from where are we viewing?) and the politics of inclusion (who has decided what is to be included or excluded from the "picture"?). Since *Naturaleza muerta con cachimba* has not yet been studied in detail, I hope my reading will demonstrate the centrality and interdependence of the issues of power and vision in that work. And, in the case of *El jardín de al lado*, my focus on the links between power and vision will lead to a new, alternative, reading of the text.

Before we look at the dramatization of power in Donoso's works, let us begin by considering our notions of power in general. As defined by the *New Webster's Dictionary*, power is the "ability to do or act." Perhaps more intriguing, the dictionary goes on to formulate power as "the *possession* of control or command *over* others" (emphasis added). As we can see in the dictionary definition, power is articulated in metaphors of spatial relations (command *over*), metaphors that suggest that power is not absolute but relative, dependent on the other and the other's position. Thus, by implication, power must be intersubjective insofar as it is contingent on where, and in relation to whom, one is located and insofar as one's power is necessarily predicated on another's lack thereof. In addition, power must be viewed as transactional; not only is it a relationship among individuals, but it also implies a working through, a (re)enacting or (re)negotiation of one's position of "power" (or lack thereof).[1] As the dictionary suggests, one both maintains and exhibits power by acting, doing. That is, rather than a static given or "possession," power is a dynamic activity (not a passive position or stance) and must be continually renegotiated—challenged anew and reestablished.

Considered in general terms, this transactional aspect of power may manifest itself in any number of ways. First, those in power manipulate space and movement through space, their own and others', as they control the location of objects or bodies (animate or inanimate, theirs or others'). In this respect, power is related to possession; those in power position valued (and thus valuable) objects (objects of desire), animate or inanimate, in proximity to themselves as they designate themselves their sole possessors (dictators of their spatial movement) in a circular maneuver that simultaneously determines which objects can be defined as desirable. In Donoso's works, the characters' desire to empower themselves (negotiate or enact a position of power for themselves) leads them to attempt to centralize themselves by surrounding themselves with visible objects (possessions). By means of those objects, the characters seek to create a mask and disguise what they perceive as the vacuity of their being, their invisibility, and powerlessness, that essential dearth into which our roots are plunged according to the epigraph of *El obsceno pájaro de la noche*. On the other hand, and again in general terms, power may manifest itself as a control over discourse (the expression of desire and the desire of expression); those in power determine who will be allowed to speak, when, and to whom, while at the same time they establish both the parameters and the validity of what will be spoken, what desires can be articulated.[2] Finally, power may manifest itself as a control over vision, as those in power decide who will see what. In its most overt form this "power" occurs negatively as censorship (internal or external), but it has far more subtle manifestations, for those in power dictate not just what but also how we shall see. The visual frames proffered by historical/political writers or realistic narrators—the most frequent objects of Donoso's criticism—establish not only what we see but how we see it and in relation to what.[3] That is to say that by determining what the focus or foreground will be, and, inversely, what will be elided and disappear into the background, the frame marks the politics of inclusion. But, if we are to judge by Donoso's works, it is precisely this background, those elements that the author/narrator would eliminate from the foreground or the frame that most threaten his/her power.

Specifically, in the case of Donoso, we find that power and its lack are both ever fluctuating and often only a *trompe l'oeil*. While power is generally visualized or articulated (as it was in the above-cited dictionary definition) as a unidirectional, hierarchal chain or pyramid in which certain individuals or groups exert control *over* those *beneath* them (note the spatial metaphor) ad infinitum, Donoso shows us that it might better be visualized in terms of nets or webs, with each character as the prey but also as the spider.[4] That is, although his characters are the objects (in the grammatical sense—direct, indirect, or prepositional objects) over whom power is exercised, at other times they also exert power as agents or subjects (also in a grammatical sense). Thus, while the metaphor I use here to describe Donoso's representation of power is still spatial, it is no longer two dimensional but multidimensional, for power operates up, down, sideways, backward, and forward. And, because it is transactional and intersubjective, power as depicted in Donoso is repeatedly deferred and displaced.[5] His works demonstrate that the notion that one has power over the other (that is, that one can possess something as abstract as power and that such a possession places one on a higher spatial level) is a *trompe l'oeil* that conceals the other's silent (if indeed transitory or unwitting) complicity. Nonetheless, what is perceived as silent complicity may well merely disguise the other's power, temporarily less visible. At the same time, Donoso repeatedly illustrates that power is always a dream, an aspiration, a deferment, never a present, here and now, tangible experience. It is always something one seeks, but something one rarely believes one has attained. But let us be more concrete and offer some specific examples of how power manifests itself in some of Donoso's works.

In *El obsceno pájaro de la noche* power (or the desire for power) is intimately linked to the questions of both space and possession. Jerónimo would control the space of the Rinconada, creating a world in a series of concentric circles (layers that envelop and mask), making others "see" as he would have them see. Surely we are meant to understand Jerónimo's desire to control space at the Rinconada as the logical continuation of his earlier attempts (both before and after his return from Europe) to find "his place," a family to "belong to," and thereby centralize and foreground himself as a/the visual focal point.[6] Thus, via Jerónimo Donoso demonstrates how one controls the other's vision by centralizing the self. By surrounding oneself with endless layers, one distances the self from the other and thus protects it, but one also removes it from direct view in a double maneuver that ensures that the self will be spotlighted and "seen" as the self would have itself seen (that is, implicitly as mask, as other). Similarly, Jerónimo's would-be mirror reflection, Humberto/Mudito, would dominate the space of the Casa (closing off sections, painting imaginary windows and doors), again creating a world in the image of his own desire. Also like Jerónimo, Mudito's efforts to dominate space in the Casa continue his earlier endeavors to centralize himself and be "seen"; for let us not forget that as a youth his principal desire was to be someone, to get a face (or a mask) and be seen by (and as) the "beautiful" people—the Jerónimos of the world. Similarly, the old women of the Casa are ever concerned with possessions, with their packages which, like Humberto's, Jerónimo's, or Inés's social masks, hide the essential dearth (the vacuity of their centers) and feign a plenitude that can never be achieved.[7]

Although it employs different metaphors, *Casa de campo* also dramatizes the passion to possess and to control space in order to conceal either meaninglessness or its equally threatening inverse, that is, the surplus, mobility, and plurality of meaning. In this novel, that surplus and mobility are epitomized in the lances, possessions whose meaning changes according to who possesses or uses them. "In the beginning," in the novel's prehistory, the lances had been viewed as instruments to protect the natives. Later, usurped by the family and used to construct a fence, they were seen as symbols of protection against the natives, while even later, after the coup d'état, they were repossessed by the natives and once more perceived as instruments of their protection. The endless dialectical oscillation among contradictory meanings results in an excess, a plurality of meaning. But an excess or surplus of meaning, which complicates the perceiver's choice of the "right" meaning, can be as forbidding as any lack of meaning. And, of course, when faced with either surplus or dearth of meaning, all eyes turn to the powerful who will decide how those signifiers will be seen and what they will mean (for the time being at least). Similarly, *Casa de campo* underscores the close connection between power and vision each time the family draws the "dark curtain" over anything that challenges their collective and self-serving "vision" of reality. What does not support the status quo as they would fashion it is metaphorically banished from the foreground, not seen.

In *La misteriosa desaparición de la Marquesita de Loria* (1980) the question of possessions again reigns supreme, but desire and power over space are also at the forefront. Not irrelevantly, Blanca's principal power is her ability to be seen and thus elicit the desire of the other. That power, having proven fatal to the other (don Mamerto), eventually proves fatal to the self as it drags her (Blanca, blank space) into the vacuum, the chasm of nothingness and nonbeing and removes her from the readers' vision.[8] Nonetheless, let us not forget that her visibility is predicated on the possessions (status symbols) with which she shrouds herself and the emptiness of her being, possessions which (like the watch and the *cloche*) remain behind after her disappearance, ready to endow temporary visibility and power on another character.

But power in Donoso's works does not reveal itself merely on the thematic level. Indeed his fiction inevitably also dramatizes struggles for *narrative* power, again a power related to the optical illusion in that it is predicated on the (erroneously) presumed superior vision of the narrator. That is, the struggle (desire) for power on the level of plot or theme (contents) is repeated in the narrative technique or structure (frame), in the narrator's struggle for power(s) over the work of art, the characters, narratees, and perhaps even readers.[9] Significantly, however, that narrative power is often exercised (as it is overtly in *Casa de campo* and *La Marquesita de Loria*) as a refusal to tell (the blank space), which draws a "dark curtain" over what readers will "see," and is again a power to control the other's vision and thwart the other's desire to see or know.

What is particularly interesting about power in Donoso, whether part of the story or the narrative (the theme or the technique), is that it is inevitably displaced and proves to be located other than where we, as readers, thought we had "seen" it.[10] Furthermore, each time we think we have relocated power, found it where it did not seem to be, we discover that it is situated still elsewhere, for in Donoso power is contextual and thus always unstable. In contrast to mimetic works that question neither the narrator's power nor that of his/her superior vision, Donoso's works continually challenge that "vision" and tacitly acknowledge that, in Jill Dolan's words, "ideology is implicit in perception" (15) and "realism is prescriptive in that it reifies the dominant culture's inscription of traditional power relations" (84). In this respect, Donoso's texts are games (power plays) that tantalize the reader with what appear to be stable positions of mastery and vision (we think we are in a position to see), only to undermine that stability and mark it as a site of misrecognition (we have not seen what we thought we were seeing).[11] For example, who is ultimately more powerful in "Chatanooga Choochoo" of *Tres novelitas burguesas* (1973): Anselmo, who smugly and confidently dismantles Sylvia when she becomes vexatious or overly independent, or Magdalena, ostensibly the least powerful character, but the one who proves to have the power to dismantle Anselmo and store him in the suitcase, thus removing him from view until she desires him? Or is the most powerful of all not the narrator? By foregrounding first Anselmo's dismantling of Sylvia, then her theft of his penis ("lo que hacía gravitar [su] unidad como persona," 54) ["the thing that endowed [him] with gravity and unity as a person" (34)], that narrator relegates to the background the more threatening subconscious fear of a less visible female power and desire. Yet even that power is located not where we expected (with the *femme fatale*, Sylvia, whose "powers" we have "seen") but rather with the wife/madonna (Magdalena). Surely, the latter's less visible power cannot be comfortably reconciled with Western society's image (dream?) of the omnipotent male/husband and the weak, powerless (undesiring) female/wife/mother. Similarly, does Mudito control the activities of the old women of the Casa in *El obsceno pájaro de la noche* or is it the reverse in that novel in which foregrounds and backgrounds are ever shifting or disappear behind patriarchal ponchos?[12] And let us not forget that although *El obsceno pájaro* opens with the subject of Brígida's funeral, a funeral to be financed by Raquel, (Brígida's employer, to whom she was ostensibly subservient and powerless), readers later discover that Raquel's power was, at least in part, an optical illusion, for, in her later years, Brígida had exercised substantial control over Raquel. Because Raquel and the oligarchy's power are foregrounded, the power of the servant class, which would contest and contravene the visible power, is pressed out of the focal frame until and unless the frame shifts. Thus, perhaps the most pertinent power relations are those between Donoso's narrators and their narratees, or even virtual readers, as the narrators control the readers' vision and make characters disappear into black holes or behind patriarchal ponchos, just out of the visual frame.

The validity of the above generalizations about power in Donoso's works could be demonstrated through a detailed analysis of any one of them. Nonetheless, it may prove more fruitful to examine power plays (in both senses of the term) in two works that are both the least directly political and the most overtly concerned with art per se: *El jardín de al lado* and *Naturaleza muerta con cachimba*. *El jardín* focuses on struggles for power in several arenas and among several contenders—Julio, Gloria, Núria Monclús—but always in relation to voice and vision as the novel implicitly raises the questions of who will be allowed to speak, whose voice are we hearing, whose words structure and frame what we see?[13] Perhaps of equal importance and in a foreshadowing of *Naturaleza muerta*, the novel also forces the question from where are we viewing? Are we viewing the other, the *objet d'art*, or from the perspective of that *objet d'art*? Where and which indeed is the subject; where and which is the object? Or is it all an optical illusion; can the contents ever be independent from the frame or the framing vision with its politics of inclusion and exclusion? In both texts, Donoso approaches the question of visual power and power over vision through paintings, visual art forms with their implicit frames, demonstrating ultimately that, in the words of Jean Baudrillard, "power *does not exist* . . . . [I]t is only a perspectival space of simulation[;] . . . if power seduces, it is precisely . . . because it is a simulacrum and because it undergoes a metamorphosis into signs and is invented on the basis of signs."[14] By "perspectival space of simulation," I take Baudrillard to mean the space within which we think we perceive power. Here and elsewhere in this essay, I have insisted on using this rather complex expression precisely because of its double emphasis on the perceptual and the imaginary. The expression highlights the fact that the space appears real or concrete but is not; it is merely perceived or imagined as such. In addition, the use of the term *simulation* acknowledges that the perceptual/imaginative quality is not fortuitous.

The simulation is deliberate even though readers often fail to recognize it as such. Someone, some agent, is instrumental in making us think we have seen power. It is this visual illusion, the "perspectival space of simulation," that I would like to examine more closely in the two works.

Specifically, I propose that the protagonists/narrators of *Jardín* and *Naturaleza* play with the politics of inclusion and exclusion by positioning themselves as both self and other, as both inside the visual sign, the work of art (the paintings in these novels), and outside it, as both spider and prey. And each does so by projecting himself into the work of art, the perspectival space of simulation, metaphorizing, repositioning, and centralizing himself in a strategy that, in the words of Barbara Freedman, "both appropriates and invalidates otherness by proving that everything strange can . . . be made to reflect a part of oneself" (163).[15] Surely, the power to make the other perceive (see) the world in one's own image or as a part of oneself (a simulacrum of possession) is the greatest power of all.

Although the second novella of Donoso's most recent work, *Taratuta/ Naturaleza muerta con cachimba*, chronologically follows *El jardín de al lado*, I would like to use it as my starting point and read backward from it to *El jardín*. Doing so will allow us to rethink the earlier work where the repositioning of the narrator/subject is less conspicuous than it is in *Naturaleza*. Nonetheless, in both the narrator (the seeing *I*/eye) is inserted into the work of art (the painting) from where it then seems to gaze back. At the conclusion of *Naturaleza muerta*, art and by implication the artist's vision conspicuously replace "reality" as they superimpose themselves on it and in turn are reflected by/in it rather than vice versa.[16] Significantly, in that work, we find that the protagonist, thirty-one-year-old bank employee turned art critic (turned artist), Marcos Ruiz Gallardo, is able to realize his dreams of power, erotic and otherwise, only after he is incorporated into (reflected in and by) Larco's painting, *Naturaleza muerta con cachimba*. As we shall see, *El jardín*'s Julio Méndez effectuates a similar outcome.

Naturaleza muerta begins with an allusion to a crime committed by the protagonist/narrator—a "theft" of paintings that echoes those of *El jardín*. In this case the "theft" is posited as a crime against a corporation, against the principles of exchange and circulation, and is by implication a subversion of "normal" webs of power. Rather than allowing Larco's paintings to circulate freely (available for possession and thus potential signifiers of power or identity), Marcos limits and controls their circulation, determining who, if anyone, will see them and what will be seen. But the alleged crime, like all else in the text, is predicated on point of view (seeing), for if readers are to trust the protagonist/narrator's rendition of events (surely a dubious stance), the only "offense" is that Marcos has "seen" and interpreted the paintings of the "difficult" painter, Larco, differently than the other members of the *Corporación para la defensa del patrimonio artístico nacional*. His vision and frame deviate from theirs in that the paintings cloaked in blue paint are of little or no value to them. Even the "originals," the drab Parisian interiors concealed beneath the coat of blue, were considered worthless until Marcos's persistence in both discovering and uncovering them (bringing them into the public eye) created an interest, made them desirable and thus valuable. In this way, Donoso ironically demonstrates how the framework (Marcos's discourse and, by implication, vision) empowers the self by creating desire in the other: surely one can only "steal" what the other desires and therefore values. Ultimately, whether Marcos or the others are the "criminals" (those who have illicitly seized another's power or possession and/or are bad readers) is left in doubt, for the fact that he is unable to recognize the "caretaker" of the paintings as Larco himself renders his "vision" dubious. If he cannot see the artist beneath the mask of the old man, how can he see/read the message or value of the painting beneath either the veneer of drab Parisian interiors or the surface of blue? Or are the message and value (power) only in the eyes of the beholder?

Revealingly, Marcos's perspective continuously shifts throughout the work as he alternately disparages and acclaims the same object or person (Larco's paintings, Hilda), depending on his focus, but generally finding reality inferior to his dreams or preconceived expectations. And even his "discovery" of the Larco museum was the indirect result of an unsatisfactory erotic encounter with Hilda—the long-awaited rendezvous that did not meet expectations. Only in the final chapter, when reality has become (interchangeable with) art and he has been projected into and empowered by the work of art as both the viewer and the viewed, the subject and the object, does "reality" (as he has created it, already an *objet d'art*) become satisfactory to him, even desirable.

After Larco's death, Marcos finds that the paintings have also been the objects of another crime. With the exception of his favorite, *Naturaleza muerta con cachimba*, they have been shrouded with a coat of bluish paint, a desecration that is the product of a double power play. First, the blue paint is an ironic response to Marcos's earlier attempt to impose (in some sense from above) his aesthetic "vision" by declaring the paintings ugly, alien to his precepts of beauty because for him they lacked color, like that bluish color so typically Chilean. Thus, Larco exercised his artistic (if indeed ironic) power *over* them and what would be seen, by overlaying them (again from above) with the layer of blue paint. (Surely there is a message here about political power and its relation to vision.) In addition, Larco was willing to deface his paintings because for him "el arte es una mierda" (120) ["art is nothing but shit" (120)] (repeated several times) and "Es la vida lo que tiene que ser una obra de arte" (120) ["It's life that has to be a work of art" (120)], a statement doubly literalized when Marcos imposes himself into Larco's already artistic world. At the same time, even the *Naturaleza muerta*, the only painting not covered in blue, is "painted over" in a different way, one that also literalizes both Larco's and Marcos's desire for power over the work of art. It was modified to include, in one corner, a portrait of Marcos and his fiancée, Hilda, idealized and depicted in keeping with Marcos's express artistic preferences, which include "perfiles de damas renacentistas sobre perspectivas de árboles o ruinas o rocas, o las frutales muchachas de Renoir disolviéndose en luz" (115) ["profiles of Renaissance ladies with a background of trees or ruins or rocks, or Renoir's fruity girls dissolving into light" (115)]. And, not irrelevantly, this modification appears within the framework of a window that had previously "opened" onto a view of stylized chimneys. Thus, we find a painting framed within a framed painting, while the former view out (as through a window) becomes a view in or back (as in a mirror). And the "new" painting is as stylized as the "old." In this manner, Larco and Donoso highlight the subterfuge of the "window of reality," art that pretends to look out or beyond but that only looks back, and specifically looks back at the "painted" in a way that doubly foregrounds the artist.

As the text concludes, Marcos will devote his life to unmasking the paintings, removing the blue paint to expose what lies beneath (that is, like Larco, he will exercise his *power over* what others see), and living the life of both the painter and the painting, reflecting the world of Parisian artists past (or his version/vision thereof) who would live their art. Thus, art replaces life, entrapping him and us in a self-reflecting mirror that purports to be a window to the exterior. It is not irrelevant that the logo Marcos designed for the corporate stationery was composed of two angels (himself and Hilda?) holding up a mirror in an ornate frame that enclosed the name of the corporation. In this text, life holds up a mirror to art rather than vice versa, but it is art (illusion, artifice, framed by and reflecting only the viewing eye) that implicitly shapes and frames (in both senses of the word) our sociopolitical expectations. In this way, Donoso subtly cautions us that the mirror is not independent of the external (if indeed invisible) power of the "artist" who positions that mirror and creates the perspectival space of simulation as he shifts the focus to himself and makes himself an *objet d'art*. At the end of the novella, Marcos acknowledges that he and Hilda are only "parte de la *visión* de un artista verdaderamente singular" (159, emphasis added) ["part of the vision of a truly singular artist" (159)]. Is that truly singular artist Larco or Donoso? Or is it Marcos himself because by now he is the "author" of his life? Thus, the text, which began with a crime, the "theft" referred to in the opening paragraph, ends with another theft as Marcos purloins Larco's life and paintings, assuming a central, visible position in his house and in his work, making himself both observer and observed, as he dictates what will be seen: himself as he would fashion/see himself, as an *objet d'art* both inside and outside the *objet d'art*—art at the service of those who would empower themselves, personally or politically.

Significantly, *El jardín de al lado* is also marked by the thefts of paintings, both metaphoric and virtual. At the beginning of the novel, Julio and Gloria move into painter Pancho Salvatierra's apartment, eat his food, drink his liquor, look through his windows, and thus on some level usurp his life (not unlike what Marcos and Hilda do with Larco). More overtly, their son's friend Bijou apparently steals one of Pancho's paintings, and later Julio himself purloins and sells one. Like Marcos's "theft" of Larco's canvases, Julio's appropriation of Pancho's painting is both metaphoric and literal, for he not only absconds with the painting itself, but he also, metaphorically at least, steals its name (identity) by giving it a new title, *Retrato de la señora Gloria Echeverría de Méndez*, and writing that new title over the old, *Retrato de la condesa Leonor de Teck*. In addition, I would suggest that his "artistic crimes" here parallel what I will call his "artistic theft" of his wife Gloria's potential power, as he twice casts her as the framed *objet d'art*, as the object of observation and the (male) gaze: first by repeatedly imaging her as the Odalisque (the beautiful slave of the Ingres painting), then by declaring her the woman in Pancho's painting. In each case, his gesture silences her and converts her into an objet, if indeed an *objet d'art*. The difference between the two paintings is significant, however, and, I suggest, points to Julio's ever growing need to objectify and disempower Gloria in order to empower himself. In the Ingres painting the naked Odalisque is surrounded by luxury and seems to look back, if indeed from only one eye, but the woman in Pancho's painting is more fetishized and disenfranchised. As described by Julio, who is fascinated by it, that painting has a phosphorescent, electric-blue background. The nude woman's lovely body is invaded by hundreds of meticulously painted insects that look like jewels and seem ready to devour her. The frame is a silver strip that decapitates the figure whose head is left out of the painting. Headless and thus visionless, the lovely lady cannot return his look (as the Odalisque seems to), and even her body, which may serve only as a felicitous background upon which to spotlight the insects that invade it, seems destined to disappear as her head already has. Furthermore, I suggest that the "theft" of power that occurs as Julio declares Pancho's painting *his* own and changes the identity of its subject to Gloria, *his* wife, foreshadows the final chapter of the text, which I shall read as another "theft" of power, also related to a change of identity, disappearance, and invisibility.

Ostensibly, *El jardín de al lado* centers on a writer's visible failure to write a novel and have it published and his wife's invisible success in the same project (invisible until the final chapter, that is). As the story of Chilean writer, Julio Méndez, exiled in Spain, *El jardín* treats the question of political power mostly on the interpersonal level. Still, personal or political, the problem in *El jardín* is one experienced by the writer himself and also dramatized in both *Casa de campo* and *La desesperanza*: a reluctance to oversimplify sociopolitical problems by endorsing reductionist solutions and by "seeing" (foregrounding) as most politically committed groups would have us see, that is, from only one perspective that validates their particular position and power. The novel that Julio wants to write would resolve political and interpersonal ambiguities and provide a "true" history with neat answers, something Donoso deems impossible or accomplished only in "bad faith," that is, by portraying (framing, foregrounding) just one or two facets of a complex reality, by drawing a dark curtain, or interposing a "please do not disturb" sign.[17]

On the other hand, Julio's problem is related to the question of exile (implicit in the title garden next door, the paradise always irrevocably lost). While exile here is presented as a specific, historical, and personal circumstance (Julio and Gloria are in exile because of the political situation in Chile), it is also a metaphor of life in general, the human condition: everyone lives expelled from the Garden of Eden that would accord the unchallenged possession of power and a position of visible centrality. The question then is how to position the self to ensure that one is seen (framed, centralized) as one would choose? On some level Julio would recreate that paradise, centralize and empower himself, with his novel: he would write a testimonial novel in which he would be both observer and observed, subject and object, and by doing so, incorporate himself into the "Boom," make himself visible (not unlike Marcos) both inside and outside his work of fiction, as the I/eye in it and as the celebrity outside it.[18]

Thus, that garden, that paradise lost, must be read as a metaphor of power. Remember, in the Garden of Eden, Adam and Eve were pretty much in control of the world, and Adam, charged with naming all the flora and fauna, might be seen as both a demigod and as the original, human writer. Nonetheless, that garden, from which we perceive ourselves as inevitably exiled, is always located elsewhere (next door) and possessed by someone else; thus even one's image of it is necessarily projection, fiction.[19] For Julio, the garden of the duke's house next door, which he "sees" voyeuristically through the *frame* of the open window, is an ideal setting (in some sense a framed blank space or page) onto which he projects the fantasies that allow him to perceive (he believes) the life of the "beautiful," powerful people next door. In this respect it mirrors the window in Larco's painting after it has been altered to include the idealized portraits of Hilda and Marcos. Still, the fact that Monika Pinell de Bray, one of the "inhabitants" of the garden next door (idealized center of power), commits suicide suggests that power (like the paradise) may be only in the eyes of the beholder. Furthermore, that "real" garden next door evokes the remembered one left behind in Chile, at his mother's house, the one from when "el mundo era edénico porque no nos proponía aún la tiránica opción de ser, tal vez, amados y célebres" (11) ["when the world was a Garden of Eden because it had not yet presented us with the tyrannical alternative of perhaps being loved and famous" (3)], that is, when one was not yet charged with producing reflections (and by implication, distortions) of multiple selves/masks and feigning the power and centrality one rarely believes one has. Thus, again Donoso focuses on the question of seeing and calls into doubt the possibility of seeing anything (including power) objectively, as other than a (desired) reflection of a (desirable) reflection.

More important, the garden next door is sometimes viewed through and framed by two living room windows, between which there is a painting, an optical illusion of a window. The juxtaposition of these two "types" of window spotlights their potential interchangeability and leads us to wonder from exactly where it is that we (as readers) are "seeing." To complicate matters even more, Julio sometimes observes the garden from the living room windows, sometimes from the dining room window, sometimes from the kitchen window, and sometimes from the bedroom window, depending on which part of the garden he would have framed, centralized, or where he would focus his gaze. At any rate, there can be little doubt that all the windows, which would theoretically afford a view of/to the external, objective reality, function here as a metaphor for the traditional, mimetic fiction that (again theoretically) affords a glimpse of a reality outside itself. But that metaphoric window (the "realistic" novel or historical, political discourse), like the one in Larco's painting, is an optical illusion. It is not a window to some unmediated, objective, external reality. On the contrary it is mediated and framed by the artist; at times it is merely a mirror that displays the observer's projections—Julio looks out the window(s) and "sees" paradise, for the I/eye is both inside and outside the frame, the *objet d'art*, just as it would be in Julio's testimonial novel. In this regard, the superior vision and (in)sight proffered by an omniscient and ostensibly omnipotent narrator is doubly undermined in this text: first, Julio is less omnipotent than he would like, and, second, neither we nor he "sees" anything but distorted reflections of reflections. As Julio comments when he finishes his novel, "No sé lo que he escrito, ni lo que a mí me ha ocurrido al escribir. No logro verme, ni 'verla'" (211) ["I don't know what I've written or what's been happening to me while I've been writing. I can't see myself or 'see it (her)'" (191)]. In spite of all indications and tradition to the contrary, the narrator/writer, the most powerful of all, does not know because he cannot see; he can only feign (the optical illusion) a superior vision, omniscience, and omnipotence, an objective I/eye outside the frame from which it would pretend it could be independent.[20]

But perhaps even more important, a second reading of the Donoso text reveals that our (the readers') "vision" has been even further manipulated (or at the very least we have not seen well), and Donoso has made an even more profound comment on art, vision, and seeing. A second reading reveals that what we had understood as an optical illusion of a window—the painting of a window to which I referred earlier, the optical illusion located between the two living room windows—is not a painting of a window at all. It is merely a painting of window curtains, a painting of that which frames the window. The representation of the window itself is missing, and thus Donoso draws attention to the very question of framing and underlines the politics of inclusion and exclusion which the artist, and perhaps even the spectator, would prefer or have been trained not to see.

In this manner, Donoso again underscores the illusory nature of the "window" of fiction and reminds us that as readers we too have been observing an optical illusion, a window that is not one but only a mirror of the narrating *I*/eye.[21] And Gloria is explicit about the self-reflecting quality of her novel: "Todos, tú, ella, Julio son sólo reflejos en mí, en nuestras subjetividades cambiantes" (259) ["All of you—you, she, Julio—are only reflections in me, in our changing subjective visions" [subjectivities] (237)]. The question of changing subjectivities evokes the repeated Donoso theme of masks and personality as an interchangeable series of masks of power with no inherent permanence. Indeed, Julio's inability to write a successful novel may be related to his inability to assume a mask, to become other, the way Gloria apparently has when she has gotten "dentro de la piel de un personaje tan distinto" (247–248) ["into the skin of a character so different" (226)]—Julio. In fact, at one point in the text, Julio bemoans the fact that Gloria has the freedom (the power) to "put on" a different face each day and determine how she will be seen, while he is doomed to a single, permanent face, reflected in the mirror of "his" novel (117) [102]. The statement foreshadows the conclusion of his narration at the end of the fifth chapter when he opts to become other, to change faces and places with the beggar and thus free himself from "esa vetusta tiranía" ["that old tyranny"] (the urge to power?) as he assumes "el fracaso como vestidura permanente" (118) [literally, failure as permanent clothing]—that is, puts on another face like Gloria. However, this is not the first time Julio refers to his desire to be (seen as) other. As he earlier explains, his "attraction" to Bijou, the bisexual friend of their son, is not so much sexual as it is "un deseo de apropiarme de su cuerpo, de ser él" (84) ["a desire to take his body over, to be him" (70)], and he recognizes that his "hunger" *to get into* Bijou's *skin* (note, these are the same words Núria uses in reference to Gloria's relation to her character, Julio) is a desire that his sorrows or pains be other than what they are—a desire to see and be seen differently. Is this not precisely what Marcos does in *Naturaleza muerta*—"become" (i.e., be seen as, mirror) the other, the artist and/or the *objet d'art*? But perhaps the most pertinent question here is, might not Julio's attraction to Gloria parallel his attraction to both Bijou and the beggar in Tangier (or vice versa) and thus be based on a desire to be her, the Odalisque—other self, other gender, other ontological status, the powerless other who is the object of the gaze, but whose gaze simultaneously focuses on and centralizes the artist/spectator? It cannot be irrelevant that Ingres's Odalisque looks back at the spectator in a way that foregrounds the act of looking and thus the spectator himself. As John Berger has noted, "In the average European oil painting of the nude the principal protagonist is never painted. He is the spectator in front of the picture. . . . Everything is addressed to him" (54). Let us add that the "he" who is the principal protagonist, the privileged spectator to whom everything is addressed, is the artist (Julio when he casts Gloria as the Odalisque) who has created and framed that nude (Gloria or Gloria as the Odalisque) in such a way that she centers her gaze on him.

Unquestionably, the notion of the mirror and the optical illusion along with the theme of "seeing" and seeing oneself in *El jardín de al lado* are directly related to those in *La misteriosa desaparición de la Marquesita de Loria.*[22] However, Gloria need not resort to Blanca's erotic acrobatics in order to be seen, for she can "see herself" (alternate between observer and observed), find a mirror, in literature and art. But, the question is, to what extent is that image already framed (in both senses of the word)? Indeed, throughout the work Gloria is frequently imaged as reading or writing. Although what she writes is generally perceived as frivolous, insignificant, or uncreative (translations)—the low key or style as the text phrases it—the topics she addresses in her "literary" endeavors are the crux of the text we read: sexism (power plays between the genders) in chiromancy (the ability to read and write the future in one's palm, an ability or a power that evokes the slip of the hand and the inversion of power that characterize the final chapter), and translation (the ability, the power, to convert oneself and one's word into another).[23] The interrelation of the topics is made explicit by Julio early in the text when he notes that Gloria returns to her work on sexism in chiromancy each time she becomes irritated with him, Pinochet, or society in general (that is, each time she feels disempowered); thus, personal politics/power are linked with (public) national politics/power.

Nonetheless, *El jardín* is simultaneously more and less unsettling than the *Marquesita*. It is less unsettling due, in large degree, to its reliance on the traditional power play of the narrator with his/her technique of "tying up loose ends," as literary agent Núria Monclús calls it (248). Those loose ends (Blanca's fate) were left dangling in *Marquesita,* hidden behind the narrator's silence, the blank space or dark curtain. Paradoxically, however, the loose ends in *El jardín* are tied up through a mis- or re-direction of attention or vision (again the question of framing) and through an act of what might be labeled "bad faith" in which the frame moves, the mirror is readjusted. In the sixth and final chapter readers are told that although failed writer Julio Méndez has narrated the first five chapters of the novel, the veritable author is not him, as we had supposed, but his wife, Gloria. Again, power is located other than where the frame had led us to perceive it. Still, in spite of this final, unsettling inversion of authorship and authority, reader discomfort is ameliorated to a large degree by the metaphoric "dark curtain" drawn with the superimposed words, "please do not disturb" (words that simultaneously do and do not tie up loose ends, for they tell us nothing). Like a metaphoric, soothing coat of blue paint, these words seem to promise, if not a "they-lived-happily-ever-after" ending, at least that the characters are going to survive and continue with some degree of peace. It is a peace achieved through literature by assuming one's proper *tono*: in Gloria's case by writing in a *tono menor*; in Julio's, by teaching literature—that is, by holding up a "lying," illusory mirror, by pretending that the optical illusion of literature is a window of vision and insight.[24]

But that reader discomfort is alleviated only by not questioning or challenging the hegemony of the vision and by feigning not to see all the unanswered questions, for, like the *Marquesita, El jardín* is still structured around a mysterious disappearance (invisibility) that is relegated to the background with another power play, an adjustment of the frame, to which the reader is not privy—we cannot see beyond the "please do not disturb" (i.e., do not question or look). I refer to the disappearance of the presumable narrator, observer, Julio, who vanishes into or is swallowed by the chaos of Tangier at the end of chapter five, after his final glimpse of Gloria, *his* Odalisque, "plácida, inclinada sobre el libro, tan confiada, que ni siquiera se molesta en levantar los ojos para ver[l]e salir del cuarto" (246) ["so calmly bent over her book, so confident that she doesn't even bother to raise her eyes to see (him) leave the room" (224)]. Unlike Ingres's Odalisque, whose gaze *is* directed back at the imagined spectator (observer or creator), this one does not look back, does not grant him existence by seeing him, foregrounding and centralizing him. That potential void—non-vision—is literalized in *El jardín de al lado* in Julio's disappearance and the subsequent imposition of Gloria as narrator. But, as is typical of Donoso's works, the text closes up around the void, around Julio's absence or disappearance, by positing that Gloria, not Julio, has been the writer behind Julio's narration all along. Indeed, by disclosing in the final chapter that the "seer," "observer," is the character presumably "seen," "observed" (Gloria, the Odalisque), Donoso undermines the premises of mimetic narrative as he calls into doubt Julio's capacity to see anything (and by implication, the readers' ability to do so, since our vision depends on the narrator's).[25] Significantly, too, the most powerful character of all and the image of the reader par excellence, Núria Monclús, is incorporated into this final chapter (again the observer observed), now inside the text, inside the window that is a lying mirror, and it is *she* who seizes power and "writes" (in some sense "writes over" not unlike Larco with his blue paint) the final words of Gloria's text, adding, superimposing, "please do not disturb."[26] Like Larco, Núria drops a dark curtain, thwarts our desire to see or know more. Thus, the power here has shifted not once (Julio to Gloria) as readers have acknowledged, but at least twice (Julio to Gloria to Núria), ostensibly resting with the character (mirror of the reader, narratee par excellence) who, while paradoxically deemed the most powerful, has nevertheless (and not unlike Gloria to some degree) been marginalized, relegated to the background, or kept just outside the narrative frame until this final chapter where she (Gloria and/or Núria) assumes center stage.

As radical and revolutionary as readers might find this inversion of authorship and authority, observer and observed, there could be yet another even more radical gesture that has been overlooked (hidden behind the "please do not disturb"): that the power (authority/authorship) and act of bad faith (failure to disclose the identity of the bona fide author[s] from the beginning) have been redoubled and located still other than where readers (with our limited view through the "window" of the text) have believed them to be. Although the reading of the text I have posited up to this point (that Gloria has authored the text, with some help from Núria, and that Julio is merely the narrator/character she has created) is certainly valid, Donoso leaves the door open for a contradictory yet equally legitimate reading that the act of bad faith is located not in the first five chapters but in the last one. Within the fiction and its enactment of ever shifting perspectival spaces of the simulation of power, it is equally plausible that in the final chapter Julio assumes Gloria's voice and mask, not vice versa. That is, rather than relocating the "author" and designating the power Gloria's, that final chapter may merely disguise that author (Julio) and by implication lure us into believing that the narrative perspective (and power) is located other than where we had believed, leading us to believe we can in fact perceive from the position of the observed, the work of art, the Odalisque. In this complex game of mirrors and windows (windows that prove to be optical illusions or mirrors), we might well interpret the final chapter as Julio's donning the mask and role (voice) of Gloria, that is, becoming her, projecting himself into the Ingres painting just as Marcos projected himself into Larco's painting and just as he (Julio) projected himself and his childhood world onto the garden next door. Recognizing that vision is predicated on the frame, we might read the last chapter as Julio's adjustment of the frame as he assumes Gloria's clothes and position, rather than those of the beggar at the end of chapter five, and gets into her skin as he earlier wanted to get into Bijou's. Julio wanted to be someone else, to be in someone else's skin. We thought the skin he would don would be the beggar's, but perhaps it was Gloria's, and specifically a Gloria whose image is repeatedly presented as framed in a painting, whether the Ingres canvas or Pancho's. And, significantly, the beggar and Gloria have several points of contact that may not be immediately apparent.

At the end of chapter five Julio seeks to be (become) the beggar and drown in his yellow eyes, "desposeído, a salvo de todas las depredaciones: el humillado, la víctima de las injusticias, no el hechor" (246) ["dispossessed, free of all its guilts: I the humiliated, the victim of injustice, not its agent" (224)]. He wants to be the one for whom revolutions are waged, outside the fight and history (powerless?). Might this description not be equally applicable to Gloria? Throughout the first five chapters she is portrayed as the insignificant wife of an insignificant writer, given to working on insignificant literature, but always with a feminist posture. Such a portrayal suggests that she is among the humiliated who have recognized gender hierarchism, the dispossession inherent to the female position in Western culture, and that she is the one outside the fight and history (outside the patriarchal frame and powerless?), the one for whom the feminist revolution is waged.[27] In this respect, surely she fits the qualities of the "skin" Julio seeks to appropriate, as do the protagonists of the two paintings with which he images her: *objets d'art*, silenced, immobilized objects of the gaze, the Odalisque or la condesa Leonor de Teck, alias la señora Gloria Echeverría de Méndez. Furthermore, earlier Gloria had complained that Julio had devoured her (201) [181], but it may be that his metaphoric "consumption" occurs, becomes visible, only in the final chapter when he displaces (and by implication dispossesses) her: first by assuming her mask, voice, and then by reframing that mask, voice, and having it centralize him, just as the Odalisque seems to focus on the spectator. (Let us not forget that "Gloria's book" is about him!) Thus, it is possible that in the final chapter we are not "seeing" from the position we believe (that is, Gloria's) but from a position of double reflection and refraction. In the Ingres painting, the Odalisque (metaphor of Gloria) seems to look back, seems to have a perspective and return the gaze, but her gaze or perspective is an optical illusion, still created and controlled by the artist (male) as well as and significantly directed toward, centered on him. By positioning the "mirror" of art, the artist focuses the optical illusion of the return gaze on himself. Is it not possible that the narrator/author of the final chapter is still Julio, doing exactly the same thing, projecting himself now in the character of Gloria and reflecting himself back? Have we not been called on in this last chapter to stop observing the Odalisque as other and to pretend to "see" from that other position, to pretend to see from a perspective that is only imaginary? But again, what Gloria "sees" is Julio as he appropriates her "viewpoint" and centers it on himself, the observer observed by himself, endless mirror reflections to aggrandize the self.

Thus, because Julio's adventures into otherness on the streets of Tangier are hidden from view, not "seen" (like the head in Pancho's painting), the possibility is left open that his "adventure" is in fact the final chapter, his "conversion" into Gloria as he hides behind her voice and mask (and perhaps even those of Núria) in what might well be a veiled comment on the political situation in Chile and the hidden, shifting power structure based on misrecognition. Perhaps he assumes her perspective and proffers yet one more "optical illusion" as he adopts the success and power he covets in the first five chapters. Surely, there is no viable reason to accept the power play and realignment of authority in the final chapter when the novel has repeatedly undermined our capacity to read or see anything accurately and questioned the stability of authority or vision (perspective). Are the novel and its structure not implicitly encouraging us to reject, or at least question, its own authority along with its authorization of a "new" reading? Ultimately, we must ask if Julio has not done with Gloria, and specifically a Gloria imaged as the Odalisque, what he did with Pancho's painting: purloin and rename it/her? And has he not done what all Donoso characters do to empower themselves: appropriate what is other and declare it their own? As the text states in the voice of Gloria or Julio (or is it Núria?): "las cosas se han apaciguado, tomando su lugar dentro de esta *perspectiva*, que *puede ser falsa* y lírica, pero que ahora me atrevo a aceptar como *mía*," (250, emphasis added) [everything has become "more peaceful, taking its place in this perspective that may be false or poetic but that I now (dare to accept or usurp) as my own" (228)]. As I suggested earlier, the ability to "appropriate and invalidate otherness by proving that everything [other] can . . . be made to reflect a part of oneself" may well be the supreme power.

The questions still pending at the end of *El jardín de al lado* are the ones with which many of Donoso's works implicitly close: Who has devoured whom by assuming the other's voice and mask? Who has overpowered whom? Is the window anything other than a mirror, and, at that, one that depends on the agency of the invisible controller who positions the frame of the mirror so that it centralizes himself or herself? It cannot be irrelevant, either, that Julio uses the money from the sale of Pancho's painting to finance the trip to Tangier and, once there, to buy Gloria a necklace of dark amber. Surely, the beads of that necklace evoke the insect-jewels of Pancho's painting while the silver filigree with which those beads are worked recalls the painting's silver frame. Furthermore, the necklace, with which Julio encircles her neck (231) [210], visually separates her head from her body as the frame of the painting did. Like Marcos, Julio can reframe reality to reflect "his" art, and Donoso again dramatizes the complexity, fragility, and illusory nature of lines of power both inside and outside the window/mirror of fiction. Finally, let us not forget that while Ingres's Odalisque seems to look back and backwards (her head is turned, looking back over her shoulder at the painter, spectator outside the frame), her face is positioned in such a way that only one eye is foregrounded while the other dissolves into the background, reminding us how necessarily partial, in both senses of the word, her vision must be.

The Bible assures us that in the beginning was the word. But José Donoso proposes that in the end there is only silence ("please do not disturb"), our complicitous silence, which has allowed all the "sound and fury" that structure Donoso's texts, the "tale told by an idiot," blind to all but his own reflections, as he and we see only the perspectival space of simulation invented by the sign, the power that is not there.

Notes

1. I use the term "transactional" with an eye to its various meanings. Etymologically it comes from the Latin *trans*, across or through, and *agere*, to drive or do. The verb form

means to conduct or carry through to a conclusion or settlement and thus suggests both a completion and a balance, compromise, or agreement between two or more parties. At the same time, transactional analysis is a form of psychotherapy that seeks to bring the three states of the ego into balance.

Jane Gallop has interestingly envisioned power as distinct from powers. The first, which she associates with the male, she defines as "a monolithic authority which would subjugate everything to its unified rule" (74); it is consolidated, consolidating (74), and "an absolute attribute of a monadic self, not contingent upon situation" (75). The second, in the plural, which she associates with the feminine, "consists of various abilities and charms that can be used strategically to influence other people's actions" (74). These strategic, tactical powers "are always powers over others, dependent upon a given intersubjective dynamic" (75). Donoso, however, seems to make no distinction between female "powers" and masculine "power" except for the fact that "female power" tends to be less overt, more silent and hidden.

2. Of course, to control discourse is also spatial to the extent that speaking and hearing depend on who is in the position to speak or hear. Little is to be gained by speaking to a nonexistent audience, an audience that is physically inaccessible.

3. These visual frames are metaphorized in a variety of ways in Donoso's works. In *Casa de campo* "dark curtains" are drawn to divert eyes from what the narrators would have remain unseen. In *El obsceno pájaro de la noche*, in the often repeated *conseja*, the landowner (patriarch) spreads his arms and poncho in such a way that the view into the room and the activities of his daughter and her nanny are hidden from the eyes of others. As a result he removes the daughter from the center of the story and shifts the attention (and the vengeance) onto the old woman, the nanny.

4. The image of one trapped in a spider web as both spider and prey is borrowed from Luisa Valenzuela (217), but it is also implied in Donoso's image of Núria Monclús's hat veil. See also the Feal study.

5. In this respect, Donoso echoes the theories of French philosopher Michel Foucault who has argued that "power must be understood in the first instance as the multiplicity of force relations immanent in the sphere in which they operate and which constitute their own organization; as the process which, through ceaseless struggles and confrontations, transforms, strengthens, or reverses them; as the support which these force relations find in one another, thus forming a chain or a system, or on the contrary, the disjunctions and contradictions which isolate them from one another; and lastly, as the strategies in which they take effect . . . . Power is everywhere; not because it embraces everything, but because it comes from everywhere" (92-93).

6. In reference to Jerónimo's return from Europe, the narrator states, "Jerónimo emprendió el viaje de regreso a su patria para ver si integrándose a algún nivel de esa *familia* lograba pertenecer por fin" (168, Donoso's italics) ["Jerónimo had set out on the return trip to see if he might become part of that *family* at some level and thus belong at last" (135)]. A few pages later, that narrator continues, "Se había venido por la guerra. Verdad. Pero más que nada porque en el último tiempo andaba con el centro de su orgullo herido. Y para que la simetría de su vida resistiera el examen de su propia exigencia debía ser distinta, nacer de una raíz propia, ineludible . . . . Cuando estalló la guerra vio que carecía de un sitio natural dentro del fragor" (171) ["He'd come away because of the war. True. But, more than anything, because toward the end he'd been going around with the

center of his pride wounded. And, in order for the symmetry in his life to withstand the test of his own high standards, his existence would have to be different, to spring from its own roots, which were inescapable . . . . When the war broke out he saw that he had no rightful place in it" (138)].

7. I discuss the question of the empty packages in detail in "*El obsceno pájaro de la noche*: Fiction, Monsters, and Packages."

8. I discuss Blanca's need to see herself and be seen in "Disappearance Under the Cover of Language."

9. Gerald Prince defines narratee as the fictive entity whom the narrator addresses, neither the real nor the implied reader.

10. Although addressing a related concept, authority, rather than power, Kerr makes an similar observation in reference to *El jardín de al lado*.

11. I am indebted to Barbara Freedman's reading of Shakespeare for these concepts.

12. See note 3.

13. Gutiérrez Mouat discusses the novel as a blend of aesthetics, ethics, and politics.

14. See Jean Baudrillard, "Forgetting Foucault," *Humanities in Society* 3 (1980): 108–109, quoted in Freedman (186).

15. This is Freedman's interpetation of metaphor.

16. In this novel, as in Donoso's earlier *El jardín de al lado*, the interartistic referents are paintings and specifically avant-garde or surrealistic paintings. *Naturaleza muerta* mentions a number of painters from surrealism, a school whose artists were determined to "live" what they proposed for art as both Larco and Marcos do: Georges Braque, Pablo Picasso, Marcel Duchamp, Juan Gris, Hans Arp, and Jacques Vaché, among others. And, in addition to evoking painting (still life), the title of the novella, with its reference to the pipe, may well be an allusion to René Magritte's 1926 painting, *Ceci n'est pas une pipe*, in a gesture that foregrounds the artificiality of all art forms and undermines the notion of art as a window to anything. Magritte is also one of the painters evoked in *El jardín*.

For an analysis of *El jardín*'s intertextuality with paintings as well as a more complete discussion of those paintings, see Rosemary Geisdorfer Feal's insightful study.

17. Montero's reading of the novel is similar to mine in this respect (452).

18. Montero has read the text in conjunction with Donoso's *Historia personal del "boom"* and viewed both as tales of desire.

The text might also be read as an ironically self-critical dramatization of Donoso's frustration during the composition (although this time successful) of *La desesperanza*, published five years later, a novel that more directly concerns itself with the Chilean political situation that *El jardín* most often skirts.

19. Meléndez likens the image of the garden to that of the text needing to be both read and written (201–202).

20. The *la* he cannot see is ambiguous here; it might refer to either his novel or his wife, Gloria, who, we are told in the final chapter, is the bona fide author of "his novel," the one that he narrates and that we read, not the one that he unsuccessfully authors. Obviously, a literary character (even if cast as a writer) cannot see the "window"/novel nor the *I*/eye that sees him anymore than he can see the system/novel that contains him since he is metaphorically inside rather than outside the frame. As Gloria's creation, he would not perceive her or her novel; he would not know what he has written because she is the writer.

21. Kerr, who analyzes in detail the play of authorship and authority in the novel, has noted that the novel thwarts the possibility of stabilizing the seemingly authoritative narrating voice or seeing eye.

22. In fact there is even a distant genealogy between Blanca and Gloria, also the daughter of Latin American diplomats who had traveled and lived in Europe. In the final chapter, Gloria bemoans the fact that her parents did not see fit to provide a university education for either her or her sisters, but rather walked/exhibited them "por los efímeros salones de Europa a donde la diplomacia [los] iba arrastrando" (256) ["in the ephemeral salons of Europe that we were steered into by his diplomat's life" (234)].

23. Accepting that the first five chapters of the text are indeed penned by Gloria, Muñoz reads her disparagement of herself and other women as her internalization of the patriarchal, phallocentric discourse which she reconceptualizes from a gynecocentric optic. On the other hand, González reads the juxtaposition of the masculine and feminine narration as a type of androgyny.

24. Swanson sees the novel as a "peaceful synthesis," in which the traditional elements convey a mood of quietude ("Donoso and the Post-Boom" [524]).

25. Julio's capacity to see anything (like Marcos's) is also called into doubt in that the last chapter "reveals" to us that Gloria's attitude was the opposite of what he had perceived (or reported to us): she immediately threw the book that, according to him, she was so "placidly reading."

26. It is also possible that Donoso has chosen specifically the word *Monclús* as the final one of the text because he intended yet another linguistic play on words. The word *conclus* is the conjugated form (I and you) of "to conclude" in French. *Mon*, of course, makes the conclusion his own.

27. I am suggesting here not so much that Gloria is powerless but that Julio would like to see her as powerless.

Works Cited

Baudrillard, Jean. "Forgetting Foucault." *Humanities in Society* 3 (1980): 87–111.

Berger, John. *Ways of Seeing*. New York: Penguin, 1972.

Dolan, Jill. *The Feminist Spectator as Critic*. Ann Arbor: U Michigan P, 1988.

Donoso, José. *Casa de campo*. Barcelona: Seix Barral, 1978.

Donoso, José. *El jardín de al lado*. Barcelona: Seix Barral, 1981. (*The Garden Next Door*. Trans. Hardie St. Martin. New York: Grove, 1992.)

Donoso, José. *La misteriosa desaparición de la Marquesita de Loria*. Barcelona: Seix Barral, 1980.

Donoso, José. *El obsceno pájaro de la noche*. Barcelona: Seix Barral, 1971. (*The Obscene Bird of Night*. Trans. Hardie St. Martin and Leonard Mades. Boston: Nonpareil, 1979.)

Donoso, José. *Taratuta/Naturaleza muerta con cachimba*. Madrid: Mondadori, 1990. (*Taratuta/Still Life With Pipe*. Trans. Gregory Rabassa. New York: Norton, 1993.)

Donoso, José. *Tres novelitas burguesas*. Barcelona: Seix Barral, 1973. (*Sacred Families*. Trans. Andrée Conrad. New York: Knopf, 1977.)

Feal, Rosemary Geisdorfer. "Veiled Portraits: Donoso's Interartistic Dialogue in *El jardín de al lado*." *Modern Language Notes* 103 (1988): 398–418.

Foucault. Michel. *The History of Sexuality. Volume I: An Introduction*. Trans. Robert Hurley. New York: Vintage, 1980.

Freedman, Barbara. *Staging the Gaze: Postmodernism, Psychoanalysis, and Shakespearean Comedy*. Ithaca, NY: Cornell UP, 1991.

Gallop, Jane. *Thinking Through the Body*. New York: Columbia UP, 1988.

González, Flora. "The Androgynous Narrator in José Donoso's *El jardín de al lado*." *Revista de Estudios Hispánicos* 23.1 (1989): 99–113.

Gutiérrez Mouat, Ricardo. "Aesthetics, Ethics, and Politics in Donoso's *El jardín de al lado*." *PMLA* 106 (1991): 60–70.

Kerr, Lucille. "Authority in Play: José Donoso's *El jardín de al lado*." *Criticism* 25 (1983): 41–65.

Magnarelli, Sharon. "Disappearance Under the Cover of Language: The Case of the Marquesita de Loria." *Studies on the Works of José Donoso*. Ed. Miriam Adelstein. Lewiston, NY: Edwin Mellen, 1990. 101–129.

Magnarelli, Sharon. "*El obsceno pájaro de la noche*: Fiction, Monsters, and Packages." *Hispanic Review* 45 (1977): 413–419.

Meléndez, Priscilla. "Writing and Reading the Palimpsest: Donoso's *El jardín de al lado*." *Symposium* 41 (1987): 200–213.

Montero, Oscar. "*El jardín de al lado*: la escritura y el fracaso del éxito." *Revista Iberoamericana* 49 (1983): 449–470.

Muñoz, O. Willy. "Confrontaciones texto/sexuales en *El jardín de al lado* de Donoso." (unpublished essay).

Prince, Gerald. "Introduction to the Study of the Narratee." *Reader-Response Criticism: From Formalism to Post-Structuralism*. Ed. Jane P. Tompkins. Baltimore: Johns Hopkins UP, 1980. 7–25.

Swanson, Philip. "Donoso and the Post-Boom: Simplicity and Subversion." *Contemporary Literature* 28 (1987): 520–529.

Swanson, Philip. "Structure and Meaning in *La misteriosa desaparición de la Marquesita de Loria*." *Bulletin of Hispanic Studies* 63 (1986): 247–256.

Valenzuela, Luisa. *Cola de lagartija*. Buenos Aires: Bruguera, 1983.

Sara Castro-Klarén

MONUMENTS AND SCRIBES: *EL HABLADOR* ADDRESSES ETHNOGRAPHY

> It seems to me that the fundamental event in the intellectual life of Peru has been the growth of the idea of the Indian.
> —Jorge Basadre

I. Introduction

No longer held to be a transparent medium, writing has emerged as a key issue in anthropology. In *Writing Culture* (1986) James Clifford foregrounds the problematics of writing in the construction of the "science of man." He proposes a cultural poetics based on fusing literary theory and ethnography. *Writing Culture* focuses on the cultural and discursive making of the ethnographic text. This approach to content challenges the ideology of immediate experience as well as the notion of unmediated symbolic representation. We can, therefore, assume in the ethnographic text, itself a cultural construct, an inextricable web of the poetic and the political. Situated at the borders of two civilizations, classes, races, and/or genders, ethnographic texts attempt to address or conjugate the area *in between* two empowered systems of meaning.

A cursory reading of Mario Vargas Llosa's *El hablador* (1987) shows that this complex question of ethnographic poetics pulsates at the core of the novel. In fact, the inquiry included in the telling of the story of Tasurinchi mirrors Clifford's description of the implications involved in considering the rhetoric and politics of ethnographic writing. Both the novel and *Writing Culture* undermine the sense of "transparent modes of authority." Both draw attention to the "historical predicament of ethnography, the fact that it is always caught in the invention of cultures" (Clifford, 2). In fact, the critique of Zuratas's ethnography woven in the plot of *El hablador* addresses this very question.

Discursive similarities between fictional narratives and ethnographic accounts are more easily detected today,[1] as we become increasingly informed by the unfolding of the post-modern stage in the West. But the incorporation into Latin American narrative of discursive features and approaches to alterity derived from the ethnographic system of knowledge can be clearly traced at least as far back as Sarmiento's *Facundo, civilización y barbarie* (1845). It is pertinent to remember here that the regionalist novel found representational strategies in the discursive model provided by ethnography. The conditions of a good many texts authored by Latin American writers have been best articulated in the *interstitial* position of the ethnographer. Moreover, recent studies on *Doña Bárbara*[2] and *Os Sertões*, for example, demonstrate the determining presence of an ethnographic model capable of allowing the representation of the "the other within."

Nevertheless, it seems that precisely because the regional novel posits a dichotomy between urban (the subject) written discourse and rural (the object) oral discourse, Vargas Llosa finds this strategy static and spent, as he has indicated in more than one recent interview. He states a preference for a symphonic intertextuality in which the velocity with which voices and points of view are mixed muffles the earlier distinctions associated with the regionalist novel. The author of *Conversación en La Catedral* (1969) thus sets his textual practice apart from the redundant taxonomy and stylistic gymnastics that the description of the "other" within or without has wrought in so many classics of the regionalist novel. Thus it would seem that *El hablador*, relying on a technique of swift splicing which blurs time, point of view, voice, and space, overcomes the subject-object dichotomy of the regional novel. What is more, by incorporating a critique of ethnography's relation to its object in the relation between Zuratas and the Machiguenga, the novel joins in the post-modern deconstruction of writing, the subject, and their verbal constructs.

However, a post-modern reading of *El hablador* also opens the possibility of reading the novel against the grain of its own manifest interpretative plan. Not satisfied with the novel's critique of Zuratas's anthropology, the reader must also delve into the novel as a master narrative that deploys the narratives of Zuratas and Tasurinchis as the "other" of its own subject. Thus Clifford's observation regarding the dynamics of writing the other, namely the idea that "every version of an 'other', wherever found, is also a construction of the self," (23) serves here as a point of departure for an analysis of the novel's poetics cum politics.

Whether we take this "other" to mean the alienating relation with the rival spelled out by Sartre (hell is the other), or the specular "other" of the mirror stage postulated by Lacan, or the "other" as primitive man elaborated by ethnography, *the other* condenses the alienating contents assigned to either the rival, the unconscious, or both.[3] In "Ethno-Graphy, Speech, or the Space of the Other: Jean de Léry," Michel de Certeau has neatly drawn the opposition between the subject and the object of ethnographic discourse. The ethnographer (subject) belongs to a cultural field characterized by writing, history, identity, and consciousness. He is the subject and object of modern historiography. The object of ethnographic discourse, on the other hand, is "primitive man" or the "savage." He appears in an ambiguous field, somewhere between nature and culture. This object is defined by the subject's four corresponding oppositions: orality, spatiality (systems without history), alterity, and the unconscious. Thus people such as Tasurinchi live within a condition "a status of collective phenomenon, refering to a signficance foreign to them and given only to knowledge originating elsewhere (209)."[4]

When it is thus defined we can see that Vargas Llosa has often responded to the call of the "other" as designated by ethnography and the regionalist novel. In fact, his novels are more often than not structured on an axial dichotomy that separates clearly the discursive space of the narrator from the space of the action in the novel. Set objects of discursive formation, such as Sarmiento's "gaucho malo," the ethnographer's guide, or Euclides da Cunha's apocalyptic rebel, have their counterparts in the fiction of the author of *La guerra del fin del mundo* (1983). But there is a very important difference between the poetics and the politics of *El hablador* and the ethnographic discourse that informs the regional novel. It is this difference that I propose to explore here.

II. Poetics.

Vine a Firenze para olvidarme por un tiempo del Perú [I came to Firenze to forget Peru for a while].
(*El hablador*, 7)

The opening sentence of *El hablador* constitutes an invitation to enter into a metafictional pact. The novel as it tells the story also reflects upon the history of its own elaboration. When Vargas Llosa published his second novel, *La casa verde* (1965), his first text on *life* in the Amazonian jungle, he also published a companion volume in which he revisited the making of this exceedingly complex book. In *Historia secreta de una novela* (1971), we find, much as in the alternate chapters of *El hablador*, the entertaining story of the adventures of Vargas Llosa as journalist. The character depicted in both *Historia secreta* and *El hablador* is an enthusiastic, amusing, decisive, and curious man who thrives within the tight circle of friends who await his return to Lima. They seem always ready to join in any new escapades that such renewal of old family and fraternal bonds may bring. In that context, Vargas Llosa the journalist makes ready for his forays into the jungle, where the possibilities for a reportage of the exotic at home abound. This reportage marks the deployment of the subject situated in Lima and other writing capitals into a "primitive" and raw, oral, outer world that closely corresponds to the object of ethnography as outlined by Michel de Certeau. Like so many other travelers who were to follow in the footsteps of Jean de Léry, the journalist brings out his literary treasure and tells the story of his encounter with Tasurinchi, the naked man.

Underpinning the value ascribed to the myths told by "primitive" people such as the Machiguenga is the notion that the culture of exotic peoples constitutes an amalgam of beliefs whose meaning is, like the feelings and verbal constructs of obsessive neurotics, inaccessible to them but decipherable to the reason of the ethnographer, the psychoanalyst, or the journalist. This assessment of the value (to us) of the culture of the so-called primitive peoples can be traced, in some literary circles, to a misreading of Freud's *Totem and Taboo* (1913).[5] For while Freud did establish a parallel between the constitution of taboo-prohibitions that condense ambivalent emotions and the logic of projection of the obsessive neurotic—a hostile impulse against someone the patient loves—(64–74), the point he made was that such hostile impulses against the authority of the father are to be found at the core of all religions. Freud's best examples were drawn from the Judeo-Christian foundational myths and their contradictory exaltation of God the Father (140–155) rather than from the less familiar Maori stories (30–35) on taboo objects. What Freud demonstrates here is the wisdom of his own working supposition: "Where there is a prohibition there must be an underlying desire" (70).

In *El hablador*, the culture within which the myths and truths that Tasurinchi tells takes its shape somewhere in an invisible and unstable divide between nature and culture. The clearing in the jungle, the place that Tasurinchi calls home, is not registered in the cartography of the journalist. This nameless place appears, allegorically, as the field of the inchoate. The disorder of Tasurinchi's performative telling of stories, themselves all too well known to his Machiguenga listeners, awaits to be traversed by the order and reason of writing so as to be made "universally" meaningful in as much as they contain a version of our subconscious. It is therefore not a surprise to see that the possible meeting with the storyteller is anticipated by the journalist with a kind of trepidation that mixes contradictory feelings of sublime pleasure and contempt, faith and disbelief, elation and disillusionment. Thus the story of the emotional ambivalences of the future author of Tasurinchi emerges as the subplot that will eventually take over the entire novel. The opening and the closing of the novel situate the author and his covalent reader in a shared place of writing from which the question of the naked storyteller is pondered as if *El hablador* were retracing the tracks left by *Tristes Tropiques* (1955).[6]

This search for the naked storyteller follows the tracks of readings and missed readings which, entwined, become the invisible map for the text of the novel as it is eventually published. But this reading map is not drawn with single road lines heading towards fixed destinations. Each road line rests on a bedding of other tracks or pre-texts. Some of these pre-texts are clearly visible, others are partly buried and others are almost obliterated. Yet all of these lines in the end weave the text of the fiction.

In *El hablador*, Vargas Llosa, playing a Cervantean game, conflates the two tracks he kept apart in *La casa verde* and *Historia secreta*. Not only does the "history" of the writing of the story appear in alternating chapters with a simulacrum of an ethnographic representation of the Machiguenga, but the "author" or subject of the novel, affirming the post-modern critique of ethnography and the current dismantling of our received notions of the truth/fiction opposition, weaves into the story of the storyteller a critique of ethnographic discourse in Peru. This critique focuses on the construction and present status of its chief object (the Indian) and its subject (the ethnographer).

It is this folding and unfolding of narratives, appearance and disappearance of discursive subjects and objects, that separates the works of Vargas Llosa from the regionalist novel mode of representing the "other" within the subject. Neither the "reality" of *La casa verde* nor the world of the Machiguenga conforms to the writing subject's personal memory of place, society, or time. Unlike the writing subject posited in Gallegos or Güiraldes, Vargas Llosa does not textualize a return to origins or to the site of childhood as does *Don Segundo Sombra*. The urban subject who reflects, nostalgically at times, the backlands of Venezuela in *Doña Bárbara*, for instance, returns, as he fictionalizes Santos Luzardo, to a personal past that is no more but will remain in the lettered memory. In inscribing the place of childhood the subject constitutes itself as such and makes possible a passage between past and present. But writing for Gallegos, Güiraldes, or Arguedas also bears witness to the alienation of the self as "other," as designated by the metropolitan system of meaning and power relations.

Somewhat less dramatized, but nevertheless similar in kind, this process of dividing the continuum of the self into the time of writing (subject) and the time of formative identity as the "other" appears already as the crux of the matter in the pages authored by Garcilaso de la Vega, Inca, and Guaman Poma de Ayala. "Autoethnography" is the name that Mary Louise Pratt has recently coined for this scission performed in the constitution of the self by writing and conquest. Pratt defines the auto-ethnographic text as one in

> which people undertake to describe themselves in ways that engage with representations others have made of them. Thus if ethnographic texts are those in which European metropolitan subjects represent to themselves their others (usually conquered others), autoethnographic texts are representations that the so-defined others construct *in response to* or in dialogue with those texts. Autoethnographic texts are not, then, what are usually thought of as autochthonous forms of expression or self-representation [as Andean quipus were (35)].

But autoethnography does not describe Vargas Llosa's fiction. The subject of enunciation in his works does not acknowledge bearing the "other," inscribed by the metropolitan gaze, within him. Nor does it perform upon itself the scission left by the deployment of self as both object and subject. Rather, the subject in *El hablador* posits a monologic discourse naturalized and secure in Western representational systems of the "other"—photography, television, tape recording, or writing. Although at times the subject engages in ironic stances of self-portrayal, this is nevertheless a subject who does not memorialize, in the story of Tasurinchi, a personal or collective past. The writing subject of *El hablador*, closer to the model provided in *Tristes Tropiques*, embarks on a voyage that departs from the center, where the subject appears anchored, and pushes out to the periphery of consciousness where the "lost world" of the Nambikwara or the Machiguenga awaits representation, recovery, existence.

Like Lévi-Strauss in Paris attending the almost secret lectures given at the Jardin des Plantes by some obscure returning traveler from the edges of humanity, Vargas Llosa in Florence partly questions the veracity of ethnographic reports and ponders the truth value of the treasured collections set in dead images. The opening scene of the novel echoes, but also distorts, Lévi-Strauss's own irritation with the travel book. While the anthropologist remarks on "how thoroughly the notion of travel has become corrupted by the notion of power" (18) and opens *Tristes Tropiques* with an uneasy sense of guilt and loss, *El hablador* embarks on a journey that will, by contrast, affirm and certify the power of writing to produce objects of consciousness that create blinding "reality effects."

If *El hablador* emulates *Tristes Tropiques* in the initial gesture of travel from the place of reason and knowledge to the outer limits of humanity in the tropics, the differences between the novel and the ethnography on the Caduveo and the Nambikwara go beyond the received generic facts that separate anthropology from fiction. Some of the more important differences can be grouped around the construction of the subject and its relation to the object. As Lévi-Strauss recollects his departure from France in the wake of World War II, with mixed emotions, he writes an epitaph to the received ethnography. In "Quest for Power" (38–46) he questions the explorer's account of "primitive" cultures. He is troubled by the "scientific status" of the traveler's account. He also finds food for thought in the interest animating the reception of the portrayal of the "primitive." Finally, of his own métier, he asks: "Are we to draw a parallel with the Marco Polos of our own day who bring back from those same territories—in the form, this time, of photographs—the heightened sensations which grow ever more indispensable to our society as it founders deeper and deeper in its own boredom?" (40).

Suspicious of the implicit commodification of the "other," *Tristes Tropiques* inaugurates the self-reflexive fieldwork account current now.[7] Far from positing the ethnographer as a character in a fictional text, as Philippe Lejeune does in *Le Pacte Autobiographique* (1975), Lévi-Strauss is nevertheless aware of the unthought dialogic relationship implicit in the production of texts in the writing of ethnographic accounts.

His paradoxical feeling of having harvested ashes instead of treasure goes hand in hand with the emerging view that "culture" is always relational and that therefore cultural accounts take place between two subjects—not subjects and objects—involved in relations of power. Faced with the impossibility of producing a completely intelligible acount of the "other," Lévi-Strauss writes:

Myself, the already-grey predecessor of these "explorers," I may well
be the only white traveller to have brought back nothing but ashes from
my journeys. . . . Either I am a traveller in ancient times, and faced
with a prodigious spectacle which would be almost entirely unintel-
ligible to me and might indeed provoke me to mockery or disgust; or I
am a traveller of our day hastening in search of a vanished reality. In
either case I am the loser .... I am the victim of a double infirmity: what
I see is an affliction to me; and what I do not see, a reproach (45).

It is this double infirmity of the impossible subject-object relation in
ethnography that Vargas Llosa drives to its own absurd limits in the
solipsistic discourse of Zuratas-Mascarita- Tasurinchi-Vargas Llosa. With
a very important local political twist, *El hablador* will make use of such
double infirmity in order to propose the idea that the naked storyteller,
and, by extension, Indians in Peru, are but the invention of ethnography.

III. The Politics of the Poetics.

Allí estaban los machiguengas lanzando el arpón desde la orilla del río
. . . . Allí estaban decorando minuciosamente sus caras. . . fermentando
la yuca. . . . Las fotos mostraban con elocuencia cuán pocos eran en esa
inmensidad de cielo, agua y vegetación que los rodeaba, su vida frágil
y frugal, su aíslamiento, su arcaísmo, su indefensión. Era verdad: sin
demagogia ni esteticismo.

[There were the Machiguengas, aiming a harpoon from the bank of a
river . . . . There they were, decorating their faces . . . fermenting
casava . . . . The photos eloquently showed how few of them there
were in the immensity of sky, water, and vegetation that surrounded
them, how fragile and frugal their life was; their isolation, their archaic
ways, their helplessness. It was true: neither demagoguery nor
aestheticism *El hablador*, 8–9; *The Storyteller*, 4–5].

As portrayed in *El hablador*, Zuratas's search and fieldwork postu-
late a Machiguenga culture that has not been, nor will ever be found.
Giving in to the force of his desire, we are to assume, Zuratas becomes
the very "hablador" that he pursues. He even allows a photograph to be
taken of his (self) impersonation. In having become the "speaker" among
the Machiguenga (as Vargas Llosa among us) he proceeds to fictionalize
the consciousness of the culture in question. Thus what he sees of the
Machiguenga is the effect of ethnographic discourse, and what he does

not see marks both the invisibility of that culture and the limits of his discourse. The Machiguenga that we do see in the novel, the circle of lost and hungry people, are the ruins of Zuratas's desire. They are not even the Machiguenga of the photographs exibited in Florence and in which we must assume Zuratas is posing as the speaker. The Machiguenga we see are a reproach inasmuch as they are portrayed as mere bodies.

Thus the novel traces a full circle, from accepting the positive gravity of Malfati's photographs, which motivate the search for the speaker, to the complete—fictionalized—deconstruction of tribal society in the telling of the story of that search. In the circumference of the circle lies hidden the preestablished objective of the narrative—which at all times is kept secret from the reader. It is the denial of the object outside the field of consciousness of the self who writes. The autonomous existence of indigenous cultures is now an idea to be debated in the fictional and fictionalizing space of novelistic discourse.

The novel's polyglossia will plot the notion that the ethnographer's discourse is but the simulacrum of his desire and that its truth status is no different from that of the fiction the novelist simultaneously crafts. The ultimate proof of this proposition is *El hablador* itself, for the novel displays a powerful command of the topoi of classic ethnography in its unmistakable kinship with Bronislaw Malinowski's *Argonauts of the Western Pacific* (1922).

But the novel not only establishes an ethnographic object of desire. It also states a pre-text in Zurata/Mascarita. It is the previous (result unknown) search of the anthropologists which provides the entry not only into the jungle but also into a previous dialogue on the relation of ethnography to *indigenismo* and of these two discursive formations to the shaping of a national future for Peru based on the identification and understanding of its historical actors.

The politics of the poetics of the novel emerge when the entire text is situated *between* two subjects engaged in relation of power[8]—Vargas Llosa the novelist and *indigenismo*. This conjunction shifts the novel's manifest discursive balance. The portrayal of the Machiguenga's cultural story can now be regarded as a *divertimento* that charmingly breaks into the development of the central theme: the interpretation of cultures. In other words, this reading of the politics of the novel renders Tasurinchi as the "gracioso," a self-deprecating alter ego, in the tragedy played by the acknowledged hero, the novelist, and the antagonist, *indigenista* ethnographers.

IV. Monuments and Scribes.

> Eres un indigenista cuadriculado Mascarita—le tomé el pelo—. Ni
> más ni menos que en los años treinta. Como el Dr. Luis Valcárcel, de
> joven . . . . ¿O sea que tenemos que resucitar el Tahuantinsuyo?
> ¿También los sacrificios humanos, los quipus, la trepanación de
> cráneos con cuchillos de piedra? Es gracioso que el último indigenista
> del Perú sea un judío, Mascarita.

> ["You're an Indigenist to the nth degree, Mascarita," I teased him.
> "Just like the ones in the thirties. Like Dr. Luis Valcárcel when he was
> young . . . . Or should we bring back the Tahuantinsuyo? Human
> sacrifice, quipus, trepanation with stone knives. It's a laugh that Peru's
> last Indigenist turns out to be Jewish, Mascarita" *El hablador*, 97; *The
> Storyteller*, 99].

El hablador could have told the story of Tasurinchi without recourse
to Mascarita. The discursive function of this symbol-ridden character
(mask for Vargas Llosa, for the author, for the ethnographer, for the
indigenistas, for Tasurinchi, for Zuratas the Peruvian Jew, for Marxist
intellectuals, for the storytelling function of the mind) is to serve, prin-
cipally, as the *indigenista* straw man. Vargas Llosa aims the plot of the
entire novel as a well-placed projectile against the immobile silhouette of
indigenismo as portrayed in the novel, for it is clear that no *indigenista*
ever advocated a "return to craneal trepanation" and that human sacrifice
has not been the exclusive practice of American indigenous cultures. The
novel's own answer to the question the character Vargas Llosa asks of his
college acquaintance Mascarita is to present his novelistic ethnographic
account of the Machiguenga. In this version, the Machiguenga appear as
an Indian culture surviving in the Peruvian Amazon. They are an ele-
mental and degraded human organization incapable of producing a
material or symbolic culture that might enable them to go on autono-
mously. If ever they were a vigorous and viable human organization with
a storyteller to keep the group's memory alive, they are now exhuasted
and have come to the point of extinction. The storyteller has lost his
bearings. Neither he nor the witch doctor knows what he is doing anymore. The rhetorical and political ploy of the novel is to attempt to substitute the image of one Indian (culture) for another. The Machiguenga, as
fact–ionalized in *El hablador*, are offered in place of the Tahuantinsuyo as
reconstructed by the work of archeology and ethnography. This process

of substitution entails an erasure of what Jorge Basadre, Peru's most distinguished modern historian, has called the fundamental event in Peruvian intellectual life: the growth of the idea of the Indian. (Tord, 193). Basadre's statement squarely contradicts the vision that *El hablador* offers from the moment the traveler and his television crew descend upon a jungle clearing and meet their guides and sources (American Baptist missionaries).

The growth of the idea of the Indian can be documented in several ways. Almost any bibliography on Peru could prove to be an appropriate vehicle. Recently there has been a greater emphasis on searching out and establishing the links between the culture of the living Peruvian population and the nation's pan-Andean past. Sustained by the work of archeology and anthropology, the ethno-historians have produced remarkable studies that document the resistance, survival, and response of pan-Andean culture in spite of the destruction brought about by Spanish colonial rule. As signposts for the purposes of this paper we should mention John Murra's *Formaciones económicas y políticas del mundo andino* (1975), Luis G. Lumbreras's *Visión arqueológica del Perú milenario* (1990), Manuel Burga's *Nacimiento de una utopía, muerte y resurrección de los Incas* (1988), Edmundo Bendezú's *La otra literatura peruana* (1986), Luis Millones's *Historia y poder en los Andes centrales* (1987), and finally *Entre el mito y la historia, psicoanálisis y pasado andino* (1987), a book written by a group of ethno-historians and psychoanalysts. This recent corpus indicates clearly that, since independence at least, a growing sector of intellectuals and academics in Peru have been working at the task of reclaiming the ancient Andes as part of the history of the Peruvian republic. Such reclamation has entailed a labor of monumentalization of the discursive object which since 1492 appears under the sign "Indian".⁹ Tangled in a polemical embrace with "grammar school" (cuadriculado) *indigenismo*, the Machiguenga of *El hablador* appears as the part that stands for the whole. This metonymy marks the beginning of the dismantling of the Tahuantinsuyo.

Pablo Macera, in his *Trabajos de historia* (1977), sees *indigenismo* as a phenomenon already observable among the *lascasiano* missionaries of the seventeenth century. Macera writes that, in spite of an already deep racial prejudice, by 1646 the image of a docile, suffering, simple, good, and quiet Indian had appeared. A rational creature, he was a free and good vassal of Spain (Macera 2:303–324). However, the monumentalization of the Indian, as a historical being capable of building a remarkable and original civilization, does not appear in Peru until scientific archeological studies begin to offer the first visible and material proof, such as in the exploratory work of José Dombey (1778–85). With the writings of Dombey the circulation of previously forgotten place names began again, but of course as part of a new discursive space. The proscribed and forgotten names of ancient temples and urban centers became infused with new meaning for a new sector of society—the literate groups. These places became sites for scientific scrutiny. Rimac, Pachacamac, Lurin, Huaura, and Lambayeque, were emptied of their value in Andean myth and worship and relocated into the space of the sciences of man. As signs they were reinvested with the prestige of the modern Western inquiry into antiquity. A temporal depth was added to the name Tahuantinsuyo. Reason and knowledge became associated with the remnants of Andean culture.

At the end of the eighteenth century, foreigners and members of the incipient Peruvian intelligentsia began the exploration of subterranean Cuzco. An Italian explorer, Coletti, wrote "Vita dei Monarchi Peruviani" (ms. 1780). And Hípolito Unanue, at the height of the Enlightenment in Peru, authored his groundbreaking *Idea general de los monumentos del antiguo Perú* (1790–94). With his articles on Tiahuanacu, Chachapoyas, Cuzco, Quito, and Lucanas, originally published in the *Mercurio Peruano* between 1790 and 1794, the idea that the "antiguos peruanos" in spite of the easily available ocular evidence regarding their descendants, could have been "irrational and unintelligent brutes" could no longer be sustained. (Macera, 2: 314).

While "discoveries" of archeological evidence increased through the nineteenth century, they reached a crescendo with the work on Chavín and Paracas by Julio C. Tello, the first "Indian" (a foreshadowing of Tasurinchi?) to write on the past of his own ancestors. A less scientific but emotionally and aesthetically charged approach is condensed in the literary and ideological writing of the *indigenistas*. It began to bridge the separation between antiquity and contemporaneity enforced by the novelty of the scientific approach and its archeological object.

Beyond the work of ethnography and the texts of the autoethnographers, the *Siete ensayos de interpretación de la realidad peruana* (1923) by José Carlos Mariátegui remains the galvanizing modern text that assumes the Indian demographic majority to be the past, present, and future of the nation. The title of a more recent work by Macera shows yet another, even more sweeping attempt to see the history of Peru as a continuum despite the gaps. *Visión histórica del Perú (Del paleolítico al*

Proceso de 1968), published in 1978, is intended to be an upper-school textbook which, like the text by Lumbreras, asserts the vitality and promise of what remains of the pan-Andean cultures (150). The power struggle for a vision of history and future of the country is clearly stated between those who, like Lumbreras or Arguedas, see the country's basic Indian roots as the foundation of all future development and those who argue that the "inferiority" and feebleness of Indian cultures spelled their own extinction before the tidal wave of Western "progress."

It is precisely this bridge between past and present that is at issue in *El hablador*. The novel stresses a break between the Indian body and a possible Indian culture. The story, which articulates the "mind" of the Machiguenga, although it plays with the notion of the "science of the concrete," in the end succumbs to the idea that tribal societies such as the Machiguenga are endowed solely with a prelogical mind. Edmund Leach, among other anthropologists, makes clear that such an interpretation is not only a misreading of Lévi-Strauss's work on the symbolic structures of "primitive" cultures, but also a misinterpretation of the worlds that "primitive" and "civilized" people alike build and experience:

> Primitive people are no more mystical in their approach to reality than we are. The distinction rather is between a logic which is constructed out of observed contrasts in the sensory qualities of concrete objects and a logic which depends upon the formal contrast of entirely abstract entities. The latter kind of logic which even in our own society is used only by highly specialized experts, is a different way of talking about the same kind of thing (88).

Further, a novel which articulates the savage mind of the Machiguenga by implication rejects the moral thesis advanced by Uriel García in *El nuevo indio* (1930). Trying to resolve the impasse posed by the idea of Indians as mere bodies without a meaningful culture and as a destroyed civilization disconnected from the present population, Uriel García, one of the *indigenistas* of the thirties, proposes the idea of a new Indian observable in current costumes and institutions. In his chapter on "Los nuevos indios" he writes on Garcilaso de la Vega, Inca, and Tupac Amaru II as exemplary figures of the dawn of a new era in whom "spirit will be predominant over race." Thus the writer and the rebel take the place of cultural heroes in Uriel García's *indigenista* account of a national foundation.

In contrast with this search for continuity, the photographs of the Machiguenga in Florence mark an unwelcome rupture for the consciousness of the author. *El hablador* introduces the Machiguenga by double layers of estrangement. They appear first in photographs taken by Gabriel Malfati and exhibited in a tiny back street gallery in Florence. Thus removed from the subjectivity that interprets the captionless photographs, the Machiguenga people are seen as "rows of seedlings" (almácigos de hombres y mujeres). According to the logic of the novel the idea that "they" may be the same as ourselves constitutes the "absurdity of *indigenismo*." For *El hablador* the past monumentalized by *indigenismo* is over and done with. Like the Machiguenga it makes for a good yarn for storytellers, but it cannot be the foundation of the future, for it is exhausted and extinct.

V. Conclusions.

According to the poetics and politics of *El hablador* the Machiguenga constitute a primitive culture which is virtually extinct. The speaker, one of the few Machiguenga institutions in which we could recognize ourselves, appears to be the invention of a maladjusted, physically deformed person, who, had he been born Machiguenga, would have been the victim of infanticide. The reality of the Machiguenga as referent, perhaps like the history of the Andean peoples, is dissolved by the transformational power of the novel's polyglossia and our current understanding of the crisis of representation. Like Saul (the apostle), Zuratas (the Peruvian Jew) experiences a conversion. Mascarita speaks a gospel. Just like Saul/Paul, Mascarita creates a logos out of a few loose and uncorroborated stories. The uncontaminated and "pure" Indians that Mascarita claims to have found appear not as a construction of self but rather as the figment of desire with no referent whatever outside language.

    In criss-crossing from the fiction to the metafiction of the ethnographic report, *El hablador* plows under two of the major branches of ethnographic discourse: Malinowski's functionalism and Lévi-Strauss's reflexive anthropology. The narrative power of the novel enacts the reality of the primitive mind and the costumes and mores of the fictionalized Machiguenga. The disciplined organization of the contents of the absorbing tale is often reminiscent of Malinowski's *Magic, Science and Religion*.[10] In fact "Baloma: The Spirits of the Dead" seems to have remarkable coincidences with the novel's rendition of the Machiguenga afterworld. The concepts of Baloma (dead man's spirit) and more specially *Kosi* (ghost of the dead man) are the objects of charming and seductive passages in Tasurinchi's confused attempts to reason beyond the bricolage of the concrete.[11]

As in previous fictions, in composing the story of the Machiguenga, together with the story of the ethnographic genre, Vargas Llosa cuts and splices a cornucopia of discourses and rhetorics at the microscopic level. And although the last chapter of the novel would close the opening into the jungle and return us to civilization in Florence, because the drama of the novel concerns the Machiguenga, the story actually ends with the scene in which the "lost" tribe, unable to produce food in their habitat, await the planeload of international donations. In this scene of abjection, the rest of the "Indian" peoples of Peru must be metonymically included for the reasons detailed above. For the Indians then, there is no history. "Para los machiguenga, la historia no avanza ni retrocede: gira, se repite . . . [han] optado por sobrevivir por el reflejo tradicional: la diáspora. Echarse una vez más a andar, como en el más persistente de sus mitos." [For the Machiguengas, history marches neither forward nor backward: it goes around and around in circles, repeats itself. . . . [they have] opted for the traditional response ensuring their survival: diaspora. Start walking once again as in the most persistent of their myths. (*El hablador*, 229–230; *The Storyteller*, 240)].

Taking into consideration the fact that the overwhelming majority of the population of contemporary Peru is classified as Indian or part Indian, a reading of the politics of *El hablador* would spell a final dispersal of a people who are portrayed as having not only lost their collective memory and territory but even their ability to speak. Though *El hablador*, resting on the critical inquiry of the West's avant-garde, would stand as the epitaph of a globalized *indigenismo*, as prompted by ethnography, it is clear from the current political struggle in Peru that the news of such a demise is highly exaggerated. If anything, what the political scene in Peru now shows is an eclosion of speakers and voices contending for power to define themselves as subjects of praxis and discourses that have previously been repressed or misrepresented.[12] Both *El hablador* and this essay were written before Vargas Llosa ran and lost in the race for the presidency of Peru. His misreadings of the self-understanding of the diverse Peruvian populace attest to the perils of writing about culture from libraries and on the basis of photographic exhibits of the exotic. Missing from the poetics and politics of his writing is a recognition of a mutual good shared by writer and "speaker."

Notes

1. For a discussion of the problematics of "literature" as a differentiated and stable set of discursive practices of unalterable value and function see Eagleton, 1–16. Eagleton argues that "Anything can be literature, and anything which is regarded as unalterable and unquestionable literature—Shakespeare for example—can cease to be literature. Any belief that the study of literature is a stable, well-defined entity, as entomology is to the study of insects, can be abandoned as a chimera" (10). "All literary works are re-written, if only unconsciously, by the societies which read them" (12), and such re-writing takes place within the dynamics of ideology, for there is no possibility of a disinterested reading. Ideology is here understood to mean "those modes of feeling, valuing, perceiving and believing which have some kind of relation to the maintenance and reproduction of social power" (15).

2. See Alonso.

3. See Jameson, 353–354.

4. de Certeau, 225. De Certeau's ethnographic features are derived from his reading of Joseph François Lafitau, *Moeurs des sauvages ameriquains, comparées aux moeurs des premiers temps* (1724), which he considers to be the first modern ethnographic work. De Certeau studies here Jean de Léry's classic *Histoire d'un voyage fait en la terre du Brésil* (1578). The chapter on ethnography appears in English in his *The Writing of History*, 1988.

5. Aware of the difference between a cultural creation such as the concept of prohibition imbedded in taboo and the individual's neurosis, Freud writes that "in maintaining the essential similarities between taboo prohibitions and moral prohibitions, I have not sought to dispute the fact that there must be a psychological difference between them . . . . But after all taboo is not a neurosis but a social institution." (70)

6. See Lévi-Strauss, *Tristes Tropiques*. In considering the entire presentation of the function of storytelling in *El hablador*, one must of course also keep in mind Lévi-Strauss's claim that storytelling is one of the primary instances of the mind. See *The Raw and the Cooked*.

7. See, among others, Rosaldo.

8. Michel Foucault writes in *Power/Knowledge* that "power is essentially that which represses . . . . If power is properly speaking the way in which relations of forces are deployed and given concrete expression . . . should we not analyze it primarily in terms of *struggle, conflict and war*? . . . Power is war, a war continued by other means." (90)

9. "The most obvious way to catalogue discursive formations would be to group together those serious speech acts which refer to a common object. This is what Foucault attempted in his book on madness, selecting for archeological study those statements which had as their object a certain experience. But by the time of the *Archeology* he realized that, far from being differentiated from their objects, discursive formations produce the object about which they speak." See Dreyfus and Rabinow (61).

10. The organization of the novel follows rather closely the chapter headings of *Magic, Science and Religion*.

11. See "The Science of the Concrete" in Lévi-Strauss, *The Savage Mind*.

12. In this light it is ironic to see that Sendero Luminoso, for totally different reasons, also rejects a good number of *indigenista* novels. See Mayer, "Peru in Deep

Trouble: Mario Vargas Llosa's 'Inquest in the Andes' Re-examined," *Cultural Anthropology* 6:4 (1991): 481.

Works Cited

Alonso, J. Carlos. *The Spanish American Novel: Modernity and Autochthony.* Cambridge: Cambridge UP, 1989.

Bendezú, Edmundo. *La otra literatura peruana.* México: Fondo de Cultura Económica, 1986.

Burga, Manuel. *Nacimiento de una utopía, muerte y resurrección de los Incas.* Lima: Instituto de Apoyo Agrario, 1988.

Clifford, James and George E. Marcus. Eds. *Writing Culture, The Poetics and Politics of Ethnography.* Berkeley: California UP, 1986.

de Certeau, Michel. *The Writing of History.* Trans. Tom Conley. New York: Columbia UP.1988.

Dreyfus, Hubert L., and Paul Rabinow. *Michel Foucault: Beyond Structuralism and Hermeneutics.* Chicago: Chicago UP, 1983.

Eagleton, Terry. *Literary Theory: An Introduction.* Minneapolis: Minnesota UP, 1983.

Flores Galindo, Alberto. *Buscando un Inca.* Lima: Instituto de Apoyo Agrario, 1987.

Foucault, Michel. *Power/Knowledge: Selected Interviews and Other Writings, 1972–77.* Ed. Colin Gordon. Trans. Colin Gordon, Joseph Mepham, Kate Sofer. New York: Pantheon, 1980.

Freud, Sigmund. *Totem and Taboo: Some Points of Agreement Between the Mental Lives of Savages and Neurotics.* Trans. James Strachey. New York: W.W. Norton, 1950.

García, José Uriel. *El nuevo indio.* 1930. Lima: Editorial Universo, 1973. First edition, 1930.

González Echevarría, Roberto. *Myth and Archive: A Theory of Latin American Narrative.* Cambridge: Cambridge UP, 1990.

Jameson, Fredric. "Imaginary and Symbolic in Lacan: Marxism, Psychoanalytic Criticism and the Problem of the Subject." *Literature and Psychoanalysis; The Question of Reading Otherwise.* Ed. Shoshona Feldman. Baltimore: Johns Hopkins UP, 1982.

Lafitau, Joseph Francois. *Moeurs des sauvages américains, comparées aux moeurs des premiers temps.* 1724.

Leach, Edmund. *Claude Lévi-Strauss.* New York: Viking, 1970.

Lejeune, Philippe. *On Autobiography*. Ed. Paul John Eakin. Trans. Katherine Leary. Minneapolis: Minnesota UP, 1989.

de Léry, Jean. *Histoire d'un voyage fait en la terre du Brésil*. Geneva, 1578.

de Léry, Jean. *History of a Voyage to the Land of Brazil*. Trans. and Intro. Janet Whatley. Berkeley: U of California P, 1990.

Lévi-Strauss, Claude. *The Raw and the Cooked*. Trans. John and Doreen Weightman. New York: Harper Torchbooks, 1969.

Lévi-Strauss, Claude. *The Savage Mind*. Chicago: Chicago UP, 1986.

Lévi-Strauss, Claude. *Tristes Tropiques*. Trans. John Russell. New York: Atheneum, 1968.

Lumbreras, Luis. *Visión arqueológica del Perú milenario*. Lima: Milla Batres, 1990.

Macera, Pablo. *Trabajos de historia*. 4 vols. Lima: Instituto Nacional de Cultura, 1977.

Macera, Pablo. *Visión histórica del Perú (Del paleolítico al Proceso del 68)*. Lima: Milla Batres, 1978

Malinowski, Bronislaw. *Argonauts of the Western Pacific: An Account of Native Enterprise and Adventure in the Archipelagoes of Melanesian New Guinea*. London: Routledge and Kegan, 1922.

Malinowski, Bronislaw. *Magic, Science and Religion and Other Essays*. Intro. Robert Redfield. New York: Doubleday, 1954.

Mayer, Enrique. "Peru in Deep Trouble: Mario Vargas Llosa's 'Inquest in the Andes Re-examined'." *Cultural Anthropology* 6 (1991).

Millones, Luis. *Historia y poder en los Andes centrales (Desde los orígenes al siglo xvii)*. Madrid: Alianza Universitaria, 1987.

Murra, John. *Formaciones económicas y políticas del mundo andino*. Lima: Instituto de Estudios Peruanos, 1975.

Ortiz, Alejandro. *De Adaneva a Inkarri*. Lima: Retablo de Papel Ediciones, 1973.

Pratt, Mary Louise. "Arts of the Contact Zone." *Profession 91*, New York: Modern Language Association, 1991.

Rosaldo, Renato. *Culture and Truth, The Making of Social Analysis*. Boston: Beacon Press, 1989.

Rostoworowski de Diez Canseco, María. *Historia del Tahuantinsuyo*. Lima: Instituto de Estudios Peruanos, 1988.

Tello, Julio C. *Chavín, cultura matriz de la civilización andina*. Primera Parte. Lima: Archivo Julio C. Tello, Universidad Nacional de San Marcos, 1960.

Tord, Enrique. *El indio en los ensayistas peruanos, 1848–1948*. Lima: Editoriales Unidas, 1978.

Vargas Llosa, Mario. *El hablador*. Barcelona: Seix Barral, 1987.

Vargas Llosa, Mario. *The Storyteller*. Trans. Helen Lane. New York: Farrar, Straus, Giroux, 1989.

Rosalía Cornejo-Parriego

THE DELEGITIMIZING CARNIVAL OF
EL OTOÑO DEL PATRIARCA

The presence of mythical discourse in García Márquez's *El otoño del Patriarca* is undeniable. The community takes on an identity based on founding events, such as "la época de la peste" [the time of the plague] and "el primer siglo de paz" [the first century of peace] and is set in a spatial and temporal framework that transcends human paradigms. We might recall in this regard the pleasure boat that gets lost in an age in which flowers have the power of thought and iguanas fly in the dark (138–139).[1] The hero, in the manner of the great figures of classical mythology, has distinguishing physical features (a huge herniated testicle, a sleek feminine hand, an authoritarian voice), and commands super-natural powers that both endow him with the ability to heal and allow him to defy Nature, ensuring his omnipresence and invulnerability.[2] Moreover, all of it is put in a language that is apocalyptic and hyperbolic, adding significantly to the mythologization.

The recurrence of myth that typifies *El otoño del Patriarca* is also found in other major novels of dictatorship.[3] As we shall see below, the reason for this recurrence is to be found in the affinity between mythical constructs and totalitarian régimes, and in their dependence on one another. As Mircea Eliade points out, myths represent the immutable values of "another world" and seek to serve as models for human con-duct in general (171). This "other world" is set in a time of plenty, and, according to Fernando Morán, it is something shared by totalitarian régimes (222). Although for myth this epoch is located in the past, while for such régimes it is in the present, both endow the archetypes with a closed, self-sufficient and invulnerable character, one that is resistent to change. For Mikhail Bakhtin both stand for absolute modes of thought, for models of total organization (*Dialogic*, 367). According to Octavio Paz, this is a means to avoid the "posibilidad de que la contradicción estalle y haga estallar el sistema" [possibility that contradiction may explode and make the system explode], because "si la coherencia se rompe, la sociedad pierde su fundamento y se destruye" [if coherence breaks down, society loses its foundation and destroys itself (*Hijos*, 47)].[4]

So it is a matter of a static world with no awareness of its own relativity, one in which everything is immutable, set, and governed by hierarchy. As a result, this world, impervious to personal experience, leaves no scope for individual perspective or assessment (Bakhtin, *Dialogic* 15–16). The stasis also explains the ahistorical side of the myth—which parallels "[el] talante ahistórico del fascismo" [the ahistorical tendency of fascism], as Morán puts it—and its break with the immediate cultural tradition (222). Besides, for the myth to fulfill its role of reviving the "pure" origins in which the perfect and paradigmatic event occurred, it must be ritually repeated so that its unchanging and absolute character is reinforced and thus "defiende a la sociedad del cambio" [it defends society from change] to quote Octavio Paz (*Conjunciones*, 27–28). Symbology—an essential part of any ritual—takes on a decisive role through its power to bring together and give identity to members of a society. The proliferation of rituals, such as parades and rallies, together with the creation and manipulation of symbols (the swastika, the yoke, the *falangista* arrows), show that totalitarian régimes have been fully aware of this and of how to take advantage of it.

Some critics, like Eliade and Campbell, share a "natural," ahistorical view of myth, seeing it as the representation of lasting and unchanging human values. This view has often been countered by others, such as Barthes and Kristeva, for whom myth is, above all, a mode of discourse, any discourse being dominated by its historical and conventional dimension.[5] In the words of Barthes, "lointain ou non, la mythologie ne peut avoir qu'un fondement historique, car le mythe est une parole choisie par l'histoire: il ne saurait surgir de la 'nature' des choses" (*Mythologies* 194) [Ancient or not, mythology can only have an historical foundation, for myth is a type of language chosen by history: it cannot possibly evolve from the 'nature' of things]. To interpret myth as in some way immanent is to turn it into a dangerous instrument from an ethical point of view. The natural and eternal justification of events has a purifying effect: it makes them seem innocent, and in the view of Barthes, suppresses all dialectics, constructing a world without contradictions (231). This makes personal judgment, dialogue and dissent impossible, as is, ultimately, any attempt at change.

The foregoing implies both the parallels between mythic and fascist discourses, and the extent to which the former can be put at the service of the latter. In the hands of a totalitarian system, myth provides a very convenient way to manipulate the populace and stop any attempt at protest or rebellion. Bearing these connections in mind, it is not surprising to find that the novel of dictatorship has frequent recourse to mythic discourse, even though its role may vary. It can be used to justify the totalitarian ideology, taking on a legitimizing function, or, as Lincoln says (25–27; 173), it can become a subversive instrument in the hands of those trying to bring about some sociopolitical change, by delegitimizing the authority of myth.[6] Following this introduction, the purpose of the present study is to identify the role of mythic discourse in *El otoño del Patriarca*.

At one point in *Politics and Poetics of Transgression*, the authors make a comment that is disturbing for Western civilization:

> The body cannot be thought separately from the social formation, symbolic typography and the constitution of the subject. . . it is rather that the body is actively produced by the junction and disjunction of symbolic domains and can never be legitimately evaluated 'in itself' (192).

To endow the body with symbolic value beyond its material identity is to acknowledge that it has a cultural importance that has often gone unrecognized. As far as Kristeva is concerned, the body is a territory in which we have been led to distinguish the clean from the dirty, the decent from the indecent, the permissible from the impermissible, thus reflecting the binary logic that underlies totalitarian thinking in the West (87). Such dichotomies require that the one be denied in the affirmation of the other, and where the duality *cuerpo/no cuerpo* [body/non body] is concerned, it is the "signo cuerpo" [sign body], as Octavio Paz calls it, that has been suppressed (*Conjunciones*, 41–48).

History, however, provides us with examples of attempts to subvert this ideological framework. In *Rabelais and His World* Bakhtin analyzes the grotesque as one of the main means of questioning the prevailing culture. The grotesque is a device capable of bringing about a significant change: it can convert a source of fear or terror into a comic monster (91). In undermining everything that is elevated or spiritual, it opens up the way, in a most exaggerated manner, to the forbidden: the body. Thus the corporal dimension acquires a delegitimizing function, invalidating authority. The General in García Márquez's novel recognizes that the greatest humiliation of all for a man is to have his body fail him (254). It is this grotesque "betrayal by the body" that becomes the main demythifying strategy in *El otoño*. Its prime realization is in the hyperbolic physical descriptions of the supposedly heroic figure of the Patriarch. Among the essential parts of his portrayal are his elephantine feet (204) and, above all, his huge herniated testicle, which is as large as an ox kidney (14) and allows him to walk only with the aid of a walker (49).

What has been glossed over most often when dealing with the human body is the waste matter that issues from its orifices. Kristeva echoes the view expressed by Mary Douglas in *Purity and Danger*, when she notes that these products, the "margins" of the body, should be considered in relation to other margins, given the symbolic importance of the body (69). The periphery turns into a serious threat for a Western mode of thought inclined to a systematic classification and hierarchization based on the notion of "center." In *El otoño*, subversion of this mode of thought means that associations are constantly made between bodily products and the figure of the protagonist. There are many references to sweat: the General wakes up soaked in sweat (71), travels the country leaving a trail of his sweaty odor (93), Francisca Linero sees him with his sweat-saturated jacket (98), and at a moment of doubt and depression concerning his authority he becomes suddenly conscious that his shirt is drenched with sweat (101). This is an element whose presence has a significant demythifying effect, for it marks the mortal dimension of the Patriarch, something he has been at pains to hide throughout his rule. A visiting stranger notes that, in contrast to his public image, in person he looked just like a common, ordinary, sweaty man (106).

But it is excrement that comes to be the dominant motif in García Márquez's novel. The hero is continually portrayed carrying out those bodily functions traditionally viewed as the "lowest," and the narrator seems rather to revel in the details. The reader learns the precise number of drops that fall during the Patriarch's bedtime urination (71), that the officers of the high command notice that he smells like a lowly soldier's uniform, reeking of skunk piss (193), and that there are rumors that during official functions he pees his pants without even being aware of it (251). The reader also learns that, after an attempt on his life, the Patriarch retires to his private apartments, locks up carefully, and delicately removes his shit-filled pants (122); that, as she teaches him to read, Leticia Nazareno washes him, moving aside the herniated testicle in order to wash off the shit from their last love making (173). The General himself is aware that he smells of shit and, significantly, one of his subjects asks him to baptize a child to see if he can cure his diarrhea (230). As he ages, his scatological side becomes ever more accentuated. It is in the toilets that the last oracles are to be found, and it is there that the General consoles himself by writing down the cries of praise that the crowds once directed at him in his youth (187, 200, 259). Also he hears such cries as "que se aparte de aquí viejo pendejo que se va a cagar en la mezcla" (223) [get away from here you old fool you'll shit in the mixture]. But nothing points more conclusively to the link between myth and excrement than does the anonymous refrain that the whole country sings, "ahí viene el General de mis amores echando caca por la boca y echando leyes por la popa" (81) [there comes my darling general issuing crap through his mouth and laws through his poop].

Even the General's personal space, which in traditional mythology would stand as an "axis mundi" (Campbell, 43–45), suffers degradation due to the excremental "invasión." Ambassador Palmerston recalls that he had to make his way through piles of torn papers, animal dung, and the leftovers from dogs' meals (89–90). And what the collective narrator encounters, on entering the seat of power at the time of the General's death, is the overwhelming stench of fermenting excrement and urine. Everything reeks of putrefaction.

During his explanation of the term "grotesque," Bakhtin calls upon a type of ornamentation found during fifteenth-century excavations. It is distinguished by unfinished or poorly defined shapes, which do not conform to the divisions of the natural world, but rather synthesize disparate or contradictory elements (Rabelais, 31–32). One such synthesis is to be found in the portrayal of the Patriarch. When "we," the collective narratorial voice, come across the corpse, it is covered with lichens and parasites, especially under the arms and around the groin (14). But earlier on Ambassador Kipling has already described him as someone made of animal, mineral, and vegetable elements: "el cuerpo tenso y lúcido de ahogado en tierra firme en cuyos resquicios estaban proliferando parásitos de escollos de fondo de mar, tenía rémora de barco en la espalda, tenía pólipos y crustáceos microscópicos en las axilas" (252) [the taut and lucid body of a man drowned on dry land in whose nooks and crannies parasites from the reefs at the bottom of the sea were proliferating, he had a ship remora on his back, and polyps and microscopic crustaceans in his armpits].

El otoño brings together what Bakhtin considers the three main acts in the life of the grotesque body: "sexual intercourse, death throes. . . and the act of birth" (353). As one discovers in the course of reading, physically grotesque features are present even at the Patriarch's birth. Evidence of this is found in his fig-sized right testicle (131). Right from the start it becomes a humiliating but distinctive characteristic, one that is even put on show, with his mother in charge of the proceedings in marketplaces (133). The distortion of his origins is also emphasized by the fact that his mother is obliged to "comer por el bajo vientre" (149) [use her lower parts for eating] and by the fact that she conceived and bore him under degrading conditions. Bendición Alvarado chooses his final moment of agony as the time to reveal to her son, "cómo le echaron su placenta a los cochinos, señor, cómo fue que nunca pude establecer cuál de tantos fugitivos de vereda había sido tu padre, trataba de decirle para la historia que lo había engendrado de pie y sin quitarse el sombrero por el tormento de las moscas metálicas de los pellejos de melaza fermentada de una trastienda de cantina . . ." (133) [how her placenta had been thrown to the hogs, sir, how it was that I could never establish which of all those back-lane fugitives was your father, tried to tell him for history's sake that she had conceived him standing up and with her hat on because of the storm of bluebottle flies around the wineskins of fermented molasses in the back room of a bar]. All this, together with her living decomposition, which is described in hyperbolic terms [the dying woman's room smelled so bad that not even lepers could bear it, and her sheets were soaked in a shiny gunk that flowed from her sores (134)], shows how bodily functions come to stand in the way of the Patriarch's claims to a glorious past after the manner of the great mythological figures (Campbell, 319).

The erotic is another dimension of the Patriarch's being to undergo grotesque distortion, even from the moment of his sexual initiation. According to one of the soldiers' whores "me quedé crispada de horror porque no encontré lo que buscaba sino el testículo enorme nadando como un sapo en la oscuridad, lo soltó asustada" (162) [I was twisted with terror because I couldn't find what I was looking for except for the enormous testicle swimming like a toad in the darkness, she let go of it in fright (162)]. Later on, Francisca Linero, the wife of Poncio Daza, speaking of the encounter\rape between her and the Patriarch, tells that "buscaba con los dedos por donde no era . . . así que él hizo por fin su voluntad . . . pero lo hizo de prisa y mal" [(he) looked for me with his fingers where I wasn't . . . so he finally had his way . . . but he did it quickly and poorly], and when it was over he cried like a lonely orphan (96–97). Furthermore, the first instance of intercourse with Leticia Nazareno, "lo convirtió en un animal degollado cuyos tumbos agónicos salpicaban las sábanas nevadas con una materia ardiente y agria que pervirtió en su memoria el aire de vidrio líquido de la tarde de lluvias radiantes del mosquitero, pues era mierda, General, su propia mierda" (165) [turned him into a beheaded animal whose death throes sprinkled the snowy sheets with a hot and sour matter that in his memory perverted the liquid glass air of the afternoon of radiant rains under the mosquito netting, because it was shit, general, your own shit].

In the context of the degradation of the hero, Martha L. Canfield sees the massive hernia as a distortion of the penis, and the fecal matter that his wife has to wipe from him after coitus, as a substitute for semen. For Canfield, the true significance of these things is that they mark a "reducción caricaturesca del machismo" (42–43) [a reductive caricature of *machismo*]. The same explanation can be applied to the androgynous hints concerning the Patriarch and his wife, which seem to suggest a certain inversion of male and female roles.[7] While his hands are feminine (17) and his crying is a dog's whimper (16)—and we need not dwell on the connotations of whimpering—hers is a man's voice (159), which shouts like a pirate (181).

Presenting the tyrant in this way again undermines the image of a classical hero, one who triumphs in all adventures, including amorous ones. But the caricature of *machismo* points to something deeper. In the first place, it attacks a phallocentric culture in which a radical opposition has been set up between the masculine and the feminine, in order to eradicate the threat of the feminine and ensure that that culture's own power is protected (Kristeva, 86). Relevant to this is a comment by Andrea Dworkin that, "In a world of male power—penile power—fucking is the essential sexual experience of power and potency and possession" (79).[8] Hence a patriarchal society does not hesitate to turn to rape in order to assert its power. In regard to this, a number of American feminists insist on "the importance of desexualizing rape by defining it as a crime of power, not of sex" (Woodhill, 170). Bearing in mind the relationships of the Patriarch with women, one realizes that every one starts with rape: Francisca Linero, whose husband is quickly done away with so that the Patriarch can satisfy himself; his many concubines, in whom the objectification of women is most patent; the seaport whores who dress up as secondary school children; even his own wife, a novitiate taken by force.

In second place the caricature of *machismo* stands for the degradation of the fascist individual who, according to Kaplan, is virile and phallic (10). These two features, as Klaus Theweleit has shown, are closely related. In his book *Männerphantasien*, he proposes that fascism can be explained not simply on the basis of a capitalist economy and the class struggle, but also taking into account the patriarchal relationship between the masculine and the feminine, and the resultant gender struggle. In this way, fascism is seen as an exacerbated form of phallocentric culture (232).[9] Thus the Patriarch asserts his absolute power not only by ferociously repressing any attempt at political opposition (one thinks of the General who is roasted and served at a banquet), but also by repeatedly raping women. According to Tobin, this is also why his sexual powers decline in tandem with his political ones (73). As his rule passes into the hands of his henchmen, so he must resort to potions designed to maintain his sexual vigour, even though his exploits leave him clinging to the toilet and weeping (259). The toilet becomes the only place where he can boast his masculinity. The demeaning picture of a dictator who cannot wield his phallic power comes, in the context of a phallocentric society, to mark the downfall of a totalitarian system.

"Agony," the third phase of the grotesque body, comes to the Patriarch in a process of progressive disintegration that undermines his ability to take on any leadership role. The so-called hero of *El otoño* becomes ever further removed from the great (almost always young) mythical figures of epic stories, and from the fascist cult of youth, of leadership, and of the body (Kaplan, 47). The large number of physical details adduced only serve to make this disintegration more pathetic and dramatic. The reader is aware of the pain resulting from his herniated testicle, which does not allow him to sleep in the winter (118), and of the lamentable state in which he was found by Ambassador Kipling: soaked in a salty matter that flowed from his skin (252).

Physical decay is accompanied by mental decay. One sees it in the Patriarch's infantilization, of which the diplomats take advantage, offering him candies and magazines with pictures of nude women in exchange for water rights (198); and one sees it above all in his loss of memory and his awareness of that loss (118). Bearing in mind that the old tyrant has shaped his own mythical identity, the retention of power and absolute authority rely to a large extent on the recollection of that "invented" identity. Reaching the point where not even he knows who he is (219) marks the self-destruction and death of the myth. But not even in death can the grotesque be avoided; instead, it is its climactic moment. The body found in the palace has been picked at by the buzzards and infested with parasites (89). This body, which opens and closes the novel, is not the body of a living person: it is a corpse, the most abject of remains. According to Kristeva:

> tel un théâtre vrai, sans fard et sans masque, le déchet comme le cadavre m'*indiquent* ce que j'écarte en permanence pour vivre. Ces humeurs, cette souillure, cette merde sont ce que la vie supporte à peine et avec peine de la mort . . . Ces déchets chutent pour que je vive, jusqu'à ce que, de perte en perte, il ne m'en reste rien, et que mon corps tombe tout entier au-delà de la limite, *cadere*, cadavre . . . le cadavre, le plus écoeurant des déchets . . . (11)

> [as in true theater, without makeup or masks, refuse and corpses *show me* what I permanently thrust aside in order to live. These body fluids, this defilement, this shit are what life hardly withstands, and with the hardship of death. . . . Such waste drops away so that I might live, until, as the losses mount, nothing remains in me and my entire body falls beyond the limit—*cadere*, cadaver. . . the corpse, the most heart-rending of wastes . . . .]

Nonetheless, the corpse in García Márquez's novel represents both destruction and genesis: the passage of time towards an inevitable death frustrates the immutable and totalitarian pretensions of myth, while at the same time opening up new opportunities in the history of a people.

Behind the grotesque show of the ill-fated myth one can hear a collective laugh at the expense of officialdom, one that has a deconstructive effect on the General's whole régime. This delegitimizing laugh, however, is not that of a single voice, but rather that of the congregation of voices that make up the community. In García Márquez's novel it is a multiple, heterogeneous, polyvalent guffaw, and in it are mingled several discourses, sometimes superimposed on one another, sometimes contradictory. One hears the "aduladores" [flatterers], the "sicarios" [henchmen], who from their location at the "center" deliberately conspire to create the dictator's myth. It is they who feed the diplomats who are trying to mediate in the conflict of the lost children with the idea that the legends about his strange illnesses are true, that he was suffering from frogs in his belly, or could sleep only if standing because of his iguana–like dorsal fins (110). It is the flatterers who contrive the farce, revealed by one of the narrators and designed to satisfy the Patriarch's desire to control time at will. To appease him they glue paper stars and moons on the windows (73). It is they who, ironically, proclaim him "descompositor de la madrugada, comandante del tiempo y depositario de la luz" (73) [undoer of dawn, commander of time, and repository of light]. As this manipulation of reality is reinforced by oral tradition (a factor of fundamental importance in popular mythmaking), the henchmen ensure the cooperation, whether innocent or interested, of the masses.[10] But as time goes by, as Tobin says, "many of his people will more or less cynically agree that these official images are untrustworthy, yet earlier these were the same folk who began to fabricate a sublime discourse around him" (67). But neither their initial support, nor their subsequent alienation from officialdom and its myths are disinterested positions; instead, they are motivated by a strong urge for power.

Also heard are the marginal sectors of the populace, with a discourse that, according to Lincoln, provides "alternative models whereby members of subordinate strata and others marginalized under the existing social order are able to agitate for the deconstruction of that order and the reconstruction of a society on a novel pattern" (8). This is the sceptical and incredulous "nosotros" [we] representing those who have not swallowed the official "truths" from the start, "los menos prudentes" who never settle for appearances (49), whose role is always deconstructive. These narrators describe the dead General as being highly decorated for imaginary victories (215). Similarly, they denounce the lack of credibility entailed in the appearance of the tyrant's image on things ranging from coins to labels on depuratives, trusses, scapularies, because they know that they are based on copies of copies that were known to be inaccurate "en los tiempos del cometa," and that the only reason the images are recognized as being of the Patriarch is that generation after generation has passed the word down (12). They also point to the falsification of his age according to the requirements of the occasion, so that at certain times he was apparently 80 years old at charity raffles, 60 at civil functions, and even less than 40 during public celebrations (89). These voices also describe how the image of the tyrant, whether physical, moral or intellectual, is magnified in official documents describing him

> como un patriarca de tamaño descomunal que nunca salía de su casa porque no cabía por las puertas, que amaba a los niños y a las

golondrinas, que conocía el lenguaje de algunos animales, que tenía la virtud de anticiparse a los designios de la naturaleza, que adivinaba el pensamiento con sólo mirar a los ojos, y conocía el secreto de una sal de virtud para sanar las lacras de los leprosos y hacer caminar a los paralíticos (52)

[as a patriarch of huge size who never left his house because he could not get through the doors, who loved children and swallows, who knew the language of certain animals, who had the virtue of being able to anticipate the designs of nature, who could guess people's thoughts just by looking in their eyes, and who had the secret of a salt with the virtue of curing lepers' sores and making cripples walk].

Thus is highlighted the vital role played in the mythification process by the media and official historiography. But the creation of this official historiography, which stoops to blatant manipulation of texts, as is the case when pages devoted to viceroys are ripped from schoolbooks so that they are eliminated from history (140), serves both the dictator's wishes to shape his life in the style of great heroes and myths, and the purpose of legitimizing his rise to and maintenance of power. As Lyotard shows, the function of mythical accounts is to legitimize régimes and institutions (38). For all his efforts, the Patriarch's wishes are doomed to failure. The implacable collective narrator unmasks the link between the mythification and falsification of historiography to give a version of history adapted to the interests of the totalitarian system. This community, which knows that the only country it has was created by the Patriarch in his own image and molded to suit his will [even space and time were changed (169)], destroys the messianic character with which the Patriarch seeks to endow his life story, and tries to lay bare the truths behind the monolithic "truth" of the régime.

Beyond that, there are voices whose precise attitude to the dictatorship is difficult to determine. When reference is made to the Patriarch's simultaneous presence, we read that "no eran un privilegio de la naturaleza, como lo proclamaban sus aduladores, ni una alucinación multitudinaria, como decían sus críticos, sino que era la suerte de contar con los servicios íntegros y la lealtad de perro de Pedro Aragonés, su doble perfecto . . ." (17) [were not a privilege of his nature, as his adulators proclaimed, or a mass hallucination, as his critics said, but a matter of his luck in being able to count on the devoted service and doglike loyalty of Patricio Aragonés, his perfect double]. Who exactly is saying this? If neither the flatterers nor the critics, then whose is this narrative voice that adds further to the deconstruction of the regime? This persistent ambiguity in the novel is evidence of an incessant refraction of the official truth through the many voices by means of which the text decomposes and fragments itself. This is a confirmation of what Foucault asserts in *La volonté de savoir*: truth is not free, it is a production pierced through by power relations (81).

In *Rabelais*, Bakhtin says that laughter plays an important part in every culture: it is an escape valve capable of unmasking and destroying the true face of an established monolithic ideology. In its unofficial literary and cultural manifestations it creates a dual, dialogic discourse that is impossible in "official" manifestations, one which renounces dogmatism and intolerance and is distinctly subversive in nature. The carnival is the best example of laughter serving as a popular device to subvert official discourse. While an official celebration tends to reaffirm and reassert the existing hierarchy of values, the established norms and truths, the carnival is a parodic celebration of liberation (albeit shortlived) from the prevailing order, with all its privileges and prohibitions. The principal carnivalesque figure in *El otoño* is undoubtedly the Patriarch, elevated into a grotesque spectacle to reflect a deep-seated collective need to subvert the political and moral system he embodies. The General himself foresees that on hearing the news of his first death (in fact, it is that of his double) his subjects will celebrate the carnival of his death (36). His enemies proceed to destroy the seat of power, and his merry widows abandon the house, taking away the cows, the furniture, and the honey. The Patriarch sees his own children dance, loot, and sing "se murió mi papá, viva la libertad" [Daddy's dead, long live freedom! (30)] and he sees a bonfire of official portraits. Also, he watches a corpse that is presumed to be his, being dragged along, doused with the spittle and excrement of the sick (36).

The confrontation of mythical and demythifying discourse, which implies the coexistence of the myth constructed by those in power and its popular burlesque replica, makes *El otoño* a carnivalesque novel. In order to go about this parodic subversion and deconstruction, the mythical language used by those in authority must first be assimilated. As Aronne-Amestoy points out, "sólo desde el interior del discurso mítico se puede destruir el mito" (524) [only from within mythical discourse can myth be destroyed]. If mythical discourse aims to establish a closed world of absolute and perfect paradigmatic values, its parody in *El otoño* denies it that perfection and proclaims its relativity.

This confrontation also marks a rejection of the monologic, the authoritarian imposition of a single discourse (Bakhtin, *Dialogic*, 335). But García Márquez's novel also avoids the dialectic dualism of dictator versus populace, and with it an oversimplification of the complex notion of power. *El otoño* follows Foucault in seeing power as a "multiplicité des rapports de force" (multiplicity of force relations) that allows us to speak of the "omniprésence du pouvoir: non point parce qu'il avait le privilège de tout regrouper sous son invincible unité, mais parce qu'il se produit à chaque instant en tout point, ou plutôt dans toute relation . . ." (122) [omnipresence of power: not because it has the privilege of consolidating everything under its invincible unity, but because at every moment it is produced at every point, or rather in every relationship . . .] García Márquez's novel confirms that power "s'exerce à partir de points innombrables, et dans le jeu de relations inégalitaires et mobiles" (123) [power is exercised from innumerable points, in the interplay of nonegalitarian and changing relations]. Therefore, one cannot speak of "le discours du pouvoir et en face, un autre qui s'oppose a lui. Les discours sont des éléments ou des blocs tactiques dans le champ des rapports de force" (134) [a discourse of power, and opposite it, another discourse that runs counter to it. Discourses are tactical elements or blocks operating in the field of relationships of force]. The Patriarch is the dictator, but what of the power wielded by his wife Leticia, by American imperialism, by other dictators who were important in their time, by the collaborators or henchmen, and so on? In other words, power is fragmented into micropowers which the novel attempts to delegitimize. First, the "fabricated" identity of the General is destroyed. As I have said, this comes about through his transformation into a carnivalesque figure, but it is also a product of the text itself: "since grammatical persons do not rule this prose, it is the furthest possible thing from being dictation—it is rather a textual web, a game of mirrors that both reconstruct and deconstruct the figure of the dictator, the missing subject" (González Echevarría, 76). All the while, the various voices from different parts of the community become confused and fragmented. It is a texture[11] woven from many power relations, into which are inserted what Foucault calls "points de résistance" [points of resistance] the dissident voices of *El otoño* whose "codage stratégique" [strategic codification] makes revolution possible (127).

The result is a text built of discontinuous segments (Foucault, 133) and dealing with the relationship between power and discourse. It is a complicated and elusive game in which discourse "peut être à la fois instrument et effet de pouvoir, mais aussi obstacle, butée, point de résistance et départ pour une stratégie opposée. Le discours véhicule et produit du pouvoir; il le renforce mais aussi le mine, l'expose, le rend fragile et permet de le barrer" (133) [can be both an instrument and an effect of power, but also a hindrance, a stumbling block, a point of resistance and a starting point for an opposing strategy. Discourse as transmitter and producer of power; it reinforces it, but also undermines and exposes it, renders it fragile and makes it possible to thwart it]. This multiplicity of functions shows how the term "discourse of power" is untenable. If power is made up of a complex dynamics of micropowers, they, in turn, weave a tangled texture of discourses. This ambiguous texture offers no single truth and has a deeply unsettling effect on the reader. Yet it also provides a challenge: the challenge entailed in scrutinizing, unmasking, delegitimizing these discourses in order to question one's position in the system's power structure. In this way, the reader may come to decide whether to collaborate or to seek a strategic point from which to participate in the subversion.

Translated by Peter Standish.

Notes

1. All translations from *El otoño* are by Peter Standish.
2. "Había sorteado tantos escollos de desórdenes telúricos, tantos eclipses aciagos . . . ." (127) [He had negotiated the reefs of so many earthly disorders, so many ominous eclipses . . .], "vimos . . . la mano pensativa que hacía señales de cruces de bendición para que cesaran las lluvias y brillara el sol y devolvió la vida a las gallinas ahogadas, y ordenó que bajaran las aguas y bajaron" (104) [we saw . . .the pensive hand which was making the sign of the cross in blessing so that the rains would cease and the sun shine, and he restored life to the drowned hens, and ordered the waters to recede and they receded].
3. *El Señor Presidente* by Asturias, *Yo el Supremo* by Roa Bastos, and *El golpe de estado de Guadalupe Limón* by Torrente Ballester, etc.
4. Translations of excerpts of works by Paz, Morán, Canfield, Aronne-Amestoy, Kristeva, Foucault, and Barthes (*Mythologies*) were made for the present volume.
5. For an account of theories of myth, see Labanyi 5–34.
6. In *Reproductions of Banality* Kaplan analyzes a number of French fascist novels in which myth plays a legitimizing role.
7. Bakhtin also draws attention to the role of the androgynous in Rabelais (323).
8. Further on she writes "The triumphal fuck is virtually synonymous with masculinity. The legitimacy of a man's civil dominance depends on the authenticity of his masculinity, which is articulated when he fucks" (149).

9. Translated into English by Erica Carter and Chris Turner as *Male Phantasies* (Minnesota: University of Minnesota Press, 1989). The author bases his theory on an analysis of certain documents of the "Freikorps," a German paramilitary organization, many of whose members were later in Hitler's SS. The novel *Their Eyes Were Watching God* by the Afro-American writer, Zora Neale Hurston, illustrates the parallels between machismo and dictatorial regimes. Note especially chapter five (32–47) in which the second marriage and the achievement of power by the husband, on becoming mayor, are described.

10. Torrente Ballester in his *El golpe de estado de Guadalupe Limón* makes fun of the same phenomenon.

11."Texte veut dire tissu . . . nous accentuons maintenant, dans le tissu, l'idée générative que le texte se fait, se travaille à travers un entrelacs perpétuel . . ." (Barthes, *Plaisir* 100–101) [*Text* means *Tissue* . . .we are now emphasizing, in the tissue, the generative idea that the text is made, is worked out in a perpetual interweaving" (65)].Translation taken from Roland Barthes, *The Pleasure of the Text*, trans. Richard Miller (New York: Farrar, Straus & Giroux, 1975).

Works Cited

Aronne-Amestoy, Lida. "El mito contra el mito: narración e ideografía en *El otoño del Patriarca*." *Revista Iberoamericana* 52 (1986): 521–530.

Bakhtin, Mikhail. *The Dialogic Imagination*. Trans. Caryl Emerson and Michael Holquist. Austin: U of Texas P, 1988.

Bakhtin, Mikhail. *Rabelais and His World*. Trans. Helene Iswolsky. Bloomington: Indiana UP, 1984.

Barthes, Roland. *Le plaisir du texte*. Paris: Seuil, 1973.

Barthes, Roland. *Mythologies*. Paris: Seuil, 1957.

Barthes, Roland. *The Pleasure of the Text*. Trans. Richard Miller. New York: Farrar, Straus & Giroux, 1975.

Campbell, Joseph. *The Hero with a Thousand Faces*. Princeton: Princeton UP, 1973.

Canfield, Martha L. *El "Patriarca" de García Márquez*. Florencia: Opus Libri, 1984.

Dworkin, Andrea. *Intercourse*. New York: The Free Press, 1987.

Eliade, Mircea. *Aspects du mythe*. Paris: Gallimard, 1963.

Foucault, Michel. *Histoire de la sexualité. La volonté de savoir*. Vol. 1. Paris: Gallimard, 1976. 3 vols.

García Márquez, Gabriel. *El otoño del Patriarca*. Madrid: Mondadori, 1987.

González Echevarría, Roberto. *The Voice of the Masters*. Austin: U of Texas P, 1985.

Hurston, Zora Neale. *Their Eyes Were Watching God*. New York: Harper & Row, 1990.

Kaplan, Alice Yaeger. *Reproductions of Banality*. Minneapolis: U of Minnesota P, 1986.

Kristeva, Julia. *Pouvoirs de l'horreur*. Paris: Seuil, 1980.

Labanyi, Jo. *Myth and History in the Contemporary Spanish Novel*. Cambridge: Cambridge UP, 1989.

Lincoln, Bruce. *Discourse and Construction of Society*. New York: Oxford UP, 1989.

Lyotard, Jean-François. *La condition postmoderne*. Paris: Minuit, 1979.

Morán, Fernando. *Novela y semidesarrollo*. Madrid: Taurus, 1971.

Paz, Octavio. *Conjunciones y disyunciones*. México: Joaquín Mortiz, 1969.

Paz, Octavio. *Los hijos del limo*. Barcelona: Seix Barral, 1987.

Stalybrass, Peter and Allon White. *Politics and Poetics of Transgression*. London: Methuen, 1986.

Theweleit, Klaus. *Male Phantasies*. Trans. Erica Carter and Chris Turner. Minnesota: U of Minnesota P, 1989. 2 vols.

Theweleit, Klaus. *Männerphantasien*. Bd. 1. Hamburg: Rowohlt, 1980. 2 Bände.

Tobin, Patricia. "The Autumn of the Signifier: the Deconstructionist Moment of García Márquez." *Latin American Review* 13 (1985): 65-77.

Woodhull, Winifried. "Sexuality, Power and the Question of Rape." *Feminism and Foucault. Reflections on Resistance*. Eds. Irene Diamond and Lee Quinby. Northeastern UP, 1988. 167–176.

Peter Standish

MAGUS, MASQUE AND THE MACHINATIONS OF AUTHORITY: CORTÁZAR AT PLAY

Time and again Julio Cortázar argued that literature could not be driven by politics, that the quest for freedom encompassed the objective of freedom of creativity, that literature compromised itself by becoming "literatura comprometida" [literature of commitment]. Freedom, he contended, also had to encompass the license to be funny, to seek liberation from the humorless intensity of political compromise, of what could, in this context, perhaps be called the *homo ludicrus*. Yet, just as those interested in maintaining the *status quo* would inevitably try to buy out Cortázar, so too his fellow socialists would subject him to pressure to display his commitment publicly:

> Y así ese justo, delicado equilibrio que permite seguir creando una obra con aire en las alas, sin convertirse en el monstruo sagrado, el prócer que exhiben en las ferias de la historia cotidiana, se vuelve el combate más duro que ha de librar el poeta o el narrador para que su compromiso se siga cumpliendo allí donde tiene su razón de ser, allí donde brota su follaje (*Ultimo round*, 189).[1]

> ["So it is that the precise and delicate balance which allows for the creation of a work with air under its wings— rather than one that turns into a holy monster, a worthy paraded around the showground of our everyday history— becomes the most arduous struggle the poet or storyteller must face if he is to ensure that his commitment continues to find fulfillment in the terrain which provides his *raison d'être*, the one in which he can flower"].

Much critical attention has been given to this dimension of Cortázar's writing, to the tension between desire for sociopolitical reform and respect for aesthetic criteria. Ironically, the author's sensitivity to this tension may itself have encouraged some critics to be quick to read his fictions as political metaphors, sometimes at the expense of oversimplifying. My main purpose here, however, is not to add to the argument about the merits of a politically committed literature, nor even to discuss many of those texts by Cortázar that come closest to being describable as such. Instead, I aim to trace some lines that I believe run through Cortázar from the earliest to the latest works, and that can be related to the exercise of power in a sense which is broader than the strictly political. The authority of the writer, the empowerment (or disempowerment) of the reader, and the implied analogy of these things with extrafictional dimensions of power (including the political) are issues that, latently or visibly, are raised by many of Cortázar's texts from *El examen* on. It would go far beyond the scope of a single essay to deal adequately with such a corpus, with so broadly defined a subject; rather, the need to confine the discussion within practical limits can be met by focusing on what I suggest is a self-defining area of that subject, and by concentrating within that area on a few illustrative texts. Thus, I am concerned here not with the whole body of Cortázar's fiction, nor yet with the writer's public persona, but with another kind of public display, with the idea of the managed, staged performance and the extent to which it can be read as a metaphor of a number of strata of authority.

Truism though it may be, all art is in some sense staged or performed for an audience. By entering the museum or theater, or by opening a book, we tacitly declare our willingness to witness the performance, to hand over the reins to the artist. Every reader of a book is, in principle, an innocent trusting the leadership of the author, a willing subject of manipulation by a writer whose function has often been seen, with reason, as Godlike, not only omniscient but also omnipotent. The paradox is that the exercise (and sometimes abuse) of such a function ultimately depends on an audience being constituted, for without a willing audience there can be no empowerment of the artist.

When Augusto Pérez appeared to stand up to Unamuno in *Niebla*, he reminded us that his own existence as character depended on the maintenance of a fragile but essential illusion of verisimilitude; by questioning the authority of his creator, Augusto Pérez was in fact undermining those essential qualities. At bottom he was being exposed and used by his author as a device to distance us from the illusion, to make us recognize it as such and be aware of the fiction at work. In the literary context of the early twentieth century, this thematization of the fictive process, the reader's *desengaño* ["loss of illusion"], may perhaps be read as purely literary and largely innovative, given the general prevalence at the time of omniscient narrative in a realist mold. As the century closes, however, self-referentiality has become commonplace and we have been seeing some reaction to its sway. Now, two questions converge, though they may seem to pull in different directions: is the fashion for writing that thematizes writing perhaps to be seen as a reflection of a modern scepticism that extends beyond art into the social and political spheres, such that the powers of the author can be held analogous to those of other authorities?; or can the fact that illusive writing has never entirely lost popularity be taken as evidence that people want to be deceived in literature and perhaps in other areas of life, too?

A rather special place in relation to all this has always been occupied by the theater, with its inherent consciousness of performance and social event. In theater, actions are quite literally elevated on stage, or focused in the round; the presence of a community is itself part of the theatrical experience; the distance between performers and audience is always apparent, even when the latter is drawn into the performance. It is for such reasons as these that theater has been called the fictive genre par excellence, more capable than any other of bringing out the "dudosa naturaleza del arte" ["the dubious nature of art"], that is, its capacity to reveal the truth through fiction (Vargas Llosa, 11). One can argue, then, that special attention is due narrative prose that in some way embeds the theatrical within itself, for it would seem to draw attention not only to fictionality, but also to the dynamics of power among the various individual and group participants involved: writer, producer, director, performers, mass audience, individual witness; in Cortázar's terms, we might perhaps refer to them all as "cómplices" ["accomplices"].

Any reader of Cortázar, especially of his short stories, will have felt (and no doubt enjoyed) the author's ability to create an intimacy between himself and his reader, between reader and protagonist. We are often drawn in and made to experience the feelings of characters in the fictions; sometimes the process of involvement is made explicit. The most succinct example of this is "Continuidad de los parques," whose metafiction makes the reader of the story become the reader in the story, but also seems to threaten that reader with an unseen presence, that of a character in the work he is in the process of reading. This is less a matter of the author using a fictional character as accomplice to steal up on and subvert an unsuspecting reader, than it is a sign that the reader, the *lector cómplice* ["reader-accomplice"], is to be held part of the process of constructing that fiction. For writing and reading, and an allied concern with the mediating function of language, are everywhere thematized in Cortázar. In the miscellanies and novels, not least *Rayuela*, this thematization is particularly overt. The book being composed in *El libro de Manuel*, and, very obviously, *62 . . .*, are in the same vein. If one looks to the short fiction, the thematization of writing and the author-reader relationship, though sometimes less overtly treated, can also be observed in many stories, such as "Las babas del diablo," "Tango de vuelta," "Historias que me cuento," and "Ahí pero dónde, cómo."

Not only is *Rayuela* a particularly illustrative example of such a thematization, it is also a book with a character called "Maga," and since I use the word "magus" in the title of the present essay, a word of clarification is called for here. As many critics have noted, the opening words of *Rayuela* allude to the nature of the search with which it deals and to the importance of La Maga in that search. She combines a large measure of down-to-earth concreteness with a certain air of the unreal; it is Oliveira, who sees in her the representation of his objective, who dubs her La Maga. Her real name, Lucía, perhaps suggests that she has the key to the quality he is seeking, that she in some sense will light the way; but she is also emphatically a character of fiction, first seen coming out of a bookshop, as if a product of all the cultural baggage Oliveira rails against. She motivates his search, as the opening words of the novel imply, and he dies (if he does die) thinking of her. Yet despite her name, La Maga is in no way the conscious manipulator in the sense I am associating with "magus" in the present study.

A first dimension of power, then, involves the performance of the author as magus, a power exerted over the reader.[2] A corollary of this authorial power is to be found in the fiction within the fiction, which may empower a (reader-) protagonist. In "La salud de los enfermos," for example, concern to protect their ailing mother leads members of her family to weave a tissue of lies covering up the death of a favored son; as the title cleverly hints, however, the sickness (the need to be deceived) is not really (or only) hers. By the end of the story the mother, now aware of the truth about her son, is actively helping to maintain the fiction which has come to be their reality, and on which their health perhaps depends. A more explicitly theatrical and earlier Cortázar text that explores some of the concerns already identified above is "Los buenos servicios." This story's protagonist, Mme. Francinet, humble and finan-cially pressed, is engaged by a wealthy family to help at a party; on arrival at their house a series of narrative signs heralds her introduction into a world of performance and histrionics. First, she nearly loses a heel, and superstitiously quotes a saying to guard against bad luck; she is then led across the threshold by "un señor de patillas grises *como en el teatro*" ["a gentleman with grey sideburns, *like in the theater*"] (my emphasis) into a world where she will be required to play various roles, taking her beyond her social station; entering into this wonderland, which "pareció mejor que ir a cualquier teatro" ["seemed better than going to any theater"] and where the lady of the house is dressed to the point where "parecía un pastel" ["she looked like a cake"]. Mme. Francinet is first made, by someone significantly called Alice, to don an oversize apron before playing one role, later to be socially elevated and more fully decked out for her star part as mother of a dead man at his wake. In this last role she comes to feel the emotions she has been contracted to perform (*Relatos*, 1, 196–221), yet as she approaches what she sees as her "escena más difícil" ["most difficult scene"], the man who has persuaded her to act the part holds her back, hurting her arm, as if to deny her complete free-dom to behave according to her instincts and to fully cross the social divide. In "Los buenos servicios" there is much emphasis on costume and appearance, associated with class in the mind of the protagonist, who seems unaware throughout of the homosexuality of other participants in the action. Another salient feature is the reiterated mention of the "arañas," referring in the immediate physical context to the light fixtures, but also conveying the image of spiders, and hence presumably intended to carry one's thoughts to the web of fiction in which Mme. Francinet is being trapped.[3]

"Las Ménades," "La banda," and later "Cambio de luces" and "Queremos tanto a Glenda" carry the theatrical metaphor a stage further. In their different ways, all speak of the possibilities for the abuse of power in credulous communities. The narrator in "Las Ménades," pleased with his own musical culture, looks condescendingly on audience reaction at an orchestral concert; he scrutinizes the behavior of orchestra and audience as if with the eye of an entomologist, using many animalistic images to chronicle their sycophantic behavior, as they advance towards an ecstatic and bloody climax. The maestro, who according to the narrator has cleverly constructed his program to pander to the middle-brow limits of his audi-ence, becomes the subject of their unbridled and unthinking adulation, until mass hysteria takes over. The fact that the narrator manages to keep his distance from the events may allude to the perils of nonparticipation in a society where things can easily run out of control; an alternative (more cynical?) reading might be that nonparticipation is the guarantee of personal safety. The maestro and the orchestra may represent some governmental structure that risks falling prey to the people it seeks to manage. The story also seems to give a foretaste of the idol worship which is dealt with in "Queremos tanto a Glenda," implying questions of faith and belief.[4] "La banda" embeds several performances: a story within a story, and a concert and a film within the embedded story. The narrator in the frame story speculates as to the possible significance of some staged events on real life, events that he then proceeds to narrate. The initial situation in the internal story is plausible, as it usually is in Cortázar: Lucio enters a cinema intending to see a film, and witnesses an absurd band concert. Here, instead of the image of the spider, we have that of the beetle; the emphasis has shifted from the web of fiction to the machinations of the band director (the coleopter), though his ineffectual gesticulations suggest that he is not the real orchestrator of the performance but rather the puppet of some overriding power. In the process of it all, Lucio, the protagonist of "La banda," is said to have glimpsed the truth: "De pronto le pareció entender aquello en términos que lo excedían infinitamente. Sintió como si le hubiera sido dado ver al fin la realidad" ["All at once he thought he understood it all in a way that went far beyond it. He felt as though at last he had been allowed to see reality for what it was" (*Relatos*, 3: 46)]. The truth has been discovered through the theatrical events; whatever that truth is, it is unpalatable, and Lucio resigns his job and flees abroad.[5]

Echoes of all this can be found in *Todos los fuegos el fuego*, particularly in one story that brings together most of the elements I have been describing so far. It is at least arguable that "Instrucciones para John Howell" can be read as a story with an implicit political message. It is surely the case that it offers a number of revealing parallels with a novel by John Fowles, *The Magus*. Following the publication of this work, Fowles was horrified to learn that certain groups in California had been enacting a scene he had written into it; fiction was spilling over into reality. The scene in question involved an interrogation, with Nazi overtones, orchestrated by a guru called Conchis; it had been conceived by Fowles as a metaphor of personal initiation into maturity and responsibility. The protagonist, Nicholas Urfe, is manipulated by Conchis through a frightening and frustratingly unexplained sequence of events, in which the rules of the game are subject to sudden change. The reader, too, identifying with the protagonist, is intentionally left unsettled, for behind the personified magus, Conchis, there lies the authorial one, playing with the reader's emotions and logical powers. "Fowles" play, cried some critics, regarding this novelist as unnecessarily manipulative, and forgetting that manipulating readers is precisely what novels are about.[6] Conchis, quite obviously, is another Prospero, and on his island he is orchestrating a world in which the real is invaded by the fantastic; as Gillian Beer argues, this sort of onslaught on the real brings with it a special relationship between author and reader, one that "liberates but also involves unusual dependency" (Beer, 8). Where, then, is Fowles leading us? While *The Magus* can clearly be read as metafiction, Fowles' ultimate aim is probably best described as moral. Using his reader's dependency, like his protagonist's, he sets out to trace a path toward mature individual responsibility. It is striking that it was to the discovery of individual identity that Fowles turned for an answer when he was asked in an interview whether he was interested specifically in political freedom: Fowles replied that "freedom . . . is unalienably bound up with self-knowledge" (Tarbox, 184).

More than a few common elements, which may be no more than coincidental, link the writings of John Fowles with those of Julio Cortázar.[7] As in *The Magus*, the protagonist of "Instrucciones . . ." is initiated by means of play-acting. Rice drifts into a London theater on a gloomy day, is drawn into the action on stage, and finally is seen running in uncomprehending fear through a maze of streets in the real world.[8] Having watched the first act of an indifferent melodrama, Rice is invited backstage and inveigled into taking over the part of John Howell. Rice receives instructions on how to play his part, as did Mme. Francinet before him, being primed for her role at the wake (*Relatos*, 1: 213–214). The invitation backstage is extended by someone identified only as "el hombre de gris" whose presence, combined with that of the "hombre alto" and the "hombre mudo," will become increasingly threatening in the course of the action. Rice's scorn for the play ["esto es una farsa estúpida" ("This is a ridiculous farce")] leads him willfully to begin to break with the prescriptions. He then becomes convinced by Eva's "no dejes que me maten" ["Don't let them kill me"], and he is emotionally compromised. As he receives his instructions for the third act he is told that it is the most difficult and the most entertaining; the "hombre alto" unhesitatingly, but somewhat cryptically, sets the parameters for action:

Ya ha visto cómo se van descubriendo los juegos. . . . En cierto modo usted ha complicado las cosas . . . yo hubiera reaccionado de otra manera . . . [pero] . . . mi opinión podría alterar sus propias decisiones, puesto que usted ha de tener ya un plan preconcebido. . . . Si le digo eso es precisamente porque no se trata de tener planes preconcebidos.

["You've already begun to see how things play out. . . . In a way, you've made things more complicated . . . I would have reacted differently . . . but . . . my opinion could influence your decisions, and you're bound to have a plan of action. . . . In saying that, I mean that having a plan of action is precisely what it's not about"].

Rice counters that he has been told he has freedom of action, which provokes a laugh from the "hombre de gris." The "hombre alto" continues: "A partir de ahora le ruego que se atenga a lo que voy a indicarle, se entiende que dentro de la máxima libertad en los detalles" ["From now on I want you to pay attention to what I say, though, of course, you retain full control over matters of detail" (*Relatos*, 2: 46-47)]. He seals his instructions with a mysterious circular motion of his finger about his open palm, and Rice is dressed in street clothes, heralding his brusque reinsertion into the real world via the stage door. Back in the audience he watches once again with scorn until Eva meets her end and the original Howell flees the stage. We last see Rice pursued though the streets of London, unable to reason why, but obscurely sensing that to cross the river is to find salvation. Upon reencountering the man who had played John Howell in acts one and four, Rice demands that he reveal his true self by removing his wig, but learns that it is not a wig, that it *is* his true self. Rice begs fruitlessly for an explanation: "No me deje ir así. . . . No puedo seguir huyendo siempre, sin saber" ["Don't let me go on like this. . . . I can't carry on running away forever, without knowing" (54)].

Given a story like this one, which cries out for interpretation, it is important to take stock of a warning piece of irony that Cortázar includes in the text a few pages before: while Rice is witnessing the final act he protests to a fellow member of the audience that the changes of actor in mid-play are outrageous; the response is, "Ya no se sabe con estos autores jóvenes. . . . Todo es símbolo, supongo" ["You never know with these young writers. . . . I imagine everything is symbolic" (50)]. Certainly many images and phrases invite interpretation, but no interpretation can be regarded as conclusive. As on many occasions, Cortázar opens up possibilities, unseats preconceptions; solutions are not offered, resolution of the picture is necessarily poor. Thus the choice of the name Eva invites thoughts of the garden of Eden and the forbidden fruit; the directorial function of the three men who instruct Howell perhaps suggests a Godlike trinity, one that allows a degree of free will on the world's stage. Crossing the river may be read in a similar vein, as a form of baptism; or perhaps it is the Rubicon or the Styx. But the fact that her name is Eva and not the more common English form Eve (the play, is, after all, being done on a London stage) must also bring to mind Eva Perón, and open the way to a more political reading of what is evidently a story about freedom and power, about a freedom unalienably bound up with self-knowledge, as Fowles put it. The labyrinthine streets and their bifurcations suggest both a constant need to choose and once again the captivating web, like the net that awaits the performer in that other arena, Marco in "Todos los fuegos el fuego"; or indeed the minotaur in *Los reyes*. The pirandellian idea of the play within the play, and the effacing of the divisions between fiction and reality, have already been noted (Quackenbush; Troiano). A concomitant interest in the nature of writing is also evident here, and has even been held to be the true meaning of "Instrucciones . . ." (Juan-Navarro).

The faceless characters who manage the events of "Instrucciones para John Howell" echo the director of "La banda," the proconsul of "Todos los fuegos el fuego," the *mayordomo* of "Los buenos servicios"; they also foreshadow the "hombre de blanco" who was to appear in the posthumous play *Nada a Pehuajó*. There he sits at a table in silence, periodically moving pieces of tableware about a tablecloth of black and white check (a confining representation of a world dominated by dualism), suggesting a grand mastery of a boardgame in which the rest of the characters are unwitting pawns.[9] In the initial stage directions the "hombre de blanco" is said to have "[un] aire de atildado *maestro de ceremonias*" ["the air of a well turned out Master of Ceremonies"] (my emphasis); the "customer" who finds himself involved with this and the other clearly symbolic characters is "de aire insignificante y ropas limpias pero raídas" ["unimportant-looking, and cleanly, but shabbily dressed"], an innocent caught powerless in the unexplained absurdities of a bureaucratic society. What is perhaps most significant for the present discussion, however, is that here, apparently late in his career, Cortázar turned for the first time to theater to provide the initial framework for the fiction, rather than making it simply an element subsumed under another fictional framework.[10]

While some of Cortázar's fictions portray characters enmeshed in the rules of a game of their own making ("Vientos alisios" is an example), others (such as *Los premios*) oblige characters to follow rules set, without explanation, by higher authority. As often as not, the characters become victims of a sense of powerlessness allied with fear. "Reunión con un círculo rojo" is a story that brings a vague, threatening presence to bear on a man dining in a restaurant; he senses that an English tourist also there is in danger, but does not know (any more than the reader does until the end of the story) that she is a party to the design, even to the point of narrating it. In this case, the fear of personal vulnerability is bolstered by the narrative deception; the author's power is used to deny access to the narrative truth, much as an authoritarian régime might control the flow of information. This sense of individual disorientation in the face of undisclosed authority is all the more intense the more plausible the narrative situations, and it is relevant to note here that with Cortázar's successive short story collections it becomes ever easier for the reader to identify with the situations in which the narratives are born. When he was asked whether he felt that his stories had evolved over the years, Cortázar answered that while his technique had hardly changed, he was dealing increasingly with situations that were less marginal to daily existence: ". . . creo que los personajes viven situaciones que, con algunas variantes lógicas, podrían ser vividas por mucha gente. Es decir, que la relación entre personajes y lectores—*como eventuales prota-gonistas*—es mayor . . ." ["I think that my characters are living in situations which, give or take a bit, could apply to lots of people. In other words, the relationship between characters and readers—as possible pro-tagonists—is closer . . ."] (my emphasis) (González Bermejo, 31).[11] In a spirit somewhat reminiscent of the one behind "Continuidad de los parques," the story with which this present discussion began, with this comment Cortázar puts the spotlight on the reader as implied protagonist, as accomplice in the drama. The increasing ordinariness of the situations being dealt with makes the reader more easily inclined to imagine him-self as "possible protagonist" playing a role in them, and thus becoming subject to poorly understood forces. Frequently a protagonist is subject to the workings of a force or design that does not reveal itself, but some-times that force or design is simply not capable of being revealed.

We have seen how Cortázar calls attention to his own control, building into his fictions other dramas, other controlling magus figures—the intra-diegetic class of managing "directors"—and how by bringing these elements into play he implies the forces beyond both, whether institutional or praeternatural. "El poeta es un mago" ["The poet is a magus"], wrote

Cortázar ("Situación . . .": 228); but in this case surely not one who is in possession of the truth, so much as one who unsettles and opens up avenues of possibility. In exerting authorial power over his reader and the characters who people his works, in the layering of authority within those works, Cortázar provides an analogy of the machinations of higher powers: the author's control comes to stand for the control of authority. The author as magus highlights his own operations and in doing so implies that there are powers operating beyond him: being trapped in a fictional web whose purpose is unforseeable is like being an individual subject to social and political pressures, to the whims of powerful individuals or the mysterious ways of gods. Just as a reader is embroiled in the authorial design, so also that reader is trapped in the designs of superior authorities: gods, chance, destiny, ways of thinking, society and its political systems; more than that, the authority of these givens is called into question. These texts are indeed in a salutary way manipulative, and self-consciously so, yet, far from being texts that function in a realm of pure self-referentiality, these speak of life itself. And if there is a lesson, it is that participation is an ineludible, if painful, duty; witness the passengers on the Malcolm, who, broadly speaking, react to the forbidden zone in one of two ways, some by acquiescing passively, some by seeking actively to challenge. Passive acquiescence on the part of a reader is met with Cortázar's derision, while the favored role of the *lector cómplice* demands active participation. Thus the reader-character caught in the web cannot see the overall design but is bound to influence it; the audience must participate in the drama; Rice, like Nicholas Urfe in *The Magus*, steps onto the stage of life, the *persona* is "unmasqued."

Notes

1. An overview of the author's stance vis-à-vis politically committed writing is provided by Peavler. Prego also deals with the subject at some length (127–145).

2. Among discussions of the thematization of the author-reader relationship are those of Sara Castro-Klarén, Kerr, and Ortega.

3. Arachne is all over Cortázar. Spiders crawl throughout, often associated with women (for example, in "Historia con migalas"). Women are sometimes portrayed as the spinners of webs in which men are victims. A little imagination applied to the name of Delia Mañara ("Circe") yields "araña" and "maraña"; she offers a victim a chocolate filled with chitinous cockroaches. The coleopter, of which Cortázar writes in "Casilla de camaleón" (*La vuelta al día en ochenta mundos*: 209–10) is associated with inflexibilty:

Llega el día en que los reporteros, los críticos, los que escriben tesis sobre el artista, deducen, esperan o hasta pretenden la panoplia ideológica y estética. Pasa que el artista también tiene ideas pero es raro que las tenga sistemáticamente, que se haya coleopterizado al punto de eliminar la contradicción como lo hacen los coleópteros filósofos o políticos a cambio de perder o ignorar todo lo que nace más allá de sus alas quitinosas, de sus patitas rígidas y contadas y precisas.

["Along comes the time when reporters, critics, writers of theses on the author, deduce, await or lay claim to an ideological and aesthetic panoply. As it happens, the artist also has his own ideas, but they tend not to come systematically, because he tends not to have become so coleopterized that he has to eliminate every contradiction as do the coleopterized philosophers and politicians, at the expense of missing or dismissing anything that extends beyond the span of their clean-cut, rigid, limited and chitinous wings"].

This also serves as a timely warning to critics inclined to rush towards a neat interpretative conclusion!

4. On "Las ménades" see Morello-Frosch, who reads the story in relation to Argentine cultural policy.

5. Certain links have been noted with practices during the Perón years; like many of Cortázar's fictions, this one is open to interpretation as political allegory (Alazraki, 77). Cortázar, of course, left Argentina because uncomfortable with Perón.

6. In the Latin American context one's thoughts must turn here to the narrative acrobatics of Donoso and Fuentes; their toying with the reader's access to information, as if abusing the reader's trust, has obvious relevance to the present argument.

7. I am not alone in making this connexion. See D'Haen.

8. An avenue towards the theatrical precedents is suggested in the dedication of the story to the director Peter Brook, who at about that time in London had been instrumental in staging plays of the so-called theater of fear.

9. The "suelo escaqueado" as found mirrored in the chess board is of particular significance in freemasonry.

10. I have no way of knowing whether *Nada a Pehuajó* is an early work published late, but the style suggests to me that it is not.

11. That comment was made in relation to *Alguien que anda por ahí*, at the time his latest collection, and one that critics have often held to contain some of his most "political" stories, such as the title story, "Apocalipsis en Solentiname" and "Segunda vez," as well as "Reunión con un círculo rojo." The fact that *Alguien que anda por ahí* was initially banned in Argentina probably says more about the sensibilities of the régime of the time than it reflects an overt political agenda on the part of the author. In fact, the reader can be forgiven for being surpised at the Argentine reaction. If, on occasions in these pieces, the sense of being subject to a superior power does indeed acquire political overtones, only rarely is this because the author himself is explicit (and when he is, he is not always at his best).

Works Cited

Alazraki, Jaime. *En busca del unicornio*. Madrid: Gredos, 1983.

Beer, Gillian. *The Romance*. London and New York: Routledge, 1970.

Bermejo González, Ernesto. *Conversaciones con Cortázar*. Barcelona: Edhasa, 1978.

Castro-Klarén, Sara. "Desire, the Author and the Reader in Cortázar's Narrative." *The Review of Contemporary Fiction* 3.3 (1983): 65–71.

Cortázar, Julio. *Alguien que anda por ahí*. Madrid: Alfaguara, 1977.

Cortázar, Julio. *Nada a Pehuajó*. Mexico City: Editorial Katún, 1984.

Cortázar, Julio. *Los relatos*. Madrid: Alianza, 1976–85.

Cortázar, Julio. "Situación de la novela." *Cuadernos Americanos* 3, 4 (1950): 23–43.

Cortázar, Julio. *Ultimo round*. Mexico City: Siglo XXI, 1969.

Cortázar, Julio. *La vuelta al día en ochenta mundos*. Mexico City: Siglo XXI, 1970.

D'Haen, Theo. *Text to Reader: Fowles, Barth, Cortázar and Boon*. Amsterdam and Philadelphia: John Benjamins, 1983.

Juan-Navarro, Santiago. "El lector se rebela: 'Instrucciones para John Howell' de Julio Cortázar o la estética de la subversión". *MIFLC Review* 1 (1991): 149–158.

Kerr, Lucille. *Reclaiming the Author*. Durham: Duke UP, 1992.

Morello-Frosch, Marta. "El discurso de armas y letras en las narraciones de Julio Cortázar". In *Lo lúdico y lo fantástico en la obra de Cortázar*. Madrid: Fundamentos, 1986.

Ortega, Julio. "Morelli on the Threshold." *The Review of Contemporary Fiction* 3.3 (1983): 45–47.

Peavler, Terry J. *Julio Cortázar*. Boston: Twayne, 1990.

Prego, Omar. *La fascinación de las palabras*. Barcelona: Muchnik Editores, 1985.

Quackenbush, H. "'Instrucciones para John Howell' de Julio Cortázar: un papel en busca de personaje." In Rose S. Minc (ed.): *The Contemporary Latin American Short Story*. New York: Senda Nueva Ediciones, 1979.

Tarbox, Katherine. *The Art of John Fowles*. Athens and London: U. of Georgia P, 1988.

Troiano, James. "Theatrical Technique and the Fantastic in Cortázar's 'Instrucciones para John Howell.'" *Hispanic Journal* 6,1 (1984): 111–119.

Vargas Llosa, Mario. *Kathie y el hipopótamo*. Barcelona: Seix Barral, 1983.

Todd S. Garth

POLITICIZING MYTH AND ABSENCE: FROM MACEDONIO FERNÁNDEZ TO AUGUSTO ROA BASTOS

Two fundamental problems present themselves when discussing the work of Macedonio Fernández (Argentina, 1874–1952) as a precursor to the mythic dimension of Augusto Roa Bastos's *Yo el Supremo* [*I the Supreme*]. One concerns the nature of precursor: it is not the objective here to consider the direct influence of Macedonio felt by Roa Bastos. Rather, this study will regard Macedonio's work along the lines of Jauss' "script of another script," one of the basic concepts underlying the idea of intertextuality. The assertion here is that Roa Bastos fashions his novels partly in the aesthetic and metaphysical space created by Macedonio Fernández and elaborated by a chain of avant-garde artists (the most obvious of whom are Borges and Cortázar) in South America's southern cone.

The idea of asserting Macedonio's impact on this chain of writers, and particularly on the work of a writer living today, in the absence of any concrete evidence of "influence," would appeal to Macedonio himself. As we will explore further on, much of the mythic dynamics elaborated by Macedonio results from his efforts to create absences more essential and enduring than any presence. This essay will discuss how both the imitation of presence by novelistic characters and the exercise of presence by the author give way in Macedonio's writing to a much weightier absence ("author" itself being exposed as an artifice). This absence, in turn, is taken up by Roa Bastos. The fact that Macedonio cannot have had direct personal influence on Roa (clearly they never met), along with the difficulty of proving a direct textual impact, would, by Macedonio's thinking, open the door to consideration of a less tangible but more enlightening kind of analysis.

The second problem in this study concerns the definitions of myth and mythology, and as a corollary, the definition of archive. As we will see, the working definition of myth for this study differs in one important respect from that of Roberto González Echevarría, who focuses on the function of myth in the explanation and expression of cultural foundations and origins. In the same vein, we will depart from González's definition of archive as the consolidation and sustenance of that myth. Nonetheless, much of what appears in the following pages is indebted to González's analysis. In particular, it stands in agreement with his assertion of both myth and archive as the author's recourse to arguably non-literary discourses in the search for authentic expression of reality in fiction (38). It also agrees with the idea that while Latin American narrative appeals to myth as part of its "struggle to free the imagination of all mediation, to reach a knowledge of self and collectivity that is easily shared . . .", the adherence to archive is intimately linked with a struggle for power (42, 24).

The argument here is largely meant to elaborate on González's observations. It will attempt to demonstrate that, in turning to myth as a means to represent and explore a Latin American reality, Augusto Roa Bastos makes use of the mythmaking space laid out in Latin American fiction by Macedonio Fernández and utilized by numerous avant-garde writers who followed him. His reliance on archive, on the other hand, places the Paraguayan novelist at odds with Macedonio's desire to reserve writing for purely metaphysical—and absolutely not political or social—expression. Roa Bastos effects, in short, a politicizing of Macedonio's antipolitical discourse.

During a digression in "Una novela que comienza" ["A novel that begins"], Macedonio Fernández makes a point of distinguishing himself from Miguel de Unamuno, his contemporary:

> Por eso yo—sigo el paréntesis por fuera para que no se me moteje de digresivo como Unamuno, que nunca escribe sobre lo que trata—, por eso yo, que a veces estoy tan poco y tenue, que me parece que me llamo Ningunamuno, digo que. . . . (17)

> [For this reason I—I continue the parenthesis outside so as not to be labelled digressive like Unamuno, who never writes about the subject—for this reason I, who at times am so slight and tenuous that I feel like I am called Noneamuno, I say. . . .]

Macedonio's repeated barbs at the Spanish author and philosopher, like so much of his prose, never fail to suggest a paradox. On the one hand, Macedonio Fernández recognizes the apparent kinship between his Belarte Conciencial and Unamuno's poetics in their radical form, their unorthodox use of the conventions of Realist writing, and, as shall be discussed presently, in their characters who fully expoit their status as fiction rather than attempt to pass as real people. On the other hand, as he suggests in his criticisms of the Spaniard, Macedonio takes the radical principles of his poetics a quantum leap further than Unamuno.

Unamuno concedes immortality of a sort to the protagonist of *Niebla* (*Mist*), Augusto Pérez, but he reserves for himself, the flesh-and-blood author, ascendency over his literary creations. Only the author can determine a character's literary existence: its inclusion in a work, its function in a text. The literary may transcend time and even death itself, Unamuno implies, but the author ultimately retains control. Macedonio Fernández, by contrast, extends his challenge to received conceptions of literature, to question not only the status and dynamics of fictional characters, but of readers and authors themselves.

Atemporality and the negation of death are two basic components to Macedonio's radical metaphysics (of which Belarte Conciencial is the principal expression). But in drastic contrast to Unamuno, Macedonio repeatedly affirms eternity not only for the entities created by the language of his writing, but for himself and all human subjects. Thus he gives us Solano Reyes, in his tale "Donde Solano Reyes era un vencido y sufría dos derrotas cada día" ["In Which Solano Reyes Was a Vanquished Man and Suffered Two Defeats Every Day"], whose death is prevented and indefinitely postponed for as long as he maintains a particular kind of relationship with the characters who help to realize his existence. Specifically, his niece must arrive at his home every evening with a genuine appetite for his leftover daily bread:

> Una vez que contó con que la sobrina tendría siempre ganas de pan a la hora en que lo visitaba, se dio a sí mismo por eterno. Su eternidad sólo flaqueaba bajo el aspecto de que podría morir la sobrina. El daría su vida por su sobrina y le interesaba asegurar la eternidad de ella más que la propia. La condición de eternidad en sí mismo la había descubierto. ¿Cuál era la condición de eternidad de su sobrina? (220)

> [Once he was able to count on his niece always wanting bread at the time at which she visited him, he considered himself eternal. His

eternity only flagged at the prospect that his niece could die. He would give his life for his niece, and was interested in her eternity more than in his own. The condition of eternity in himself had been found. What was the condition of his niece's eternity?]

Further on, the question is answered:

He aquí que la vida de la sobrina depende de dos cosas: 1) Que ningún cuentista la nombre (el lector, creo, se conformará fácilmente con esta fácil omisión del nombre de la sobrina en esta novela de un tío en obsequio de su eternidad en ella) y 2)—lo que ya se comprende que descubrió muy fatigosamente y después de mucho tiempo don Solano—: Que las pinchaduras de aguja tenían que hacer con la no eternidad de la sobrina, en tanto que el dedicarse todas las mañanas a coser era esencial a su eternidad. Moriría si dejaba de coser, pero también moriría si cosiendo padecía más de un pinchazo de aguja por semana (221).

[So it is that the niece's life depends on two things: 1) That no storyteller name her (the reader, I believe, will easily resign himself to this easy omission of the niece's name in this novel of an uncle out of respect for his eternity in her) and 2)—and it is understood don Solano discovered this after a long time and with great difficulty—: That needle pricks had to do with the noneternity of the niece, whereas devoting herself every morning to sewing was essential to her eternity. She would die if she stopped sewing, but she would also die if while sewing she suffered more than one needle prick per week.]

These two characters take their places in an infinite, eternal web of human interdependencies, sacrifices, and symbioses, which make up the fabric of Macedonio Fernández's cosmos. It is a cosmos, we will argue presently, with a strong mythical dimension. Macedonio himself, however, is no less subordinate to this web than they. The author (indeed, the reader, too) must agree to cooperate in the eternity of the characters; the characters cooperate in affirming the identity—and ultimately the eternity—of the author.

Macedonio's plays on negation and eternity are a repudiation of Unamuno's ultimate reaffirmation of the ascendency of the individual human subject over linguistic creation: a suggestion that both he and his antithesis Unamuno are, in opposing ways, at the mercy of their writings; a refusal, in other words, to acknowledge the possibility of death for Augusto Pérez.

In *Museo de la novela de la Eterna: Primera novela buena* [*A Museum of the Novel of Eterna: The First Good Novel*], the most extreme of Macedonio's major works, characters confront the author (usually to take issue with him), much as Augusto Pérez confronts Miguel de Unamuno. But they also will confront the reader, who is no less a part of this web than they (174). And naturally, therefore, "the reader" occasionally appears and takes issue with the whole lot (181). Characters, like Nicolasa the cook, may elect to excuse themselves from the work; others, such as "Frederico, el chico del largo palo" ["Frederico, the Boy with the Big Stick"], beg to be admitted but are refused (80–83). But at any given point in Macedonio's narrative opus, the particular function or functions of a character, relative to the others (including author, narrator, reader, and so on) is unmistakable. Even the book itself is subordinate to this mythic cosmos; accordingly, the author of *Museo* discusses with one of his anonymous characters the merits of characters' "transmigrations" among various novels (63). In this sense, all perform roles in a cosmos to which the author, reader, and all other individuals are subordinated: an essentially mythic one.

Although Macedonio Fernández never uses the terms myth or mythical with regard to his own work, a strong argument can be made for terming as mythical the characters who people the metaphysical landscape of Macedonio Fernández's fiction. In discussing Macedonio's radical, metaphysically oriented approach to fiction, critics have not labeled it mythmaking. But they have remarked on his unmistakable interest in the permanence of entities constituted by language, and thus in the eternalizing power of a metaphysics constituted by such entities. Nélida Salvador, in particular, demonstrates how part of the permanence Macedonio strives for is the constant frustration of absolute and terminal definitions and an interminable, unceasing "movement" (113). This constant movement is in effect an attempt to realize the eternity and permanence of a mythic discourse. Macedonio is not expressly interested in myth, and does not openly intend to create a new mythic cosmos. But in his efforts to establish a metaphysical space that refuses the structures of time, materials, perception, and consciousness, he ends up articulating what is effectively a mythmaking space. On the other hand, he also expresses a refusal of that which *mythos* becomes when it is archived or written down, merged with *logos*, and thus made into mythology: rigid, unchanging, and authoritative. In essence, Macedonio turns to a reinvention of a mythic metaphysics as a rejection of all that the old mythological cosmos has evolved into: Western literature in all of its monolithic stature.

In fact, as regards aesthetic creation, Macedonio's energies are mainly focused on the immediate task of dismantling the book: undoing the structures and strictures of language and literature, what will be referred to here as "archiving" structures. Thus his mythic *Museo de la novela de la Eterna*, the "first good novel," is offered as a tandem work to *Adriana Buenos Aires: Ultima novela mala*, the "last bad novel" and a masterpiece of deconstructive prose. (Both of these novels were published posthumously, in different years. Macedonio, however, wrote a single foreword to be included in both, suggesting they were meant to be received jointly, refusing the reader the definitive knowledge as to which was the "última mala" and which the "primera buena.")

Adriana makes use of a great number—indeed, an extravagant number—of the conventions and structures of Realist literature. But Macedonio works to negate such structuring by persistently refusing his characters the presence of a stable identity, personality, or individuality. Even though the characters in *Adriana* take the form of realistic fiction—of an archive of reality—the author repeatedly frustrates this archiving impulse. The same is true of his agreement not to name the niece in "Solano Reyes"—not to archive her—and thus similarly his insistence that his characters in Museo must not strive for status as flesh-and-blood humans but must maintain identity in terms of their *spiritual* function with regard to other characters. This basic principle of Belarte is suggested by the description of one of these characters, Deunamor:

> Por eso juraría que Deunamor dejó de ser una conciencia personal desde hace muchos años, y yo mismo observo que su conducta en la novela es la de un hombre que nada siente, piensa ni ve, en actitud de espera, pero sin sentir la espera, de volver a reunirse con la amada y ser feliz, o sea que es actualmente una insensibilidad con perspectiva de ser una sensibilidad. (*Museo*, 61)

> [So I would swear that Deunamor stopped being a personal conciousness many years ago, and I myself observe that his conduct in the novel is that of a man who neither feels, thinks nor sees anything, one who seems to be waiting, but without feeling the wait, once again to be reunited with his beloved and to be happy, in other words that he is currently an insensibility with the perspective of being a sensibility.]

In other words, Macedonio's characters do not conform to the characters of Romantic or Realist fiction, each with an individual identity and consciousness, each with its own isolated complex of needs, talents, failings, and circumstances. Each of Macedonio's characters can only have meaning or identity in its interaction with others (Deunamor's function, in this regard, is to wait to be reunited with his beloved). Nor do they undergo "development" or "growth" or "revelation," such as we expect of the characters in most Western prose since the Renaissance. They simply exist to define each other and to articulate a mythic universe. This mythic universe, moreover, although always there, has been obscured by the constructions that, in Macedonio Fernández's view, Western culture has come to accept as "reality." These are the cultural constructions—individualistic, measurable, and limited—largely constituted and perpetuated by Realist literature. The mythic, he implies, without referring to myth at all, is inherent in all human existence, and should be explicit in all literary creation. It is archive, the assertion of the finite, concrete, limited, mortal individual, that impedes the realization of the mythic in all of us.

Macedonio attests here to the power of language to create entities that are not only real and palpable, but arguably permanent, just as a particular idea or fantasy may remain a constant fixture in the consciousness of an individual whose life in the world of objects is in constant flux. It is a simple truism that what has been said cannot be unsaid; what language creates cannot be uncreated. But the essence of myth requires atemporality; the subjects of myth are permanent and eternal, absent—in the accepted physical sense—from the realm of human time, as it were. They may evolve, but they do not die and arguably are not ever born, thus they are never really present. They are rather the products of language's own limitless generative and self-sustaining power: the very essence of language creating itself and, consequently, sustaining humans while it is sustained by them.

There is myth evolving in our presence, evolving as we speak and write, both in the literary creation of people and in the people themselves. It is not an exaggeration, really, when we speak of historical figures as having mythical qualities or proportions. These are people who, although "absent" to ordinary physical sensibilities—indeed, in part because of their physical absence—are, in a very real sense, alive, evolving, and exerting great power on our concrete world, well after their recorded and acknowledged historical deaths. It is this kind of weighty absence constituted by myth—so much more important to Macedonio Fernández than personal presence or the imitation of it—that pervades his work, his metaphysical cosmos, and the aesthetic legacy taken up by more recent novelists such as Roa Bastos.

Macedonio Fernández was an anarchist in the most fundamental sense of the word. He was opposed to organized government not out of political conviction but out of metaphysical vision. When he ran for the presidency of the Argentine Republic in 1927, it was not as pure "burla," not merely to parody what he felt to be a system harmful to the people subjected to it. It was a campaign of absence, conducted in earnest. Unofficial and unrecorded in periodicals of the day, the campaign, as Leopoldo Marechal describes it, attempted to transgress and dismantle those structures and boundaries most basic to what Argentines assumed to be their everyday reality: utensils, measurements, spaces, pathways; all disrupted ". . . para introducir luego el nombre de Macedonio Fernández como la única solución" [". . . so as then to introduce the name Macedonio Fernández as the only solution"], in the words of Germán Leopoldo García (23).[1] It was a campaign entirely in keeping with Macedonio's persistent call for the "Individuo Máximo en el Estado Mínimo" ["the Maximum Individual in the Minimum State"]. Moreover, this fantastic project, dreamed up and disseminated among friends (though to what extent carried out will never be clear), is also presented in *Museo*. The resident characters of "The Novel," drafted for the purpose by an entity named "the President" (who spends most of his time thinking and writing), undertake to "introduce beauty" to Buenos Aires by much the same means as ascribed to Macedonio's presidential campaign.

Such an example helps demonstrate how Macedonio's desire to bring his metaphysical vision to bear on Argentine reality is evident in every word he wrote. His writing is not so much a prescription for reality as an effort to bring to life his personal metaphysical vision. On the one hand, he is aware, like any good anarchist, of the revolutionary nature of this endeavor; thus *Museo de la novela de la Eterna* is the *primera novela buena*, the first time authentic metaphysics is expressed in novel form. On the other hand, Macedonio acknowledges his inability to achieve the ideal "novela futura," as Noé Jitrik describes it: permanently open, alive, evolving (Jitrik, 42, 47, 49). In effect, he signals his failure to attain completely the mythic as we have defined it here; he does not entitle his work *Novela de la Eterna* but *Museo de la novela de la Eterna*: an unwilling artifact by virtue of being printed on paper, placed between two covers and archived on a shelf for the public to view.

Macedonio Fernández carries his negation of the author's ascendency and his adherence to a mythic cosmos to their utmost consequences. Repeatedly and doggedly, he insists on demolishing the contemporary conception of the individual subject as the focus of all creation and replacing it with a metaphysics resting on the concept of an all-embracing, interindividual spirit. The "Individuo Máximo," a concept articulated by Macedonio in tandem with his anarchic proposal for an "Estado Mínimo," is precisely the rejection of all reference to an objective reality hinging on the perceptions and sensations of the individual self ("Brindis a Marinetti," 74). It is not, however, a concurrence with the Surrealist expansion of the individual consciousness and subconscious. Belarte, in fact, strives against Surrealism's transcription of consciousness to an aesthetic and metaphysical status equal to empirical reality. On the contrary, Macedonio calls for an expansion of the spirit and soul of the individual—most pointedly not the isolated consciousness—to the point of maximum, perhaps infinite, sympathy with all other individuals, a process accomplished only through the power of love. It is the Individuo Máximo who is just that realization of our mythic possibilities; thus the mythic, atemporal, eternally absent maximum individual replaces the delineated, defined, but ephemeral present self, the "yo." This transindividual aesthetic and metaphysical vision, however, necessarily rests on the writer and reader as organic and integrated individuals. Writer and reader are ascendent beings of thought, feeling, and dreaming (ascendent to the extent that they are part of a transindividual phenomenon and in cooperation with the characters of a mythic cosmos, not as individual identities). They stand in contrast to entities whose identity or integrity ultimately are subordinate to the society in which they participate or the material objects of the physical environment they inhabit. Thus the anarchic "Estado Mínimo," the disruption and ultimate eradication of political structures, must accompany his "Individuo Máximo."

Like Macedonio Fernández, Augusto Roa Bastos, in his *Yo el Supremo*, strives to liberate writing from the bonds of received literature and he turns to the mythic potential of language to do so. But it is precisely in this aspect of literature that Roa parts company with Macedonio; for in addition to working in the mythic space elaborated by Macedonio and the subsequent chain of avant-garde writers leading to the present day, Roa concerns himself with the mythology already current in Paraguayan cultural discourse. Moreover, Roa's very conception of the mythic differs in one crucial way from the discourse defined here as Macedonio Fernández's mythic space.

Roa wastes no time in establishing el Supremo's eternity and demonstrating the eternalizing powers exercised by language. But the "eternalizing" measures in Roa's work, measures that also serve to refuse closure and linear structure, are part of an ultimate ambition rather different from that of Macedonio Fernández. Roa attempts to apply this reinvented mythic discourse to concerns of political and social nature. This is obvious in the very choice of focus: the Paraguayan dictator of mythological proportions, José Gaspar Rodríguez de Francia.

For the most part, the devices that Roa uses to redefine the space of the novel resound of the metaphysical space Macedonio stakes out in his works. Roa employs these devices candidly, with little reticence concerning the tricks he plays on readers of the Realist tradition. The passage in which el Supremo discusses the endless, torturous parade to which he subjects visiting dignitaries is an example. Addressing the reader directly, he affirms with a minimum of linguistic acrobatics that he has simply collapsed time into a single plane:

> Escuchen, Aún está sonando la charanga del mismo, solo, y único desfile que brindé a la turbamulta de enviados imperiales, directoriales, provinciales, urdemales. En desagravio del país. Año 1811, 1813, 1823.
>
> Superpuestos los enviados plenipotenciarios de Buenos Aires, Herrera y Coso, y del Imperio del Brasil, Correia. Transpuestos a la dimensión que les obligo mirar. Sentados unos encima de las rodillas de los otros. En el mismo lugar aunque no en el mismo tiempo. Miren, observen: Les ofrezco el despliegue de la parada que cubre dos primeras décadas de la República, incluida la última década de la Colonia (394).
>
> [Listen. The fanfare of the same, sole, and only parade that I offered the mob of imperial, directorial, provincial, conspiratorial envoys. To compensate the country. Years 1811, 1813, 1823.
>
> The plenipotentiary envoys of Buenos Aires, Herra and Coso, and the Empire of Brazil, Correia, superposed. Transposed to the dimension upon which I oblige them to gaze. Sitting on each other's knees. In the same place though not at the same time. Look, observe: I am unfolding before you the parade that covers the first two decades of the Republic, including the last decade of the Colony (248)].[2]

Using this negation of time as the most obvious device, el Supremo sets before the reader his mythicizing technique. The parade is an endless, timeless, creation that places absent foreign dignitaries in a determined relationship within the "republic" created by the mind and words of el Supremo.

With equal candor, el Supremo claims for himself another, even more fundamental phenomenon basic to Macedonio Fernández's metaphysical vision: the negation of birth and death.

> Yo no tengo familia; si de verdad he nacido, lo que está aún por probarse, puesto que no puede morir sino lo que ha nacido. Yo he nacido de mí y Yo solo me he hecho doble. (250)

> [I have no family; if indeed I was really born, which has yet to be proved, since only what has been born can die. I was born of myself and I alone have made myself double (133)].

But whereas Macedonio's negation of birth and death as temporal and spatial phenomena is integral with his overall argument for the existence of an interindividual spirit based on consciousness of human emotion, the assertions of el Supremo have the opposite effect. The refusal of limitations of time and space, here put forth as a mythicizing principle, when conflated with the affirmation of the individual self, the "yo," as the only valid gauge of reality, results in the most extreme megalomania conceivable: the conversion of the self into a god:

> Negado el azar por un anacronismo, de los muchos que empleo en mi batalla contra el tiempo, soy ese personaje fantástico cuyo nombre se arrojan unas a otras las lavaderas mientras baten montones de ropa limpiándola de la suciedad de los cuerpos. Sangre o sudor, lo mismo da. Lágrimas. Humores sacramentales, excrementales; qué más da. **YO** soy ese **PERSONAJE** y ese **NOMBRE**. Suprema encarnación de la raza. . . .

> **YO** soy el **SUPREMO PERSONAJE** que vela y protege vuestro sueño dormido, vuestro sueño despierto (no hay diferencia entre ambos) que busca el paso del Mar Rojo en medio de la persecución y acorralamiento de nuestros enemigos . . . (479–480)

> [Having ruled out chance through an anachronism, one of the many I use in my battle against time, I am that fantastic personage whose name the washerwomen bandy back and forth as they pound the filth of bodies out of mountains of clothes. Blood or sweat: it makes no difference. Tears. Sacramental, excremental humors: all the same. **I** am that **PERSONAGE** and that **NAME**. Supreme incarnation of the race. . . .

I am the **SUPREME PERSONAGE** who watches over and protects
your sleeping dream, your waking dream (there is no difference
between the one and the other); who seeks the passage through the Red
Sea amid persecution and entrapment by our enemies . . . (320–321)].

Thus, two fundamental changes are necessary to convert the aggressively antipolitical metaphysical space staked out by Macedonio
Fernández into a space for the forging of the political and social discourse of Roa Bastos's novel. First, as illustrated above, Roa must shift
from Macedonio's elaboration of a metaphysical vision expressed by
means of the author's personal consciousness (which in turn constitutes
participation in a transindividual spirit, thus rendering the author more
absent than present) to a self-mythicizing vision by a third, historically
depicted and established individual: el Supremo.

The second, and related difference, is the use as raw material of an
already existing mythology—already fashioned, written down, archived.
This mythology is rooted in history and politics and closely tied to the
constitution of a Paraguayan national identity, a socially delineated
collective consciousness, entirely different from Macedonio's interindividual spirit. Macedonio rejects out-of-hand all such prior material
and all suggestion of a socially constituted discourse. Even for *Adriana
Buenos Aires* he allows only the form and conventions of the Western
storytelling tradition, the signs cut off from their expected or received
meaning. But Roa Bastos, rather than disposing of what precedes him, is
provoked by it. One of the missions of *Yo el Supremo* is specifically to
expose and dismantle what has come before. It aims to question the
national Paraguayan mythology so intimately intertwined with the life
and presence of Dr. Francia, elucidating the distinctions between the
mythic and the mythological. The novel can only accomplish this task
within the metaphysical space of mythmaking.

There is a further, and subtler, distinction between the poetics of
Macedonio Fernández and Augusto Roa Bastos and between their
elaborations of mythic discourse. The mythicizing context of the parade
discussed above allows for the bringing to life of another myth, this one
existing prior to the inventions of the narrator, in which the governor's
daughter is carried off by a serpent native to the myths of the Guaraní
people. And as if to emphasize the point that this is indeed a living myth,
the text notes the absence of written references to this mythical creature
(Roa Bastos, 388–393, [243–247]). Although attempts have been made

to mythologize the serpent—in effect to kill him by archiving him, setting him down in written words—he remains a living, unwritten myth. It is important to note here, however, that even this myth, albeit distinguished from archive by Roa Bastos, still does not satisfy Macedonio's requirements for his Belarte Conciencial, specifically because of its identification with an acknowledged cultural group. It remains by Macedonio's standards a cultural artifact rather than authentic fiction.

Fernando Moreno Turner has pointed out that the monstrous egomaniacal dictator portrayed in *Yo el Supremo* in fact comprises, on the one hand a historical, individual "yo," and on the other hand a mythic "él" (Moreno, 15–20). El Supremo invests the presence of his "yo" with this "él," sustained by the atemporal, immeasurable, immortal, mythic discourse of the Paraguayan people (thus empowering his presence with a far weightier absence). In doing so, el Supremo also effects the mythologizing—or archiving—of Paraguay's heretofore mythic discourse. Roa Bastos attempts to counteract or dismantle that mythologizing by means of exposing and breaking the empowering bond between "yo" and "él." He does this in part by exposing the *process* of mythologizing, the method el Supremo uses, with his scribe, Patiño, as instrument—by means of writing, of archiving—to appropriate for his "yo" the mythic discourse of the countless generations of the multitude.

This re-creation of an "ecisión" (as Moreno calls it) between "yo" and "él," between self and collectivity, is one that Macedonio Fernández would never permit. Macedonio's primary purpose in reforming narrative is to achieve the ultimate fusion of the individual with the collective. On the one hand, he denies the existence of all fundamental concepts based on the idea of self as a grounded subject and as a perceiving presence in the world: linear space, ordered time, birth and death are among these banished concepts. Roa Bastos, in contrast, utilizes these negations to facilitate first the representation, then the dismantling of mythology. On the other hand, Macedonio refuses legitimacy to any organized or delineated collectivity; the concepts of nationality and race as well as governments are, in his eyes, fictions. As a result, even Roa's mythic serpent, identified as it is with a specific national culture, fails Macedonio's test for a truly metaphysical discourse. Even Roa's idea of authentic myth would constitute, for Macedonio, a sort of mythology.

While Macedonio dismantles the fictive self, the "yo," Roa takes this operation a step further to dismantle the historical fictive self created by the mythology of el Supremo. Thus both challenge the domain of the self, but Roa acknowledges the power of the word to create political realities spawned by (or constituted by) the mythology of the self, while Macedonio strives to destroy that power by refusing it acknowledgment. The vacuum left by the denial of politics in Macedonio's work—by the Estado Mínimo, an "absence" according to received, rational thought—is filled by another absence, one authentic to Macedonio Fernández's thinking. This absence is the Individuo Máximo, the definition of which exceeds all possible boundaries of subjective self-hood and individuality. Just as Francia's individual historical "yo" would be termed a falsehood by Macedonio, so would his mythic "él," to the extent that it constitutes the expression of a politically defined body.

As Salvador Bacarisse points out, Roa does not concede to language the absolute autonomy and nonreferentiality propounded by numerous avant-garde writers, among whom we can include here Macedonio Fernández (Bacarisse, 153–161). Macedonio's attempt to realize a metaphysics freed of the constraints of objective reality, of presence, demands that language be no more nor less than the consciousness of creation—most pointedly not the consciousness of the self. Roa, committed as he is to reforming history—and reforming present reality—cannot adhere to such avant-garde purism. Indeed, Bacarisse compares Roa's "mythification of history," his use of the mythic dimension of recounting, to Unamuno's concept of "intrahistoria" (156). He thus reminds us that like Unamuno, Roa ultimately does not relinquish the ascendency of the empirical author. While he does distinguish the function of "compiler," arguably an identifiable, present individual, from the collective authorship of myth constituted by absent generations of the Paraguayan people, language itself and the myth it constitutes remain subordinate to the people who express it.

But Roa does utilize the principles of avant-garde aesthetics towards his ends: the exposure of el Supremo as a historical self, a "yo" who appropriates—archives—mythic discourse to create a mythological presence, a legendary monster. Roa endeavors to expose the objective reality corresponding to the mythological, and by exposing it to liberate society from it, replacing it with the *myth* generated by the historical and social collective consciousness of Paraguay; or in Roa's own words:

De lo que se trata entonces es que el mito formal de la libertad sea reemplazada por la imaginación auténticamente libertadora, y que el universo imaginario, más libre y creativo que nunca emerja de las fuentes mismas de la realidad y de la historia ("La narrativa paraguaya," 139).[3]

[What is attempted, then, is to replace the formal myth of liberty with authentically liberating imagination, and to make the imaginative universe, freer and more creative than ever, emerge from the very sources of reality and history.]

This consciousness, however, by virtue of its very historicity, proves to be more present than absent according to the standards of Macedonio Fernández's thinking.

In attempting this liberation of myth from mythology, in replacing the presence of a "yo" with the absence of a more pervasive "él," Roa does not only make use of Macedonio's mythic metaphysical space to address a social and political agenda, entirely contrary to Macedonio's purpose. He also reveals the one feature that is inherently pernicious in Macedonio's vision: it is precisely the void left by the dismissal, or empirical "absence" of politics in Macedonio's Belarte that el Supremo has appropriated as his own and filled with his self-consciousness, his construction of a personal identity, his presence, his "yo," suppressing all possibility for the expression of the Individuo Máximo. Roa's response to Macedonio's poetics is, in effect, to affirm the value and authenticity of its metaphysical principles but, at the same time, to insist on a social foundation, on a politics of absence—for its very protection. Privileging the social dynamics—the political *presence*—of cultural creation, Roa implies, is the only viable way to protect the space of absence, of myth-making, of cultural creation, from the presence of individual identity and the self-ish structures imposed by it.

The above conclusion suggests that Macedonio Fernández's "novela futura" is largely a failed project. Indeed, failure weighs heavily in Macedonio's writing whenever it approaches moments of closure: forgetfulness overpowers love at the end of *Adriana*; the President disbands the residents of the "Novela" at the end of *Museo*, having recognized the failure of his project to transform Buenos Aires into a world of beauty (a failure we have already suggested is signaled in the novel's title). Of course, the identification of failure with closure is inevitable in writing that strives for perpetual opening and unceasing movement. But it is the enduring space of opening and movement upon which the mythic cosmos of Roa Bastos's writing is built. The inherent paradox of a "novela futura," a source of some anxiety for Macedonio, is accepted and put to use by Roa Bastos. Indeed, one way to summarize Macedonio's importance as "precursor" to contemporary Latin American novelists is to attribute to Macedonio's "ungrounding" exploration of that paradox the existence of ground upon which contemporary writers elaborate myth.

A fundamental difference between this contemporary mythic ground and Macedonio's ungrounded "novela futura" is their responses to a further modern paradox: the nature of subjectivity. Much of Macedonio's radical poetics, his striving for the "Individuo Máximo" and his anarchistic ideas are expressions of his anxiety concerning this paradox. On the one hand, Macedonio relentlessly attacks the concept of individual as subject; on the other hand, he confronts the fact that to write is, to an extent, to make oneself subject. Contemporary writers like Roa, having recognized and accepted this paradox, are able to exploit it. While much of that exploitation, its utilization in concerns of political and social nature, is anathema to Macedonio Fernández, its success in bringing to life the "universo imaginario" of contemporary works like *Yo el Supremo* attest to the endurance—the weighty and productive absence—of Macedonio's vision in Latin American letters.

Notes

1. García here paraphrases—but does not cite—his interview of Leopoldo Marechal; Jorge Luis Borges, et al., *Hablan de Macedonio Fernández* (Buenos Aires: Carlos Pérez Editor, 1986), 70–71.

2. All quotations in English of *Yo el Supremo* are from Helen Lane's translation, *I the Supreme*; page citations in brackets refer to that volume.

3. Where Roa speaks of "mito formal" I would substitute "mitología."

Works Cited

Bacarisse, Salvador. "Mitificación de la historia y desmitificación de la escritura: *Yo el Supremo* de Augusto Roa Bastos." *Bulletin of Hispanic Studies* 65 (1988): 153–161.

Fernández, Macedonio. *Adriana Buenos Aires: Ultima novela mala.* Vol. V of *Obras Completas.* Buenos Aires: Ediciones Corregidor, 1974.

Fernández, Macedonio. "Brindis a Marinetti." In *Papeles de Recienvenido/Poemas, Relatos, Cuentos, Misceláneas.* Buenos Aires: Centro Editor de América Latina, 1966. 74.

Fernández, Macedonio. "Donde Solano Reyes era un vencido y sufría dos derrotas cada día." In *Papeles de Recienvenido/Poemas, Relatos, Cuentos, Misceláneas.* Buenos Aires: Centro Editor de América Latina, 1966. 218–225.

Fernández, Macedonio. *Museo de la Novela de la Eterna: Primera novela buena.* Vol. VI of *Obras completas.* Buenos Aires: Ediciones Corregidor, 1975.

Fernández, Macedonio. "Una novela que comienza." In *Relato: cuentos, poemas y misceláneas.* Vol. VII of *Obras completas.* Buenos Aires: Ediciones Corregidor, 1987. 17–42.

García, Germán Leopoldo. *Macedonio Fernández: la escritura en objeto.* Buenos Aires: Siglo Veintiuno Editores, 1975.

González Echevarría, Roberto. *Myth and Archive: A Theory of Latin American Narrative.* Cambridge: Cambridge UP, 1990.

Jitrik, Noé. *La novela futura de Macedonio Fernández.* Caracas: Universidad Central de Venezuela, Ediciones de la Biblioteca, 1973.

Moreno Turner, Fernando. "Escritura, mito e historia: A propósito de un episodio de *Yo el Supremo.*" *Hispamérica,* 14.40 (April 1985): 15–20.

Roa Bastos, Augusto. *I the Supreme.* Trans. Helen Lane New York: Alfred A. Knopf, 1986.

Roa Bastos, Augusto. "La narrativa paraguaya en el contexto de la narrativa hispano-americana actual." In *Augusto Roa Bastos y la producción cultural americana.* Compiled by Saúl Sosnowski. Buenos Aires: Ediciones de la Flor, 1986: 138–146.

Roa Bastos, Augusto. *Yo el Supremo.* Madrid: Ediciones Cátedra, 1983.

Salvador, Nélida. *Macedonio Fernández: precursor de la antinovela.* Buenos Aires: Editorial Plus Ultra, 1986.

Unamuno, Miguel de. *Niebla.* Ed. Mario J. Valdés. Madrid: Ediciones Cátedra, 1984.

José Carlos González Boixo

THE UNDERLYING CURRENTS OF "CACIQUISMO" IN THE NARRATIVES OF JUAN RULFO

Rain falls on the graves of Comala. It is the end of a story whose characters, branded by solitude, cannot even find peace in the quietude of the cemetery. In their graves they toss and turn, pursued by their memories: such is the case of Susana San Juan who restlessly continues with her love-induced ravings; or further away, the anonymous character who has not yet been able to forget the fright of an unfortunate encounter with Pedro Páramo. Nearby, in another grave, Juan Preciado and Dorotea listen to those murmurs and tell each other about the shattering of their illusions. But the rain, an unmistakable symbol of hope in Rulfo's novel, falls insistently on these graves.[1] Does this mean that the novel is leaving the reader with a final sign of hope? Would not such a hopeful ending, written about a place where "sadness makes its nest," be paradoxical? The answer is no. It was an illusion that drove Rulfo to tell these stories, just as it motivated his characters: Juan Preciado, Dorotea, Susana, Pedro Páramo. The illusion that a happy world might exist, although denied by reality, caused him to leave the door open for hope: but Comala cannot embody that hope because her arid lands have turned into the image of hell and her inhabitants are dead. Can Comala rise again from her ashes? Does a happy world perhaps exist? Rulfo did not find it, but with his symbolic rainfall he left the hope that there might be such a place. He had no choice but to tell us of a harsh reality, one filled with sorrows, the only one he could observe about him.

In dealing with the theme of "caciquismo"[2] in the works of Rulfo, one must keep in mind that his fictions reflect the reality of rural Mexico, more specifically, that of the region of Jalisco. One should also recognize that Rulfo rises above any regionalisms and manages to infuse his literary work with universal value, transmitting to the reader a world characterized by solitude and anguish. But one should not forget that that anguish and that solitude, universal characteristics that any reader can associate with his or her more immediate realities, emerge literarily, through characters and an environment that are precisely defined: the characters are "campesinos," the space re-created is that of the Jalisco region of Mexico—although Rulfo avoids a precise location, in his work real places mix with other fictitious ones, creating a coherent, fictitious geography—and the chronology, intentionally imprecise in many cases, undoubtedly has the Mexican revolution and its subsequent years as a temporal point of reference.

When Rulfo published his collection of stories, in 1953, literary critics had no difficulty categorizing him as a "regionalist" writer, although with the passage of time literary qualities that were vastly superior to those of any other writer with whom he might be compared within the regionalist mold began to become more and more evident. The big surprise came two years later, when his novel appeared, stupefying many because of the way it broke with the traditional system of narrative technique and because in its very complexity it acquired a symbolic value that exceeded the regionalist connotations of the story narrated. In effect, with the passing of time, symbolic interpretations have been plentiful, which is hardly surprising in the case of such an overtly symbolic novel, but, given that some interpretations flatly contradict others, at least some must surely be erroneous. Such appraisals of Rulfo's work—which have basically focused on his novel—should not blind us to the local or regional component upon which Rulfo bases his literary work: only a literary analysis that keeps in mind that reality can be considered correct.[3]

Naturally, a direct consequence of the reality that Rulfo reflects in his narratives is the presence in that reality of the theme of "caciquismo." It would be as easy as it would be useless to enumerate here the instances in which this theme appears in Rulfo's work. It is not, therefore, a question of isolating a theme, but rather of observing what importance it has from a narrative point of view, identifying how it aids in shaping Rulfo's narrative world. Before beginning a detailed analysis, it is necessary to pose a twofold question: what are the conceptual limits of the terms "cacique" and "caciquismo" and what is their place in the narrative setting that Rulfo writes into his works.

With regard to terminology, there is a series of words that bear some relationship to each other and that respond as much to a social reality as to their usage within a literary context. Literary criticism has been able to distinguish, in an explicit manner within the area of the Spanish American novel, a significant number of works grouped under the heading of "novels of dictatorship." In fact, such literary works, essentially narratives, classified together because of their common themes of dictatorship and other related issues, such as the "caudillo," or the "cacique," are justified because they project reality itself. It is certainly true that that reality is not exclusive to Hispanic America, although there it has had a special impact. Given that these things are so well known, it is hardly necessary to establish a detailed typology for each of these groups of characters[4]; one need only recall that all of them are characterized by the unlawful retention of abusive power, generally by violent means, a power wielded over diverse spheres of their reality. Thus, the *dictator* moves in the area of politics and wields his power on a national level, the *"caudillo"* is a local version of the dictator, and the *"cacique"* is distinguished from the others in that he normally has no political dimension, even though he wields a certain degree of local power. In a general sense, the "cacique" is a wealthy landowner, a person who is powerful because of his economic resources, one who uses his social position to his own advantage and maintains his hegemony on the strength of the many individuals who depend upon him. This is the case of Pedro Páramo.

The beginnings of Hispanic American narrative constructed around the figure of the dictator go back to the romantic period, precisely when the independence movement was giving birth to new countries and favoring the appearance of the first dictators. The Argentine ruler Juan Manuel Rosas was the focus of Esteban Echeverría's "El matadero," José Mármol's *Amalia*, and Domingo Faustino Sarmiento's *Facundo* (in which the biography of the "caudillo" Facundo Quiroga was also narrated). What all of these works had in common was that literature became a personal testimonial, a direct means of denouncing reality, with visible signs of Manichaeism, and very much in the tradition of what is known as "thesis" literature. These characteristics persisted throughout the first half of the twentieth century. And, as far as narratives about the "cacique" are concerned, the typification of this character can be seen in the indigenist narratives of Alcides Arguedas, Jorge Icaza, or Ciro Alegría, or even in so paradigmatic a novel as *Doña Bárbara* by Rómulo Gallegos. Although in this last example the characterization of the protagonist breaks boldy with the ironclad typology that had been serving as a framework for such characters, it is in the second half of the twentieth century that the literary characterizations of dictators or "caciques" achieve true autonomy. Compare, for example, the cases referred to earlier with the interior projections of dictators as resuscitated by Augusto Roa Bastos in *Yo el Supremo*, by Alejo Carpentier in *El recurso del método*, or by Gabriel García Márquez in *El otoño del Patriarca*. It is in this more recent line that the treatment given by Rulfo to the figure of Pedro Páramo should be considered.

Focusing now on Rulfo's narrative, we must clarify certain things. The complexity of *Pedro Páramo* is well known, and this is not the place to take up the multiple perspectives of the novel, given that the reader will already be sufficiently familiar with that aspect of this classic of contemporary narrative. In light of the work's complexities, if we take *Pedro Páramo* to be a member of the group of "cacique" novels we may risk employing a reductive criterion that devalues its literary qualities. Nonetheless, bearing in mind the work's sophistication, if one pauses to reflect on the characterization of Pedro Páramo as a "cacique" one is not lapsing into an analysis that is anecdotal in nature because the story narrated is centered on a character who is a "cacique." Moreover, nor is it possible to reduce the presence of "caciquismo" in Rulfo to this novel alone, since in his stories it is a thematic constant, even though a superficial reading might fail to detect it. Finally, the theme of "caciquismo" acquires its full importance in the context of the world created by Rulfo as a manifestation of violence; the relationship of "caciquismo" to other forms of violence that determine Rulfo's reality is evident.

Pedro Páramo, the "cacique" of Comala

While reading the novel, the reader comes to visualize its story, and the characters of necessity will take on a certain physical dimension. How does the reader's mind picture Pedro Páramo? That is a curious question, one that could be equally well be asked with regard to the rest of Rulfo's characters, and one that would presumably yield a wide variety of answers. The contemporary novel is not exactly characterized by the presence of an omniscient narrator who helps the reader "imagine" the narrated events (remember, by way of contrast, the minute physical descriptions of the characters of the realistic novels of the nineteenth- and early twentieth-century novels). In the case of Rulfo narrative is founded on the use of the first-person and, failing that, on a third-person narrator who adopts the perspective of the character in question (technically known as an equiscient narrator)[5]; one finds such extremes of absence of information that it would be difficult for any two readers to agree on the physical appearance of a character.

In fact, in the whole of the novel there is not one description of Pedro Páramo, and it is difficult to know how old he is at critical points of the story. All of this, despite the fact that he is the character around whom the entire story revolves. We note in this regard that Rulfo had in mind two totally different titles for the novel before it finally appeared as *Pedro Páramo*. It might be an interesting interpretive exercise to try to explain the final title in light of the others. However, this is not the place to venture into the kind of hypotheses that are always difficult to defend, but instead to ponder a palpable matter that directly affects the topic in question: without devaluing the possible symbolic interpretations that some readings of the novel might evoke (I refer essentially to the symbolism of the "quest" of Juan Preciado),[6] one must keep in mind that the figure of the "cacique" conditions the entire story, and that his presence is a constant throughout the novel.[7] In fact, he is the center toward which all the stories of individuals converge, and all the characters "exist" only through their dependence on the nuclear personage of Pedro Páramo.[8]

Given that Pedro Páramo is so important to the novel, his status as "cacique" should not be set aside. Perhaps those critics who have concerned themselves with the novel have barely stressed this fact since it is so evident. Nonetheless, it is demonstrable that all the action originates as a result of Pedro Páramo's status as "cacique": through scenes that collect together diverse moments in the life of Pedro Páramo (and bearing in mind the fragmentary nature of the novel and the chronological ruptures in the narration (discourse) of the "story") the reader can gradually reassemble the figure of the "cacique" and quite easily see that his presence fills the entire novel. On a denotative level, the "story" in *Pedro Páramo* clusters into a series of units: a) the childhood of Pedro Páramo; b) the different episodes that affirm his status as "cacique": the marriage to Dolores, the murder of Toribio Aldrete; c) the death of Miguel Páramo; d) the story of Susana; e) the death of Pedro Páramo. All of these narrative blocks (which group together different fragments or sequences[9]) center upon the "history" of Pedro Páramo; but the story of the cacique of Comala is also enhanced by means of the novel's other narrative level, the first-person narration of Juan Preciado.

In order to analyze the figure of Pedro Páramo as "cacique" one must keep in mind the dual perspective that Rulfo gave his novel: on the one hand, the note of ambiguity arising from the universal character that the "story" acquires on the symbolic level; on the other hand, the Mexican essence in which the narrated events are steeped, which gives the novel an inescapably concrete nature. *Concreteness* and *universality* are the two poles (complementary, not opposing) that characterize the narrative discourse of the novel, so that in sketching the personality of Pedro Páramo as a "cacique" one can also carry out an analysis that progressively proceeds from the particular (Mexican) to the symbolic (universal).

Rulfo devotes a good portion of the novel to characterizing Pedro Páramo as a "cacique." From a critical point of view, we find ourselves on a level that we might consider to be "particular." The numerous scenes that describe the violent means used by the protagonist to achieve power, converting him into the "cacique" of the region, do not merely provide the reader with a characterization of Pedro Páramo as "cacique"; they also demonstrate great efficiency in the creation of other characters, whose own separate stories, as they intertwine, accumulate into the complexity that typifies the narrative world created by Rulfo. From this perspective, the characterization of Pedro Páramo as "cacique" makes it possible to discern the creation of two types of characters, distinguished by the nature of the relationship they establish with him. In one group are those who have no relationships other than with Pedro Páramo: such is the case with Fulgor Sedano, Damasio, and the lawyer, Gerardo. The presence of each can, for the most part, be justified only through their involvement with Pedro Páramo's activities as "cacique." In the second group are the more complex characters, such as Susana, Juan Preciado, or Father Rentería, all of whose relationships are much more extensive but who nonetheless are linked to Pedro Páramo through his "caciquismo" (even though this link may not be the only one present, as in the case of Susana San Juan). One can thereby conclude that the characterization of Pedro Páramo as a "cacique" is in fact essential to the development of the narrated story; thus, to simplify greatly—and without betraying the truth as a result—one can say that the novel tells the story of a "cacique" who violently seizes power over lands that are not his and who, at a given moment, decides that the village must die. Thus the reader can distinguish a Comala in three distinct realizations: the idealized village evoked through memories that Dolores passes on to her son, Juan Preciado; the harsh reality of a village under the yoke of Pedro Páramo; and, finally, the hellish Comala visited by Juan Preciado. At this level, Juan Rulfo's purpose of denouncing "caciquismo" in rural Mexico is quite evident.

From this standpoint, it might seem that Rulfo's novel is not greatly different from the numerous others of previous decades dealing with the subject of "caciquismo." The differences, however, are so obvious as not to deserve comment, given that Rulfo's work is situated within the novelistic tendencies that mark a sharp break with the traditional novel. It is from this enriching perspective that one should always approach the detailed study of the characteristics of "caciquismo" in *Pedro Páramo*. The complex universal symbolism of the novel arises from this very specific foundation constructed from details of local Mexican reality. To cast aside this localism would be to falsify the novel and, without question, to hinder a satisfactory reading: hence the need for a preliminary interpretation focusing on this local aspect, in which "Mexicanism," as an interpretive key, impinges in a special way on the theme of "caciquismo."

The reader perceives the geographic space of the novel clearly: a rural zone in Mexico that authentically reflects the region of Jalisco, where Rulfo came from, which serves as a point of reference for the creation of the fictitious environment of Comala. The fictitious work finds a home in the Mexican frame of reference. Let us remember that near Comala lies Sayula, a real place, and that the novel mentions other towns that exist in reality. Consequently, the same relationship exists between the reality of "caciquismo" and the fiction of a "cacique" named Pedro Páramo, and on a chronological level, between a real time and a fictitious one. I will dwell for a moment on this last aspect because it serves as a clear example of Rulfo's narrative technique, and its discussion provides a clearer characterization of Pedro Páramo.

The fact that the whole of Rulfo's literary work is concerned with a few very concrete themes (situated in a specific time and place) lends an evident testimonial or denunciatory character to his narrative. The temporal point of reference, easily identifiable in the majority of his stories, is that of the Mexican revolution, whose mention in the novel serves as a means of establishing the chronological limits of the narrative. In fragment 45, Susana returns, and Pedro Páramo remarks: "Ya para entonces soplaban vientos raros. Se decía que había gente levantada en armas" [There was already something unusual in the air. People said there were some who had taken up arms; (152)].[10] He is referring to the beginnings of the revolution, in other words, to 1910. That date serves as a reference point enabling us to situate one of the "interpolations" of Pedro Páramo: "Esperé treinta años a que regresaras, Susana. Esperé a tenerlo todo." [I waited thirty years for you to come back, Susana. I waited to have everything (51)]. There is no possible reason to deny that sentence its referential value; it takes us back to 1880, a time when Pedro Páramo would have been roughly between 10 and 15 years old. This conjecture is based on considerable circumstantial evidence: Pedro Páramo's oldest memories (presented by means of "interpolations"), correspond to the period of childhood/adolescence; hence the approximate calculation of 10 to 15 years of age. His play with Susana at that age is documented by Pedro Paramo in fragment six, and by Bartolomé San Juan in 46. Susana must have left Comala at about that time, since Dorotea tells of her departure after the death of her mother, in fragment 43. "Ahora recuerdo que ella nació aquí, y que ya de añejita desaparecieron." [Now I remember that she was born here and she was already getting on in years when they disappeared (147)]. Moreover, Susana remembers the moment of her mother's death in fragment 42, and points out that "en mis piernas comenzaba a crecer el vello entre las venas." [On my legs down was beginning to grow between the veins. (145)]. In other words, Pedro and Susana are about the same age, and it is during the period of childhood and adolescence that Susana left Comala. This means that, if Susana's return takes place thirty years later, both characters are about 40 to 45 years old in 1910. Susana dies around 1914 (in fragment 63 we are told that more than three years have passed since she arrived, already ill). From that moment on, Pedro Páramo "se pasó el resto de sus años aplastado en un equipal. . . . Le perdió interés a todo." [spent the rest of his life slumped in a chair. . . . He lost interest in everything (149)] and we are told the time of his death—"cuando le faltaba poco para morir vinieron las guerras esas de los 'cristeros" [not long before he died, we had that Cristero War (fragment 43, 150)]; that is to say, in 1926 when he was between 55 and 60 years old. Data such as these, defining the chronology of the story told, are particularly important when one comes to consider characterization. From a narrative point of view, they show how carefully Rulfo weaves his web, what a wealth of detail lies behind certain apparently ambiguous moments in the novel (for example, behind its final scene in which Pedro Páramo and Damiana are put to death by Abundio, a scene related in an eliptical manner, but one that a careful reading shows is quite unambiguous). This kind of chronological detective work, therefore, allows us to arrive at a clearer picture of the "cacique"; having a vague idea of the love of Pedro for Susana is not the same as finding out how that love brings suffering to a man's life throughout his forties and fifties and until his death. It brings the image of the heartless "cacique" up against a one of a human being whose suffering equals that of his victims.

The reader has less information to help imagine the physical appearance of the "cacique." There is only one direct allusion to the matter, in fragment 60, where "el cuerpo enorme de Pedro Páramo" [Pedro Páramo's huge body (175)] is mentioned, an image corroborated by two others that are heavy with symbolism: "Quedaba él, solo, como un tronco duro comenzando a desgajarse por dentro" [There he was, alone, like a hard tree-trunk starting to come to bits inside (178)] and "Dio un golpe seco contra la tierra y se fue desmoronando como si fuera un montón de piedras" [Hit the ground with a dull thud and began to crumble as if he were a pile of rocks (195)].

The lack of physical description is compensated by the richness of the character's interior life, which carries us far beyond "caciquismo." The important thing is to appreciate the fact that Pedro Páramo is, in effect, a "cacique," but that in his portrayal Rulfo did not limit himself to copying a type that, though based on reality, had been disseminated in literature. The character of Pedro Páramo achieves individuality by means of his relationships with other characters, and the fact that he is a "cacique" is not something that serves as an initial point of departure, but is rather a consequence of the very development of the narrative.

The novel contains a clear image: that of an ambitious youth who surprises Fulgor Sedano by demanding that the latter address him as "Don," a youth who will build an empire out of nothing, who will employ boundless violence, and who behaves amorally and without scruples. It is the image of the powerful "cacique" who can afford to spare the three hundred men he sends off with the revolutionaries in order to be able to control the course of events. But, unlike the traditional model of the "cacique," Pedro Páramo acts out of motives other than the simple exercise of power, or the accumulation of wealth. The novel clearly enunciates what seems to be his fundamental motivation: by being powerful he hopes to win the love of Susana and, in fact, when she dies, as Dorotea indicates, "[Pedro Páramo] le perdió interés a todo. Desalojó sus tierras y mandó quemar los enseres" [lost interest in everything. He abandoned his land and gave orders for all the equipment to be destroyed (149)]. The hellish world that Juan Preciado will find is the result of the loss of Pedro Páramo's "illusion," even more than of his personal revenge ("—Me cruzaré de brazos y Comala se morirá de hambre," [I will sit back and Comala will die of hunger (187)]), a revenge he exacts because of the improvised and incoherent celebration that marks the end of the villagers' mourning for Susana (fragment 66).

But there is still another explanation for Pedro Páramo's great violence, and one that will justify Abundio's defining him as "un rencor vivo" [living hatred; 68] and Bartolomé San Juan's indicating that he is "la pura maldad" [evil incarnate (153)]. In effect, Juan Rulfo has created in him a symbol of human evil, portraying even in his personality an unjust society in which a few play the role of executioner and the many that of victim. Rulfo needed to create a character that would embody the most extreme violence, an evil presence that, in religious terms, might be considered demonic in the face of divine good. The religious symbolism of the novel, and of the rest of Rulfo's work, is one of the fundamental elements that must be kept in mind in order to arrive at an adequate interpretation of the world created by Rulfo, and the image of God the *Father* is opposed to the concept of fatherhood embodied by the figure of the "cacique." The difficulty mentioned so many times above does not lie in the apparent complexity of the novel's narrative technique so much as in the enormous complexity of the thematic framework in which the extremes of the local Mexican scene and a universal concern merge, developing their respective symbolism in tandem.

The religious symbolism of the novel and its relationship to the theme of "caciquismo" can be seen in the following:

1. In an explicit manner, and with paradigmatic value, two spheres are set against one another: heaven and hell. Dolores has filled Juan Preciado's mind with paradisiac images of Comala, but when he arrives there he finds a dead village, an infernal place. Rulfo thus symbolically opposes good and evil, utilizing traditional Christian concepts such as heaven and hell. It is not surprising that he should use these symbols, given that religion is a constant point of reference for the novel's characters; a reflection, moreover, of the very Mexican reality that the novel recreates.

2 The behavior of Pedro Páramo as "cacique" destroys the possibility of a happy world. The image of heaven is associated with that of God the Creator, God the Father, according to Christian tradition. Consequently, within this tradition appears the image of Paradise Lost as a consequence of original sin. As a matter of fact, the inhabitants of Comala wander about the village, converted into expiators, a situation produced by a moral sense of sin that in

essence is related to the original guilt that humankind, descended from Adam and Eve, must bear. The presence of this theme in the novel is key to the work's interpretation, but to follow it would be to wander far from the theme of "caciquismo." What is important here is that the image of God the Father is closely related to that of the "cacique" as father.

3. The "cacique" is a univeral figure whose presence may be found in any kind of society (although the term that designates it may vary considerably). The common characteristic is that for personal benefit the local tyrant exercises immoral or illicit power over a definable social group. In the Mexican setting to which Rulfo refers, a special element of a sexual nature is also part of the picture. Traditional Mexican society is based on the hegemonic role of the masculine to the detriment of the feminine. This fact, one which is generally discernible in the majority of societies, reaches special proportions in Mexico, where traditionally, as a result of the Spanish heritage, "machismo" has been prized. While the wife withdraws into domestic matters, the husband assumes the role of social protagonist in a world in which success is measured by means of certain standards, such as strength or bravery, that are associated with masculinity. Thus two spheres that are divergent from one another are clearly defined: the familial nucleus (the private world made up of mother and children) and the social world in which the adult male has to demonstrate those masculine attributes that have been mentioned, leading thereby to "macho" behavior. Unquestionably, social acceptance of the "cacique" depends on the fact that "caciquismo" represents the epitome of "macho" values.

The split of the family nucleus into mother-and-children/father is reflected in the mythification of the personality of the Mexican. The duality of Malinche-Virgin of Guadalupe, as analyzed by Octavio Paz in *El laberinto de la soledad*, reflects this situation in mythic form. The Spanish conqueror, exemplified by Cortés, provides the model for "machismo": the woman, forced to yield to the virile male, is interpreted mythically in the relationship between Malinche and Cortés. In contrast, the Virgin of Guadalupe—the most authentic and popular adaptation of Christianity to the Mexican setting—represents the opposite pole: she plays the role of Mother to all Mexicans. The "cacique," the supreme embodiment of "machismo," is the violator who does not recognize or who abandons his own children. Thus the conflict between fathers and children will result in the shaping of the myth of the Mexican as orphan.[11]

From this standpoint, the concept of paternity is of fundamental importance for the interpretation of the figure of the "cacique." In the novel, just as in Rulfo's short stories, the ever-conflictive relationship between fathers and sons is a constant. In *Pedro Páramo*, Juan Preciado travels to Comala guided by the "illusion" of finding his father. The legitimate son of the "cacique," he does not bear his father's name, and this paternal abdication symbolizes the relationship Pedro Páramo has with Comala. Miguel Páramo is one of the "cacique's" illegitimate sons, but his father has made him legitimate by giving his last name to the one who will turn out to be a faithful reflection of the faults of the father. Abundio Martínez, another of Pedro Páramo's sons, will be the unwitting patricide who symbolically avenges all of the other Abundios and Juans. But the paternal image of the "cacique" permeates Comala in its entirety. However, unlike the sheltering image represented by God the Father, Pedro Páramo's is an inverted image: God the Father is the Creator; Pedro Páramo is the evil destroyer.

In his novel and in his short stories Rulfo created a literary world that is uniform, without fissures. His world is desolate, a place in which hopes are dashed, as symbolized in Comala. In using the figure of the "cacique," Rulfo created a meditation on his immediate reality, but it is also a meditation on good and evil, on the duality that dominates human reality: truth and falsehood, or life and death.

The Predominance of the Theme of "Caciquismo" in the Short Stories

Apart from this novel, there appears in the literary works of Rulfo no "cacique" whose portryal is comparable to that of Pedro Páramo. Nonetheless, several characters do indeed reveal aspects of the "cacique" and numerous situations in the stories reflect a society dominated by such a figure, or by "cacique"-like behavior. The physical violence that Pedro Páramo represents in the novel is reproduced in the stories in the relations between small landowners or, at the other extreme, through the power of the government, which is always generically mentioned and whose actions are those of a great invisible "cacique."

The injustice and the abandonment with which the government treats its peasants are criticized in several stories. Rulfo avoids any direct reference that might make it possible to identify a specific government or any precise time in Mexican politics. Thus, in "Nos han dado la tierra," the reference to the mythical "30-30" carbines of the revolution allows the reader to place the story in the final years of the revolutionary process, making the allusions to agrarian reform evident. This means that Rulfo does not criticize a particular government, but a situation that for Mexico had all the significance of the historical break that the revolution caused. It is true that Rulfo could just as well have set his stories in any other historical period, because what he is trying to reveal to his readers has universal value: anguish, solitude, the hopes of humankind. In speaking of the government, Rulfo speaks, quite simply, of power. Therefore, the characters in the story refer to it abstractly: "Espérenos usted, señor delegado. Nosotros no hemos dicho nada contra el Centro." [Wait, Mr. Delegate, Sir. We haven't said anything against the Center (42)]. But, whether it is called "government" or "cacique," the same reality is represented: that of the defenseless villager faced with the authority that emanates from an abstract power such as the government, or with the violence of a "cacique."

Fighting in the revolution has gained nothing for the peasants of "Nos han dado la tierra." The government has despoiled them of everything, and symbolically, their belongings have been reduced to the single chicken one of them carries. The promises of arable fields have turned into the concession of arid lands, a cruel joke with which the government's representative dismisses the peasant's claims.

In "Luvina," where historical references are very vague (one might be able to identify the story with the period of Cárdenas, bearing in mind the effort that was made at that time to establish rural education), Rulfo offers us a fantasmal and inhospitable village, whose few inhabitants refuse to leave. It is one of the most precise images created by Rulfo to express the feelings of peasants who identify with the land of their birth, even though that land may have nothing at all to offer. The cry of rebellion that Rulfo composed in the form of a litany to accompany the images of peasants emerging from fissures in an arid land in his film script for "La fórmula secreta," in "Luvina" becomes a simple lament in the face of a reality that offers no future. When the teacher advises the peasants to leave, and tells them the government will help them, they answer: "¿Tú conoces al gobierno? . . . . También nosotros lo conocemos. Da esa casualidad. De lo que no sabemos nada es de la madre del gobierno." [You know the Government? We know it too. It just so happens. What we don't know anything about is the Government's mother (127)]. For them the government is "el señor ése" [that gentleman (127)] who remembers them only to persecute them. The personification of such an abstract entity as the government allows its identification with the "cacique." The presence of the governor in "El día del derrumbe" should be interpreted similarly, this time with a touch of black humor: he is the great "cacique" who must be entertained royally, even though the tribute exacted is far too great for a village ruined by an earthquake. Without question, the "cacique" as well as the government are depicted by Rulfo as agents of violence, exercised from a position of power against helpless peasants. The ultimate image that the reader perceives in Rulfo's narratives is that of an unjust world in which a small number of individuals abuse the majority, who, because of a fatalistic view of history, seem resigned to accepting the situation.

To a lesser degree, as compared with the power of a "cacique" of the stature of Pedro Páramo, Rulfo laid out several plots that fit under the heading of "cacicazgo." In "El despojo," one of his film scripts, he specifically mentions the "cacique" of the village; a peasant who has lost everything, including his son, dreams of killing him. In "La Cuesta de las Comadres" we find a similar situation to the one in *Pedro Páramo*: the Torrico brothers are not exactly "caciques," but are rather bandits who have managed to terrorize the people living in the area with their killings. Their resemblance to the stereotype of the "cacique," nevertheless, is patent: "ellos eran allí los dueños de la tierra y de las casas que estaban encima de la tierra, con todo y que, cuando el reparto, la mayor parte de la Cuesta de las Comadres nos había tocado por igual a los sesenta que allí vivíamos" [they were the owners of the land around there and of the houses that were on the land, and everything, and when it came to parceling it out, most of Cuesta de las Comadres was divided equally among the sixty of us who lived there (45)]. Again, in this story agrarian reform has been unable to solve the problems of the peasants (although in this case not through fault of the government), thus producing a situation analogous to that of Comala when Pedro Páramo stops working his lands: the area eventually becomes uninhabited. The background for the story "¡Diles que no me maten!" also reminds us of the theme of "caciquismo": "Don Lupe Terreros, el dueño de la Puerta de Piedra, por más señas su compadre. Al que él, Juvencio Nava, tuvo que matar por eso; por ser el dueño de la Puerta de Piedra y que, siendo también su compadre, le negó el pasto para sus animales" [Don Lupe Terreros, the owner of Puerta de Piedra, and his compadre, what's more. The one who he, Juvencio Nava, had to kill because of it, because he owned Puerta de Piedra and because, even though he was his compadre, he wouldn't allow his animals to graze (112)]. The reader will surely picture Don Lupe as a small landowner, behaving like a "cacique," and even though Juvencio is his "compadre," the title of "Don" (remember that Pedro Páramo demanded its use by Fulgor Sedano) establishes the difference between the two men. Similarly, the "Don" characterizes the rancher in the story "En la madrugada": "don Justo era el dueño de la luz" [don Justo was lord of light (75)], thus establishing the distance that exists between the powerful man and the humble peasant. A final example that attests once more to the "caciquil" basis of the society that Rulfo portrays: in the story "La herencia de Matilde Arcángel," one of the main characters, Euremio Cedillo, is "el dueño de las Animas" ["the owner of Las Animas," also translatable as "lord of Souls" (161)].

In all, one can conclude that the theme of "caciquismo" is of great importance in Rulfo's narratives. In *Pedro Páramo* it is, after all, one of the primary axes of the plot. In the stories, its presence is more dispersed, but equally significant; although none of them features a "cacique," various characters and situations remind us that the reality of the setting is a society ruled by oppression, and typical of "caciquismo." Rulfo took advantage of the figure of the "cacique" to portray a society dominated by violence: a violence that can be institutional (that of the state) or individual (that of the "cacique" or similar beings). In both cases, it sufficed for Rulfo to reflect on the closest reality he knew, that of his own homeland Jalisco, a rural society traditionally based on "caciquismo." But Rulfo did not limit himself to telling stories whose plots were confined to Mexican local color. His stories transcend the local and become symbols of a humanity dominated by solitude and subjected to injustice and violence. Nevertheless, the pessimism with which Rulfo observes reality does not mean that he is fatalistic in his view of it: the symbolism of the rain falling on the graves of Comala, alluded to at the beginning of this essay, is a clear indication that utopia is feasible and that humankind cannot reject the hope of achieving a happy world. I have insisted on this hopeful interpretation of *Pedro Páramo*, despite the fact that existing criticism tends to insist on the note of desolation. That "hope," it is true, is not present in the world of Comala, but it is projected toward the future through the image of a sought-after happy world, one that would be Comala's opposite.[12]

Translated by Terry J. Peavler

Notes

1. Rodríguez-Alcalá (1965: 191–193) analyzes the symbolism of the rain on two fronts: positive (the paradisiacal image of Comala) and negative (the world of death reflected in the agony of Susana San Juan and in the cemetery of Comala). In my opinion, however, the overtly symbolic association of rain with Comala has nothing to do with the clearly referential use of rain in fragments 48 and 49 (during which Susana's illness is recounted): these are not to be read symbolically. By contrast, the rain falling on the tombs is indeed laden with symbolism, and is to be accorded the positive connotations found elsewhere in the novel. It should be borne in mind that Rodríguez-Alcalá only notes some characteristics, and does not go into great detail.

2. This theme has been specifically addressed by Rosales (1978), Arango (1978), González (1974) and Avila (1985), who study the generic form of the figure of Pedro Páramo and his relationship with the reality of rural Mexico in which the "caciques" rise to power. For her part, Canfield (1989) analyzes the archetype of the Terrible Father, comparing its formulations in *Pedro Páramo* and in Gabriel García Márquez' *El otoño del Patriarca*.

3. The critical bibliography on Rulfo is so abundant that it is almost impossible to take it all in. The bibliographies of González Boixo (1985) and Ocampo (1992) are useful, and Martin's (1992) panoramic vision of scholarship on Rulfo provides a useful overview.

4. Numerous studies have been made of the "dictator" from a literary point of view. On the other hand, those that deal with "caciquismo" are rare. The "Présentation" in Verdevoye (1978: 9–36) is very useful in identifying related concepts; and the same book contains several articles that analyze the theme of "caciquismo" in specific works.

5. Oscar Tacca distinguishes three types of third person narrator: *omniscient* (N>P), *equiscient* (N=P) and *deficient* (N<P). The degree of *equiscience* (of equality between narrator and character) is defined as follows by Tacca: "Si el narrador, en cambio, en lugar de acordarse de un punto de vista privilegiado para su información, se ciñe a la que pueden tener los personajes; si renunando a la mirada omnisciente opta por ver el mundo con los ojos de ellos, la narración gana vibración humana" [If the narrator, on the other hand, instead of settling upon a privileged point of view for his information, restricts himself to that which the characters might have, if renouncing the omniscient view he chooses to see the world through their eyes, the narration gains in human vitality (77)]. This is an important characteristic because it presumes, even from the use of the third person, a preference that the form of expression be in agreement with the mentality of the characters. For more on this, see González Boixo (1983: 138–141).

6. Symbolic interpretations have been the most common ones in Rulfian criticism. They are listed and commented upon in Martin (1992).

7. This aspect was clearly highlighted by Escalante (1986: 296): "*Pedro Páramo* es y seguirá siendo la historia de un cacique y de su decadencia inevitable; la historia de un pueblo, Comala, sumido en la ignorancia y la superstición, incapaz de sacudirse los yugos espirituales y materiales del sacerdote Rentería y del cacique que todos conocen." It is evident that this type of socio-historical reading must always be kept in mind, even though critics—legitimately—tend toward the mythic and symbolic.

8. Of particular significance is the special manner in which this dependence affects the symbolic Juan Preciado, a character without a personal history, the reader's "alter

ego," whose special quest into the hell of his own conscience ends only when he finds his own identity reflected in the mirror of Pedro Páramo.

9. More information on the novel's structure can be found in González Boixo (1983: 182–205) and Peavler (1988: 45–116).

10. Quotes are from the Cátedra edition (Madrid, 1983). The Cátedra edition is also used for *El llano en llamas* (Madrid, 1985).

11. Panebianco (1973) has analyzed the figure of Pedro Páramo within the parameters of a "chingón," a Mexican term that stresses the qualities of "machismo."

12. In this regard I must point out what I believe to be a correct, optimistic interpretation, that of Bell (1966: 239) who observes: "The crumbling of Páramo, after having been dominated by one of God's creatures, is tangible evidence that the paralysis caused by the *cacique* is finally coming to its termination. Therefore the exalted death of Susana San Juan and the disintegrating image of Pedro Páramo represent forward progress in time and new hope for Mexico."

Works Cited

Arango, Manuel Antonio. "Correlación social entre el caciquismo y el aspecto religioso en la novela *Pedro Páramo* de Juan Rulfo." *Cuadernos Hispanoamericanos* 341 (1978): 401–412.

Avila Rodríguez, Benigno. "La familia, metáfora de la realidad social en la novela *Pedro Páramo* de Juan Rulfo." *Educación y Ciencia* (Tunja, Colombia) 1 (1985): 208–221.

Bell, Alan S. "Rulfo's *Pedro Páramo*: a Vision of Hope." *Modern Language Notes.* 81 (1966): 238–245.

Canfield, Martha L. "Dos enfoques de *Pedro Páramo*." *Revista Iberoamericana* 148–149 (1989): 965-88.

Escalante, Evodio. "Lectura ideológica de *Pedro Páramo*." *De la crónica a la nueva narrativa mexicana.* Ed. Merlin Forster and Julio Ortega. Mexico: Oasis, 1986. 295–303.

González Boixo, José-Carlos. "Bibliografía de Juan Rulfo." *Cuadernos Hispanoamericanos* 421–425 (1985): 469–490.

González Boixo, José-Carlos. *Claves narrativas de Juan Rulfo.* León, Spain: Universidad de León, 1983.

González, Alfonso. "Onomastics and Creativity in *Doña Bárbara* and *Pedro Páramo*. *Names* (New York) 21 (1974): 40–45.

Martin, Gerald. "Vista panorámica: la obra de Juan Rulfo en el tiempo y en el espacio." *Toda la obra.* By Juan Rulfo. Ed. Claude Fell. Madrid: C.S.I.C., 1992. 471–545.

Ocampo, Aurora M. "Una contribución a la bibliografía de y sobre Juan Rulfo." *Rulfo,* 1992. 891–943.

Panebianco, Cándido. "Struttura e mito nel romanzo di Rulfo: *Pedro Páramo*." *Siculorum Gymnasium* (Catania) 26, 2 (1973): 331–348.

Peavler, Terry J. *El texto en llamas: el arte narrativo de Juan Rulfo*. University of Texas Studies in Contemporary Spanish American Fiction 1. New York: Peter Lang, 1988.

Rodríguez Alcalá, Hugo. *El arte de Juan Rulfo*. Mexico: Ediciones de Bellas Artes, 1965.

Rosales, Nilda. "El tema del caudillismo en *Pedro Páramo* de Juan Rulfo." *"Caudillos", "caciques" et dictateurs dans le roman hispano-américain*. Ed. Paul Verdevoye. Paris: Editions Hispaniques, 1978.

Rulfo, Juan. *Toda la obra*. Ed. Claude Fell. Madrid: C.S.I.C., 1992.

Tacca, Oscar. *Las voces de la novela*. Madrid: Gredos, 1973.

Verdevoye, Paul, ed. *"Caudillos", "caciques" et dictateurs dans le roman hispano-américain*. Paris: Editions Hispaniques, 1978.

Terry J. Peavler

CABRERA INFANTE'S UNDERTOW

Guillermo Cabrera Infante's declarations (and declamations) on the subject of politics, particularly vis-à-vis the writer, are perhaps only slightly more extensive than his denials of its importance in his own writings. Scholars, for the most part, follow his suggestions on how to read his works, stressing their apolitical nature, while acknowledging the political content only of *Así en la paz como en la guerra*, a book that the author himself has faulted repeatedly for being misguided (nonetheless he recently collaborated in the English translation, *Writes of Passage*, which omits only the highly charged vignettes of the original). Even though the historical sweep of *Vista del amanecer en el trópico* is widely recognized and commented upon, it too is generally discussed in aesthetic rather than social or political terms. Nonetheless, if one accepts the idea that even highly aesthetic literature may seek to advance a social agenda, although that agenda may be presented indirectly (e.g., the depiction of a situation that can no longer be endured), then Cabrera Infante is as blameworthy (or praiseworthy) as any author, including in the pages of *Tres tristes tigres* and *La Habana para un Infante difunto*.

Such an affirmation does not contradict Cabrera Infante's insistence that literature can never aspire to be anything other than literature: ". . . la literatura debe exclusivamente tener que ver con la literatura. Cualquier otra preocupación es totalmente extraliteraria y, por tanto, desde mi punto de vista actual, condenada al fracaso" [literature should be exclusively about literature. Any other concern is totally extra-literary and therefore, in my present way of thinking, condemned to failure (Rodríguez Monegal, 64)], nor, for that matter, the Cuban's perception that literature should never seek to be anything other than play: "Literature can *never* be experimental. Literature can and must be a game" ("Cain by Himself," 9). Rather, it acknowledges that while the primary purpose of Cabrera Infante's writings may indeed not be messianic—"No creo que el escritor sea un misionero, ni siquiera creo que el escritor tiene deberes como tal. El único deber, si hay uno del escritor, es escribir lo mejor posible" [I don't believe that the writer is a missionary—I don't even believe that the writer as such has any obligations. The only obligation, if a writer has one, is to write the best he can (Rita Guibert in Ortega, 19)], some of his purportedly most apolitical works offer strong critiques of the societies in which they are set.

Of course the author acknowledges the political intent of some pieces, but apparently only for the purpose of the harshest imaginable repudiation: *"Vista del amanecer en el trópico* (not the collection of vignettes published in 1974, but the original version, which, once purged of its political demons became *Tres tristes tigres*) "es un libro que yo moralmente repudio" [is a book that I morally repudiate (Rodríguez Monegal, 66)]; "Personalmente lo [*Así en la paz como en la guerra*] considero total y absolutamente fuera de mi canon, que debe comenzar con *Un oficio del siglo XX*" [Personally, I consider it totally and absolutely outside of my canon, which should begin with *Un oficio del siglo XX* ("Viaje verbal," 54)]. The works that the author most values are, in his mind, free from political taint. His masterpiece, *Tres tristes tigres*, is in fact "the most apolitical book ever published by a Spanish American author" ("Cain by himself," 10).

The reader, under such heavy-handed guidance from the author, can easily, too easily perhaps, envision a rather shy, somewhat reclusive Cabrera Infante, living comfortably and contentedly in London, crafting his pyrotechnic puns. The truth of the matter is, or at least seems to be on the basis of each of the author's texts, including *Tres tristes tigres* and his more recent success, *La Habana para un Infante difunto*, that Cabrera Infante suffers deeply. He suffers most certainly from exile, most probably from solitude, perhaps from a sense of grief and guilt at a grand political experiment gone sour, and quite possibly from what seems to be a sort of writer's block: the promised books never seem to materialize. *Cuerpos divinos*, for example, has been promised since 1968, and a book of essays has been underway for several years.

Meanwhile, some of the more interesting writings may well be the overtly political outbursts (most of which have been collected in the very recent *Mea Cuba*) that have appeared from time to time on the pages of *Vanidades*, or *Vuelta*, or *El País*. The "literary" offerings seemed for many years to be filled with the same tired puns—was he capable of mentioning Karl Marx without a Marx brothers pun? True, *La Habana para un Infante difunto* (1979) seems fresher than *O* (1975) or *Exorcismos de esti(l)o* (1976), but its repetitions of its own cleverness also become somewhat wearisome—should the hero not go blind after the first few dozen pages?

Cabrera Infante's meticulously sculpted chronologies ("a la manera de Laurence Sterne"), readily available in a number of books and special issues of journals dedicated to the author, clearly demonstrate his preoccupation with his political past, and with the historical events that shaped his future. More than half of the entries covering the 55 years chronicled in "(C)ave Attemptor!" contain specific references to historical and political events, and clearly reveal his concern with the poverty and injustices of his youth, as well as those events, particularly in Cuba, that have continued to affect him and his Cuban friends.

His successes in literature and in film have brought him financial security and international recognition, which, coupled with his biting sense of humor, have spared him from many of the ravages of exile. Yet he has remained keenly aware of the plight of his countrymen, both at home and abroad, as his preoccupation with the deaths (particularly by suicide) of fellow Cubans attests.[1] One senses the presence—the passion, the frustrations, the anger—of the real Cabrera Infante more in his spirited rebukes of Gabriel García Márquez ("Nuestro prohombre en La Habana") and Hermann Bellinghausen ("El escritor y la aspereza") or in his compassionate portrayal of Nicolás Guillén ("Nicolás Guillén: Poet and Partisan") than one does in his often vacuous word plays.

In a stirring commentary, written some fifty years after the murder of Federico García Lorca, Cabrera Infante, who had had the foresight and the common sense to flee political oppression, chided the Spaniard for his romanticized vision of Havana:

> I could have told him that I've known all kinds of poets in Cuba. Poor poets and sick poets, poets pursued and poets in prison, dying poets and dead poets finally: all dead as the dodo in the end. Poets I've known who were treated not like princes but like scum—called scum, in fact. Called worms also. Poets as pariahs on the island. Poets considered untouchable, poets suffering from political leprosy. But Havana was for Lorca a moving feast, and I don't want to rain on his parade of beauties. I don't want to contaminate his poetry with my experience ("Brief Encounter in Havana," 522).

Furthermore, whether Cabrera Infante likes it or not, in *Así en la paz como en la guerra* he published some of the finer short stories ever penned by a Spanish American. A few, such as "Josefina, atiende a los señores," "Abril es el mes más cruel," and "En el gran ecbó," are superb. While it is true that "Resaca," which suggested the title for this essay, is coincidentally not only one of the more political but also one of the weaker stories, and that a number of the more heavy-handed vignettes may not be worth saving, their presence hardly justifies throwing out the whole lot. "Josefina," for example, is both one of the best and one of the most political. In fact, it bears a strong odor of "socialist realism," a type of literature that the author would come to abhor, although he admitted that "I am not so much against socialism as I am realism. . . ." ("Talent of 2wo Cities," 18).

More important than the literary value of the individual selections from *Así en la paz* or the passion of various newspaper and magazine pieces, however, is the political subtext that characterizes Cabrera Infante's best literary work, including, and especially, *Tres tristes tigres*, the novel he considers to be free from contamination:

> *TTT* resultaba un libro político por su ausencia de política: las pocas referencias políticas: aludir a la dictadura de Batista de soslayo, llamar a Fidel Castro un fiasco, sólo reflejaban que el libro ocurría argumen- talmente en 1958, pero su escritura se hacía en 1965. Pero de veras hay pocos libros más apolíticos en América Latina. Aunque por supuesto siempre es posible una lectura política, todas las lecturas son posibles en la literatura, es la escritura la que es única.

> [*TTT* became a political book because of its very lack of politics: the few political references—sly allusions to Batista's dictatorship, calling Fidel Castro a fiasco, did no more than reflect that the story line was taking place in 1958, although it was being written in 1965. But in fact there are few more apolitical books in Latin America. Although it is always possible, of course, to read politically—all readings are possible in literature—the process of composition itself is unique (Pereda, 101)]

This masterwork, which is best and most widely known for its play, its puns, its verbal pyrotechnics—even the most devoted readers may often despair of ever understanding all of the allusions and double entendres—is also an immensely sad book, a book that is caught in the powerful and irresistible undertow of the author's despairing vision, which in turn is forged from Cabrera Infante's personal, often political or politicized history.[2]

As Alfred MacAdam, one of the few critics to focus on this aspect of Cabrera Infante's literature, has pointed out, "There is no separation between life and art for Cabrera Infante, because any reflection he makes on life involves a verbal formulation of it, and any formulation entails a stylization" ("Seeing Double," in *World Literature Today*, 543). Many, including Cabrera Infante, have commented on the fictionality of all of the author's characters, not only in *TTT*, but even in *La Habana*, a novel that seems totally autobiographical. Even so, despite the author's vehement denials of any personal presence, especially in the earlier work, the vision projected is pure Cabrera Infante, and can be found throughout his writings.

Few readers can have failed to notice, for example, the author's antipathy to racism. In a review of *Carmen Jones*, written in 1955, he wondered if the cruelty of segregation depicted in the film might not have made a more tragic theme than the traditional story of Carmen (*Un oficio del siglo XX*, 68), and he saw *Gone with the Wind* as a monument to racial segregation (69). He was disturbed by the portrayal of the Japanese as animals in American films, when they are in fact "una congregación humana no mejor, pero tampoco peor que cualquier otro pueblo de la tierra" [a human congregation that is no better, but neither is it worse than any other people on the earth (87)]. In *TTT*, the mulatto Ribot cannot expect to develop a relationship with Vivian, because "Entre Vivian y yo había más de una calle que atravesar" [Between Vivian and me there was more than one street to cross (106)]; "ella *nunca* se acostaría con él porque es mulato, y pobre para colmo" [she would never go to bed with him because he is a mulatto and poor to boot (433)]. Laura dreams she is raped by a black worm (271); Arsenio Cué cannot be attracted to mulatto women: "¿Cuándo tú has visto que me gusten las mulatas?" [Since when have you seen me going for colored women? (425)].

Furthermore, the entire novel takes place under the shadow of fear cast in 1962 by the possibility that Cuba could become the point of ignition for a nuclear holocaust (Edward Teller, father of the atomic bomb, is mentioned by name on page 417). Laura's psychiatric sessions overflow with images of a world engulfed in a nuclear conflagration. Excerpts from her second session are illustrative:

> . . . hacía un sol terrible. El camino estaba blanco del resplandor y la
> yerba se veía quemada. . . . En la orilla había un perro jugando . . .
> metió el hocico en el agua y vi que echaba humo: echaba humo por el
> hocico y por el lomo y por el rabo que era como una antorcha.

[the sun beat down something terrible. The road was white with its light and the grass looked burnt. . . . On shore a dog was playing . . . he stuck his muzzle in the water and I saw that he was smoking: smoke was coming out his muzzle and his back and his tail which was like a torch (80)]

Much later in the novel, when Silvestre relates the dream of his friend (clearly Laura, although not specifically identified) to Arsenio Cué, the imagery is again unmistakable:

El brazo le crece y crece y atraviesa el cuarto (ella lo siente, cree que lo ve más negro en la negrura del sueño-realidad) pero lento, muy lenta, l,e,n,t,a,m,e,n,t,e y mientras el brazo viaja hacia la luz, en dirección del botón de la luz, alguien, una voz en el sueño, cuenta al revés, del nueve abajo, y justo cuando la cuenta llega al cero su mano alcanza el conmutador y se hace una luz blanca-blanca, increíble, de un blanco terrible, pavoroso. No hay ruido pero teme o sabe que hubo una explosión. . . . Toda la Habana, que es como decir todo el mundo, arde. Los edificios están derruidos, todo es destrucción. La luz de los incendios, de la explosión (ahora está cierta ella de que hubo un estallido apocalíptico . . .) alumbra la escena como si fuera de día.

[The arm grows longer and longer and crosses the room (she feels it, she believes that it looks even darker in the darkness of the dream-reality) but slowly, very slowly, s,l,o,w,l,y and while the arm travels toward the light, toward the light switch, someone, a voice in the dream, counts backward, from nine down, and just when the count reaches zero her hand reaches the switch and there is white-white light, unbelievable, a terrible, frightening white. There is no noise but she fears or knows there was an explosion. . . . All Havana, which is like saying the entire world, is on fire. The buildings are demolished, everything is destroyed. The light from the fires, from the explosion (now she is certain that there was an apocalyptic blast . . .) lights up the landscape as if it were daytime (420–421)].

Cué has his own dreams of the atomic apocalypse:

la playa—y no sólo la arena blanca sino el mar que ya no es azul, sino blanco, no sólo la tierra, el agua también se levantan—se repliega y sube sobre ella misma. El sol es tan fuerte que el vestido negro de mi compañera comienza a arder y su cara invisible es blanca y negra y ceniza de un golpe. . . . Cuando veo que la sombra de la sombrilla se borra con una luz blanca, es el momento en que distingo también que la columna no tiene la forma de una sombrilla sino de un hongo, que no es una protección contra la luz asesina, que es ella misma la luz.

[the beach—and not just the white sand but the ocean which is no longer blue, but white, not only the land, the water too rises up— withdraws and then rises over itself. The sun is so strong that my companion's black dress catches fire and her invisible face is white and black and ash instantly. . . . When I see that the shadow of the umbrella is erased by white light is precisely when I also see that the column is not shaped like an umbrella but like a mushroom, that it is not protection against the killer light, it is actually the light itself (313–314)].

Cabrera Infante had written previously on the horrors of nuclear destruction in his review of the film *Hiroshima* (*Oficio*, 85–89) in 1955. *Tres tristes tigres*, clearly, although set in the swinging fifties, was written under the incandescent silhouette of an impending atomic cloud, under the fear that gripped the world in the fall of 1962, a fear that must have been almost unbearable in Cuba, where Cabrera Infante resided, and an island at which were aimed the most terrible weapons the United States had in her possession. It is a mistake to attribute the empty banter and the senseless, seemingly endless partying that affects and infects all of the book's significant characters to a nostalgic view of the "good old days" or even to the excesses and abuses of capitalism. The Havana it depicts, and the Havana that Cabrera Infante so clearly remembers and preserves, is not a carefree city of continual barhopping, it is a world perched on the edge of the abyss—and all of the characters, even though their story precedes the crisis of October by several years, are keenly, although only subconsciously through their creator, aware of the events of 1962.

This fear of impending doom—not just the emptiness of life without purpose—helps explain the existential absurdity felt by many of the characters, whose goal is simply to disappear: "quería seguir borracho y caminar borracho y vivir borracho que es como decir borrado" [I wanted to stay drunk and walk drunk and live drunk which is like saying eradicated altogether (275)] yet be remembered: "porque la única cosa por que siento un odio mortal es el olvido" [because the only think that I really detest is being forgotten (287)].

Two passages are critical to this reading of *Tres tristes tigres*. One is the epilogue, comprised entirely of the ravings of a madwoman. What seems at first to be only nonsense is, in fact, a final reminder of the profound seriousness of the book:

Hers is the plaintive cry of a woman driven mad by the moral corruption of her environment. Now for the first time, the lack of political freedom—'Que viene el mono con un cuchillo y me registra' [the ape comes with a knife and searches me (*TTT*, 451)]. . . .—is united with a sense of existential chaos. Like the other narrators, this woman represents the despair and the suffocation which we have seen in the other characters. She also represents victimization by a regime whose corruption has given birth to a state in which political repression and decadence are the natural order of things. Her life, as Cabrera Infante described it to me in an interview, is one "trapped between politics and history—a life which kept getting more sordid and difficult" (Alvarez-Borland, "Readers," 556).

Play, which as mentioned earlier is in Cabrera Infante's view the only legitimate role of literature, is offered to the characters in *Tres tristes tigres* as their best and perhaps only defense against that sordidness and difficulty. The vast majority of the book, as all readers quickly discover, is devoted to verbal pyrotechnics. Apart from the endless streams of puns, the fine art of storytelling constantly interjects itself while simultaneously calling the reader's attention to its presence as pure artifice. Thus, within the steady flow of embedded narratives we find in the notorious case of William Campbell a story with emendations made by another character that are actually a part of the original story, the totality of which was then translated (badly) into Spanish, and then corrected yet again by still another character.

Most of the important characters are artists, professional creators of illusions. There are actors, models, photographers, writers, musicians, and singers. The goal of all of these professions, and all of these conversations, is clearly to communicate, to interpret, to represent. Yet such communication is the one activity that never quite seems to take place. Language in particular, the primary instrument of the actor and the writer, must be shared by both sender and receiver before it can be interpreted. The codes manipulated by Cué and Silvestre, actor and writer, respectively, become so personal that only the two of them can be included in the communicative act—and even they do not always understand one another.

Thus the play of language and literature, rather than serving as a defense by uniting the characters and by allowing them to ignore momentarily their desperate situations, serves rather to drive them ever more deeply into isolation and despair. Particularly illustrative is the scene in "Bachata" in which they try to show off their cleverness for the benefit of Beba and Magalena:

—Buenas noches, señoritas—dijo Cue....Perdonen que las llame señoritas, pero no las conozco todavía.

Adrenalina, 0. Glóbulos rojos, 0. Reacción Marx-negativa. Humores, no se aprecian.

["Good evening ladies," said Cue, " . . . . pardon me for calling you ladies but I don't know you yet." Adrenalin, 0. Red corpuscles, 0. Reaction Marx-negative. Sense of humor, no visible sign (379)].

Throughout the episode, try as they may, they are unable to penetrate the armor of ignorance of their companions: "Te juro muchacho que no entendí ni papa" [I swear to you boy I didn't understand a word (379)]; "No se rieron. No entendían. . . . Seguimos" [They didn't laugh. They didn't understand. . . . We went on (383)]; "No se reían" [They didn't laugh (383)]; "Hubo algo que podían ser risitas" [There was something that might pass for a giggle (383)]; "Ni hablaban" [They didn't even say anything (384)]. "Nada nada nada. . . . Nada de nada" [Nothing nothing nothing . . . nothing but nothingness (384)]; "Nada y nada y nada [Nothing and nothing and nothing (385)]; "Nada que estás en la nada nadificada sea tu nada. Un último intento" [Nothing who art in nothingness nothinged be thy nothing. One last shot (385)]; [after which] "Se hizo un silencio total" [There was total silence (386)].

These brief references to the two women remind the reader of their presence, a necessity, since the passages are separated by at times lengthy word plays, reenactments of scenes from movies, etc. The language and the allusions—which include a delightful reenactment of Abbott and Costello's "Who's on First" routine, here rendered as "What is the title of the song" (389), come from the world of the two language artists. Finally freed from their burdensome and unappreciative companions, Arsenio Cué and Silvestre take one more plunge into Havana's nightlife, after which Silvestre returns very much alone to his apartment, and to the other key passage in the novel, now carefully set up by the previously described banter, and which begins, significantly "En el silencio" [In total silence (444–445)].

Earlier portions of the text have revealed the degree to which language can often be no more than meaningless noise. Even Bustrófedon's brilliant linguistic games, we are led to believe, may have been the result of a brain tumor. And, whenever the characters make a genuine attempt at serious communication, they are unable to make contact, as illustrated by the pathetic attempts at self-revelation in "Bachata." Every significant issue—should Silvestre marry Laura; should Arsenio go to the Sierra—becomes a pretext for more linguistic humor.

The episode that speaks loudest is, ironically, the one in which the professional wordsmith is surrounded by nothing but silence. After being dropped off by Cué, Silvestre enters his apartment:

> En el silencio que dejó el carro detrás subía las escaleras flanqueadas por dátiles en flor y atravesé el oscuro pasillo solo y en silencio y sin miedo al hombre-lobo ni a la mujer pantera y cogí el elevador en silencio y encendí la luz de la cabina y la apagué de nuevo para subir a oscuras y en silencio entré en casa y en silencio me quité la camisa y los zapatos en silencio y en silencio fui al baño y oriné y me saqué los dientes en más silencio y en silencio y en sigilo. . . .

> [In the silence that the car left behind I climbed the stairs bordered with blooming dates and I went down the dark corridor alone and silently and fearing neither the werewolf nor the panther woman and I entered the elevator silently and turned on the light and turned it off again so I could ascend in the dark and silently I went into my apartment and silently I took off my shirt and shoes silently and silently I went to the bathroom and urinated and took out my teeth silently and silently and secretly . . . (444)].

In twenty-eight lines, silence is mentioned thirty-six times before Silvestre goes to his window and begins to contemplate the vastness of the universe and his own insignificance. Finally, he falls asleep and dreams of bad literary translations, ending the passage with the now famous "Tradittori" (a play on the Italian proverb, "traduttore, traditore"—to translate is to betray, 445).

In many ways, Cabrera Infante's displays of verbal brilliance are like those of the characters in his masterpiece: dazzling, entertaining, at times illuminating, but occasionally tiring. In the end, as the reader comes to recognize that they are often no more than failed attempts of speakers to assert their existence, they are even depressing to some degree. There is a clear rupture between words and meanings, signifiers and signifieds, as words and phonemes dance to their own tunes, playing off and against one another. The novel clearly has its darker side: characters suffer from loneliness, from their inability to communicate, from boredom, from a quiet sense of desperation that they seek to hide behind their very loud language use and abuse, even from a pronounced sense of impending doom—the end of an era, the end of a lifestyle, perhaps the end of the world, with Cuba going first.

Like his characters, Cabrera Infante seems to fear silence, particularly his own, above all else. And, like his characters, he seems to feel isolated, cut off from fellow writers, countrymen, the world at large. While he enjoys far greater prestige and success than most members of the Cuban diaspora, he clearly and understandably longs for his homeland; although he moved to London in 1966, he states in his chronology that he came to terms with the weather some eighteen years later, in 1984 ["(C)ave Attemptor!" 519]. His magazine and newspaper articles suggest both the frustrations and the fears that boil to the surface from time to time.

Cabrera Infante has been, since the 1950s, disempowered politically, culturally, and personally. In fact, his almost obsessive attention to textual detail suggests that he feels he can control nothing beyond language, and that he wields that power with a vengeance designed to compensate for his sense of helplessness and frustration in other areas. His chronology, for which he has carefully selected only a handful of events to portray his entire life, reveals the significance, to him, of being disenfranchised: "1952: El infame segundo golpe de Estado de Batista echa por tierra sus esperanzas de votar por primera vez en su vida. Su pesar será eterno" [The infamous second coup d'état of Batista destroys his hope of voting for the second time in his life. His grief will be eternal (Ortega et al., 13)]. 1952 is also the year in which he was imprisoned for publishing a story containing vulgarities ("Balada de plomo y yerro"). Since that time he has exercised power only over his words, and since his words can be neither read nor heard in his homeland, he has been forced to direct them toward himself. The masturbation motif, which overwhelms *La Habana para un Infante difunto*, and which, revealingly, appears throughout *Tres tristes tigres* as "masturhablar" [an untranslatable pun combining "masturbate" with "to speak," suggesting speaking or writing only for one's own personal gratification] reveals the degree to which he has turned inward, with his back to the world. He writes, as he has repeatedly said, only for himself.

His withdrawal is hardly due to lack of courage. Even during Batista's regime, Cabrera Infante was eager to publish vignettes from what would become *Así en la paz*, but despite the absence of official censorship, none of the established presses in Cuba dared publish them (Rodríguez Monegal, 65). His confrontations with Fidel Castro, embodied in his work as editor of *Revolución* and particularly in the publication of *Lunes*, his role in provoking Castro's infamous "conversations" with the intellectuals, and his involvement in the early Padilla affairs, are well known. As Carlos Franqui reveals, long before his self-imposed exile, Cabrera Infante's humor hid a very sharp set of teeth: "in an egalitarian division of a steer, who gets the filet mignon?" (90).

Furthermore, he used those outlets available to him tirelessly in an effort to continue to be heard. *Un oficio del siglo XX* gathered into book form all of the film critiques he had previously published in *Carteles* and *Revolución*, many of which contained thinly veiled social and political commentaries. His review of *Mau Mau* (written in 1957, *Oficio*, 183–184), as MacAdam points out in "Seeing Double" (547), is more a condemnation of the political situation in Cuba during the last years of Batista and a defense of Castro's guerrilla war than a review of the film (see also the review of *Something of Value* for a further development of the same theme. *Oficio*, 198–201). Reviewing *Twelve Angry Men* gave the opportunity to condemn social inequalities, as he accused the jurors of "frivolidad, ligereza, ausencia de humanidad, racismo y hasta psicosis larvada" [frivolity, shallowness, lack of humanity, racism, and even latent psychosis (226)], and praised the film for its "culto a la verdadera democracia" [tribute to true democracy (227)]. In his "Manuscrito encontrado en una botella," written in 1962 and included in *Oficio*, he described Charles Chaplin's *Monsieur Verdoux* as "el único film verdaderamente marxista que ha dado el cine" [the only truly marxist file that the cinema has yielded (243), this after he was relieved of his duties at *Revolución*]. He also used reviews to attack U.S. Senator Joseph McCarthy for his assault on basic rights (255, 259, 292) during the final years of Batista, when the dictator owed his power directly to a United States that was grateful to him for his rabid anticommunism.

Only after Cabrera Infante found refuge in London and turned his energies to writing film scripts did he seem to lose the edge on his humor. His "literary" books (*O*, 1975; *Exorcismos*, 1976) were filled more and more with empty and repetitive puns, while his "political" writings were increasingly devoid of humor.[3] *Vista del amanecer en el trópico*, in many ways the most political book yet,[4] provides a sort of watershed between the author who was sometimes angry, sometimes merely frustrated, but always keenly involved in historical and political events, particularly in Cuba, and the creator of verbiage for its own sake that seemingly flows through many pages of *O* and *Exorcismos*.

Vista is a very significant book.[5] It apparently began as a sort of therapy: Cabrera Infante had sunk into a deep depression while working on a film script for *Under the Volcano*. During his recovery, which included shock therapy, he received the devastating news that his old friend, Alberto Mora, had committed suicide in Cuba. The book, dedicated to Mora and to Plinio Prieto (another friend, who had been executed in 1960) is a sort of catharsis, a hymn to Cuba and its violent history. Though absolutely devoid of humor, it is the author's most poetic work, and may someday be judged to be one of his best.

Significantly, *Vista* is in many ways a throwback to *Así en la paz*, the book Cabrera Infante would like to purge from his canon. While it is even more "committed," it is somewhat cleansed by being made more abstract, more epic. *Vista* is devoid of the short stories of its predecessor, which served, frequently, as a respite from the horrors of the vignettes. Instead it offers a series of 100 such horrors, stretching from precolumbian Indian tribes that sought to dominate and destroy each other, to scenes of imprisonment, torture, and murder under Castro.[6] Numbers 99 and 100, which relate the death by hunger of a prisoner of some twelve years and the agony of his mother respectively, are hauntingly reminiscent of vignettes in *Así en la paz*, making it perfectly clear that the atrocities commited under Castro are indistinguishable from those under Batista. In fact, the mother's monologue, presented as her half of a telephone conversation that is cut off abruptly (one supposes by Castro's henchmen), is disturbingly like the ravings of the madwoman in *Tres tristes tigres*, or the rambling account of the young girl in "Un rato de tenmeallá," in *Así en la paz*. All three reflect a sense of helplessness and despair brought on by constant suffering and repeated abuse by those in positions of authority.[7]

Through the pages of *Vista* run Cabrera Infante's old obsessions, including racism and suicide. And for those readers too insensitive to decipher the book's message, the final vignette provides a poetic gloss:

> Y ahí estará. Como dijo alguien, esa triste, infeliz y larga isla estará ahí después del último indio y después del último español y después del último africano y después del último americano y después del último de los cubanos, sobreviviendo a todos los naufragios y eternamente bañada por la corriente del golfo: bella y verde, imperecedera, eterna.

[And there it will remain. As someone said, that sad, unhappy and
lengthy island will be there after the last Indian and after the last
Spaniard and after the last African and after the last American and after
the last Cuban, surviving all the shipwrecks and forever bathed by the
gulfstream: beautiful and green, imperishable, eternal (233))].

While *Vista del amanecer en el trópico* may never challenge *Tres
tristes tigres* for a place atop Cabrera Infante's canon, one cannot but
sense in its pages that the author cares and cares deeply about his
homeland, his people, and his profession. In that regard it is of a piece
with *Así en la paz como en la guerra*, *Tres tristes tigres*, and *Un oficio
del siglo XX*. His insistence that he wrote it not for political, nor parochial, nor historical, but for aesthetic reasons (Hernández Lima, 141) is
also true of the other volumes mentioned, probably including *Así en la
paz* in its time.

The same is also true, no doubt, of the volumes not mentioned: *O*,
Exorcismos del estilo, and *La Habana para un Infante difunto*, but these
works lack the passion and the commitment of the others. *La Habana*
recounts some of the unhappy episodes of Cabrera Infante's childhood—
his parents used and abused by the Communists and persecuted by the
"Batistianos," for example—, or the observation that certain youthful
extortionists would some day become assassins, but would call themselves revolutionaries (208). For the most part, however, these books
become as personal as the humor of Cué and Silvestre in *Tres tristes
tigres*. They seem at times to be little more than mental masturbation (to
go with the physical marathons described in *la Habana*). It is one thing
to write purely for oneself, as Cabrera Infante repeatedly claims to do (as
do most writers), and quite another to shut out one's readers.

One suspects that Cabrera Infante sometimes writes only so that the
echo of his words, and the reviews of his books, will reassure him that he
has not disappeared. In a telling piece, first presented at a conference in
1987, he spoke at length about expatriation. There, under the title "The
Invisible Exile" and the epigraph "I was born in Cuba, and I hope to die
in England," he described how the warmth of his creature comforts
contrasted with his state of invisibility.

Cuban exiles, he argued, are not even "exilados" like other Spanish-
speaking exiles, they are "exiliados." They are also "gusanos" [worms]
and "escoria" [scum], words that echo back to Goebbels' use of "vermin"
for all Jews. He went on to point out that "exiliado" has no place in the

authoritative dictionary of the *Real Academia*, i.e., the "exile" (as designated in Cuba) does not exist.[8] He further described how, in a long article on political exiles in Latin America, a Uruguayan literary critic (one assumes Angel Rama)[9] mentioned only one exile from Cuba: José Martí. According to Cabrera Infante, Gabriel García Márquez (also not named in this piece but specifically attacked in "Nuestro prohombre en La Habana"), spoke of the horrors of Pinochet, of the exile of over one million Chileans; yet the Nobel laureate never mentioned Cuba, which apparently has no exiles, only some ten million individuals who no longer exist.

The tragedy of Cabrera Infante and so many other Cuban intellectuals who comprise the Cuban diaspora is that, since they fled a socialist regime that once attracted support from intellectuals around the world, they were forced not only into exile but into invisibility. They were not accorded the prestige that has been granted other exile groups, such as the intellectual refugees from the Spanish Civil War or World War II. The fact that the Cuban revolution has gone sour and lost its international support has not restored to its exiles their rightful visibility and acclaim. According to Cabrera Infante, Julio Cortázar[10] once said that "there are no exiled writers from Cuba. There are only worms abroad" ("The Invisible Exile" 38). While such an assertion may come as a shock to those familiar with the highly visible and organized Cuban communities in the United States and Europe, Cortázar's remark would have been an echo of the "official" Cuban position: those who fled the island ceased to be Cubans. Cabrera Infante concluded his remarks with a quote from *The Invisible Man*, by H.G. Wells, the one in which the stranger removes his bandages and reveals that he is totally invisible.

In another ostensibly "nonliterary" piece, his introduction to Carlos Franqui's *Family Portrait With Fidel*, Cabrera Infante is preoccupied with an "official" Cuban photograph, one with two versions. The first shows Castro speaking into a microphone held by an unidentified man, with Carlos Franqui in the background. The second version has the same Castro speaking into the same microphone, held by the same unidentified man—but Franqui has "disappeared," thanks to some anonymous but "official" Cuban censor. The cause of this disappearance was simple: Franqui, like Cabrera Infante before him, not only worked for *Revolución*—in fact he was its founder and editor—but also fled the revolution when he saw it turning sour, and was consequently, in that (ig)noble soviet tradition, "erased." Cabrera Infante's dread of erasure also appears in vignette 85 of *Vista del amanecer* in which a photographer dodges away[11] a face in order to make the photograph more compact. The face is that of a comandante who is later "eliminated."

In his introduction to Franqui's book, Cabrera Infante observes that Cubans have managed to create their own unique prose, distinct from Spanish or even South American prose. The authors he mentions, with the single exception of Martí, all wrote after the revolution. Some (Lezama Lima, Carpentier, Piñera) died in an at best uneasy relationship with the government that was forced to recognize them while holding them under great suspicion, if not in outright contempt. Others perished in exile— some by suicide (the ultimate expression of impuissance). All have been "erased" to at least some degree. Their fates have weighed heavily on Cabrera Infante, who has written many articles on suicide, particularly among his countrymen.[12]

Cabrera Infante himself, however, has been incredibly active and visible. In fact, his pen has rarely been still since he left Cuba. In addition to writing numerous screenplays (including "Weekend," "Vanishing Point," "Under the Volcano," etc.) and essays, he has published nine volumes since 1971 (one, *Holy Smoke*, on cigars and cigar smoking) and has collaborated on several translations. Not only is he a prolific writer, he has been vitally important to the advancement of Cuban prose. His irreverence, his humor, and his biting insights have also made him one of the most innovative and significant authors of the "Boom." Unfortunately, he is also a man who seems at times to be drowning in frustration and helplessness, whose bitterness becomes so great that rather than writing, as did Machado de Assis, one of his literary idols, with "a pena da galhofa e a tinta da melancolia" [the pen of mockery and the ink of melancholy (Machado de Assis, 23)], too often he manages to grasp only the same tired language games. When he is at his best, his barbs fill the reader not only with laughter, but with a heightened awareness of injustice and even evil; when his anger exceeds his creative powers, as has been the pattern in recent years, then he seems all the more impotent. He would no doubt argue that his situation and that of his homeland allow room for nothing but bitterness; his devotees might reply that that is all the more reason to distance himself and to treat the issues with a generous dash of humor.

Notes

1. See especially Alvarez-Borland, "Viaje verbal," 56, and "Entre la historia y la nada: notas sobre una ideología del suicidio."

2. Siemans argues that *TTT* "is severely apolitical, but only in its subtle yet emphatic rejection of the *authoritative voice* that tends to dominate political discourse in Latin America . . . the book is highly political in offering a written text characterized by radical multivalence as an alternative to such an authoritative voice. . . ." (107).

3. He continued to be active in a certain way, through his extensive contributions to Hugh Thomas's massive history, *Cuba: The Pursuit of Freedom*.

4. For a concatenation of the vignettes and their historical antecedents, see Hernández Lima.

5. For a fine analysis of the book's more literary aspects, see David William Foster's "Guillermo Cabrera Infante's *Vista del amanecer en el trópico* and the Generic Ambiguity of Narrative" in Foster, *Studies in the Contemporary Spanish American Short Story*.

6. For a correlation between the vignettes of both books and specific historical events see Hernández Lima, 112–140.

7. "por qué me va a imponer su ley su asquerosa ley" ["why are you trying to sic your law on me your dirty law" (*TTT* 451/487)]; "Ésta es la vida . . . ésta es la libertad en este país" [This is life, this is liberty in this country (*Vista* 227)]; "y el hombre le dice que no la coja con el que no tiene que ver nada y que el hace lo que le mandan y que para eso le pagaban y mama le dijo que estaba bien que ella comprendia todo pero que si no podian esperar un mes mas y el hombre dice que ni un dia y que mañana vendrian a sacar los muebles y que no oponga resistencia porque seria peor porque traerian a la policia y entonces los sacaraian a la fuerza y los meterian en la carcel" [and the man says to her not to get on him about it he doesn't have anything to do with it and he just does what he is told and that is why they were paying him and mama said to him ok that she understood and all but couldn't they way one more month and the man says not a day and tomorrow they were coming to get the furniture and not to put up a fight because it would be worse because they would bring the police and throw them out by force and put them in jail (*Así en la paz*, 14)].

8. Cabrera Infante was clearly in error on this point, and modified it in the reprint of the essay in *Mea Cuba*. The Academy did, in fact, accept "exiliado" as an alternative for "exilado" before he wrote his essay. While "Exilado" is still the preferred term for many native speakers, María Moliner (*Diccionario del uso del español*, 1: 1254) predicted that since the Academy established "exiliado" as the standard over "exilado," the older form will eventually disappear. Such quibbling over detail, however, misses the point: Cuban intellectuals who live in exile are "invisible" to the intellectual community at large, which tends to be liberal and hesitant to embrace foes of the Cuban revolution.

9. Cabrera Infante specifies that the critic was Uruguayan, and that he died in a plane crash. Angel Rama, a leftist Uruguayan critic, was killed in the crash of an Avianca Boeing 747 on November 1983.

10. Like the other authors alluded to in "The Invisible Exile," Cortázar is not mentioned by name. However, Cabrera Infante provides sufficient details to make each identification easy for the informed reader.

11. Dodging is a darkroom technique by which a photographer removes unwanted material from a photograph. Light rays are blocked after they leave the negative, but before they fall on the print paper. A skilled darkroom technician can effectively "erase" any portion of a photograph without leaving any evidence that it was ever present on the original negative.

12. The most extensive piece is "Entre la historia y la nada: notas sobre una ideología del suicidio," which was followed by "Más sobre el suicidio en Cuba."

Works Cited

Alvarez-Borland, Isabel. "Readers, Writers, and Interpreters in Cabrera Infante's Texts." *World Literature Today* 61 (1987): 553–558.

Cabrera Infante, Guillermo. *Así en la paz como en la guerra.* Barcelona: Seix Barral, 1971.

Cabrera Infante, Guillermo. "Brief Encounters in Havana." *World Literature Today* 61 (1987): 519–525.

Cabrera Infante, Guillermo. "Cain by Himself: Guillermo Cabrera Infante, Man of Three Islands." *Review: Latin American Literature and Arts* 28 (1981): 8–11.

Cabrera Infante, Guillermo. "(C)ave Attemptor! A Chronology (After Laurence Sterne's)." *World Literature Today* 61 (1987): 513–519.

Cabrera Infante, Guillermo. "Conversación de *Tres tristes tigres.*" With Rita Guibert. *G. Cabrera Infante.* By Julio Ortega et al. Caracas: Fundamentos, 1974. 19–46.

Cabrera Infante, Guillermo. "Entre la historia y la nada: notas sobre una ideología del suicidio." *Vuelta* 74 (1983): 11–22.

Cabrera Infante, Guillermo. "Guillermo Cabrera Infante." With Emir Rodríguez Monegal. *El arte de narrar.* By Emir Rodríguez Monegal. Caracas: Monte Avila, 1968.

Cabrera Infante, Guillermo. *La Habana para un Infante difunto.* Barcelona: Plaza & Janés, 1986.

Cabrera Infante, Guillermo. "The Invisible Exile." *Literature in Exile.* Ed. John Glad. Durham: Duke UP, 1990. 32-40.

Cabrera Infante, Guillermo. "Más sobre el suicidio en Cuba." *Vuelta* 79 (1983): 50–51.

Cabrera Infante, Guillermo. *Mea Cuba.* Barcelona: Plaza & Janés, 1992.

Cabrera Infante, Guillermo. "Nicolás Guillén: Poet and Partisan." *Review: Latin American Literature and Arts* 42 (1990): 31–33.

Cabrera Infante, Guillermo. "Nuestro prohombre en La Habana." *Vuelta* 78 May 1983: 51–53.

Cabrera Infante, Guillermo. "Portrait of a Tyrant as an Aging Tyro." *Family Portrait with Fidel.* By Carlos Franqui. Trans. Alfred MacAdam. New York: Random House, 1984. vii–xix.

Cabrera Infante, Guillermo. *Un oficio del siglo XX.* Barcelona: Seix Barral, 1973.

Cabrera Infante, Guillermo. "Talent of 2wo Cities." *Review: Latin American Literature and Arts* 35 (1995): 17–18.

Cabrera Infante, Guillermo. *Tres tristes tigres*. Barcelona: Seix Barral, 1970.

Cabrera Infante, Guillermo. "Viaje verbal a La Habana, ¡Ah vana!" With Isabel Alvarez-Borland. *Hispamérica: Revista de Literatura* 11 (1982): 51–68.

Cabrera Infante, Guillermo. *Vista del amanecer en el trópico*. Barcelona: Seix Barral, 1974.

Cabrera Infante, Guillermo. *Writes of Passage*. Trans. John Brookesmith, Peggy Boyars and Guillermo Cabrera Infante. London: Faber and Faber, 1993.

Foster, David William. "Guillermo Cabrera Infante's *Vista del amanecer en el trópico* and the Generic Ambiguity of Narrative." *Studies in the Contemporary Spanish American Short Story*. Columbia: U of Missouri P, 1979. 110–120.

Franqui, Carlos. *Family Portrait with Fidel: A Memoir*. Trans. Alfred MacAdam. New York: Random House, 1984.

Hernández Lima, Dinorah. *Versiones y re-versiones históricas en la obra de Cabrera Infante*. Madrid: Pliegos, 1990.

MacAdam, Alfred. "Seeing Double: Cabrera Infante and Caín." *World Literature Today* 61 (1987): 543–548.

Machado de Assis, *Memórias Pósthumas de Brás Cubas*. 5th ed. São Paulo: Editôra Cultrix, 1968.

Moliner, María. *Diccionario del uso del español*, Vol. 1. Madrid: Gredos, 1966. 2 vols.

Ortega, Julio et al. *G. Cabrera Infante*. Caracas: Fundamentos, 1974.

Pereda, Rosa María. *Cabrera Infante*. Madrid: EDAF, 1979.

Siemens, William L. "Guillermo Cabrera Infante and the Divergence of Revolutions: Political Versus Textual." *Literature and Revolution*. Ed. David Bevan. Amsterdam: Rodopi, 1989. 107–119.

Thomas, Hugh. *Cuba: The Pursuit of Freedom*. New York: Harper & Row, 1971.

David William Foster

OF POWER AND VIRGINS: ALEJANDRA PIZARNIK'S LA CONDESA SANGRIENTA[1]

From a radical feminist perspective it is clear that "Father" is precisely the one who cannot exorcise, for he is allied with and identified with The Possessor. The fact that he is himself possessed should not be women's essential concern. It is a mistake to see men as pitiable victims or vessels to be "saved" through female self-sacrifice. However possessed males may be within patriarchy, it is *their* order; it is they who feed on women's stolen energy. It is a trap to imagine that women should "save" men from the dynamics of demonic possession; and to attempt this is to fall deeper into the pit of patriarchal possession. It is women ourselves who will have to expel the Father from ourselves, becoming our own exorcists. (Daly 2)

The fundamental challenge presented by a literature of the horrible is for the reader to accept how what it is describing has anything to do with historical reality. One feels safe in saying that this literature is never taken seriously by the majority of its readers, for whom it represents a thrilling form of escapism from the humdrum texture of the everyday social world, rather than a cultural product that allows them insightful access to the inside of historical reality. The impression that the horrible is not really a truth about the world, that it may deal with the hidden and terrible forces of the human psyche, but not really with the dynamics of social relations, leads to a margination of the horrible. Such a margination may be performed by readers whose tastes drive a consumerist production of popular writing and film production and by critics who are neither interested in popular writing nor, beyond Romanticism, much interested in treatments of the horrible.

In those cases in which the horrible is tied to specific sociopolitical events like the disappeared in Argentina during recent military dictatorships, the slaughter between government and guerrilla forces in El Salvador, or the massacre of indigenous tribes in the Brazilian jungle in order to facilitate the construction of the Trans-Amazonian Highway, the horrible is processed as the ugly face of tyranny that has suddenly been revealed to decent people. The implication, of course, is that they should repudiate it as inhuman, as a debasement of what is naturally right. The ethics of such a disjuncture allows readers both to confirm their own decency and to repudiate the horrible that is being exposed to them in the name of sociopolitical denunciation. In this relatively circumscribed arena, the horrible is separated from the dark recesses of the human soul where the Romantics had discovered it and attributed to repudiated individuals, who are then seen as "amoral," "degenerate," and "sick."

It would seem that the first move in the attempt to reinstall horror in an interpretation of historical reality must be in terms of how what is presented is horrible. This presentation is in some way a dense concentration of an integral facet of human experience, and not something that is viewed as a character supplement that takes possession of only some individuals and turns them into a threat to putatively normal people. In order to function as a perception of the materially historical, the horrible has to be installed in the center of what is being viewed as human experience, where it will be shown to be a dominant factor in the configuration of a social reality individuals know as their world and against which they struggle for liberation. In this sense, the horrible is an index of historical necessity, and it can only have meaning in a sense beyond the gratuitously fantastic or escapist as an index of the confines of history that individuals must repudiate in order to avoid psychological and physical degradation.

The bloody countess of *La condesa sangrienta* (1976) by Alejandra Pizarnik (1936–1972), the real-life Hungarian Erzébet Báthory (d. 1614), is the focal point for a meditation on the horror of absolute power. This power is expressed in sexual terms, specifically in the figure of a woman who tortures (as a form of displaced rape) and kills over six-hundred young women, whereby the ability to fulfill completely one's erotic fantasies bespeaks an absolutist social system. Pizarnik frames her brief narrative (eleven vignettes in a sparse and highly controlled poetic prose) with two quotes that on first impression appear to be contradictory. The first is from Jean-Paul Sartre, who in *Saint Genet*, on the criminal/writer Jean Genet, defended the individual condemned as a criminal threat to society as in reality a privileged outsider to the structures of bourgeois repression (Sartre literally saved Genet from execution as a recidivist with his eloquent argument). Pizarnik quotes Sartre as an epigraph to her text:

El criminal no hace la belleza; él mismo es la auténtica belleza (7) .

[Beauty is not made by the criminal; he is himself authentic beauty (my translation)].

After seventy pages of relentless descriptions of the sufferings inflicted on the bodies of young women placed in the countess's charge as hand-maidens, Pizarnik closes with the following reflection: "Como Sade en sus escritos, como Gilles de Rais en sus crímenes, la condesa Báthory alcanzó, más allá de todo límite, el último fondo del desenfreno. Ella es una prueba más de que la libertad absoluta de la criatura humana es horrible" [Like Sade in his writings, like Gilles de Rais in his crimes, Countess Báthroy attained, beyond all limits, the depths of her excesses. He is one more proof that absolute liberty for the human being is horrible (my translation); (76)].

Yet, these two propositions need not be viewed as contradictory. In the first place, one can assume that Sartre engaged in a deconstruction of the concept of beauty, not only in the sense of an absolute value but as an aesthetic category divorced from a grounding in lived experience. It is possible to imagine that the thrust of this declaration is that, to the extent that the criminals are totally circumscribed by the materiality of life (both in the historical necessity that makes them criminals and in the ways in which the forces of society provide the definition of their existence and control their bodies, ultimately through incarceration), they are the most authentic indexes of the quality of our collective life and, hence, its most "beautiful" exponent. By contemplating them we can most know about ourselves, most experience the sort of transcendental self-knowledge traditionally attributed (at least in bourgeois aesthetics) to the beautiful that is outside our lived experience. But Sartre's object of beauty does not lead us outside the materiality of our historical circumstance and into an ineff-able realm we seek to inhabit as a release from the social realm we cannot handle. Rather, it leads us squarely back into sociohistorical reality because what is being called the beautiful is exactly what is most bound (literally by the chains of the criminal, figuratively by the network of signifiers that define the criminal) by sociohistorical reality. The concept of the beautiful is now, from the perspective of Sartre's formulation, that which most brings us to an awareness of the substance of our lived social experience.

From this point of view, then, the story of Erzébet Báthory does not belong to a realm of the abstractly beautiful, even when that beauty may be based on the systematic inversion of the primes underlying the notion of the beautiful as ennobling—seen in these terms, Báthory would be the point-by-point refutation of the figure of woman as soul-fulfilling beauty for her masculine contemplator, something like a negative image of the Virgin Mary tradition of feminine representation. Not only is Báthory the *belle dame sans merci* inversion of the Virgin Mary sign (in the tradition of Mario Praz's "romantic agony"), but her corporeality which is incarnated by the horror of her sexual conduct leads to a regrounding in historical materiality: Báthory embodies masculinist violence, the rape of the Other. In her activities as a rapist she is both a symbol of the absolute power of the aristocrats of her own historical period (she is saved from execution, despite the threats of a peasant uprising, because of the protection of her family by the Hapsburg crown), and as a symbol of the absolute power of the persecutions of the military tyranny in Argentina at the time in which *La condesa sangrienta* was written. For this reason, it would be a mistake to see Báthory as exemplifying the patriarchy's myth of feminine evil that Mary Daly has denounced in her writings: the countess's apparent crossing over the boundaries of civilization into the realm of the Wild Hag is, as I will argue in what follows, not the sort of transgression advocated by radical feminism, but is in fact a confirmation of the terrible masculinist violence of the patriarchy whose martyrs are betokened by the countess's hundreds of female victims. Báthory may have been a woman, but her relationship with the girls who came under her authority is the confirmation of the masculinist establishment she paradigmatized because it had created her and given her the terrible abusive power she exercised: "Each of [the] subcultures of sadism has its own hierarchy, apprenticeship, initiation rites, and its own language. . . . Moreover, women have a special role in these subcultures as subservient token torturers of other women. The 'bitch of Buchenwald' and female torturers of female political prisoners in such countries as Argentina are illustrations of this traitor-token syndrome" (Daly 96).

If Pizarnik's novel became an underground classic in Argentina and is now one of the rarest items in the bibliography of contemporary Argentine poetry, it is in large measure because the historical necessity she describes for the victims of the bloody countess is a typological figure of the historical necessity experienced by the thousands of victims of the *guerra sucia* [dirty war].[2] The sadomasochism Pizarnik attributes to Báthory, which is to be sure part of the legend of the Dracula typus and the Sadean legacy of the continuum of sex and power, is a constant motif in treatments of the psychology of the torturer as *he* confronts a victim over whom he exercises complete power, particularly when that victim is a woman (cf. Partnoy for one woman's personal testimony). See, for example, the novel by a psychologist who works with victims of torture, Ana Vásquez, *Abel Rodríguez y sus hermanos* (1981) and Eduardo Pavlovsky's play *El Sr. Galíndez* (1973), where a group of bored torturers entertain themselves with a couple of prostitutes with whom, for the men, sex means playfully torturing them. If the victims of Báthory are young girls, the emphasis of lesbianism added to her sadomasochism only enhances the sense of horror for her readers whose conventions are likely to find lesbianism in itself horrible enough, just as the fictional treatments and documentary reports on male torturers and their male victims may emphasize homoerotic dimensions (e.g., Beatriz Guido's *El incendio y las vísperas* [1963]).

It is immaterial whether "real" homosexuality is involved: one could insist that sexuality to one degree or another is involved in all human relations, and hetero- versus homosexuality is only a matter of calling attention to the gendered identities of the conjugation of participants of the moment (see Foster on the lesbian dimensions of Pizarnik's text). Nor is it a matter of documentary reports versus fictional accounts, since one presumes that the latter bear some sort of reasonable correspondence to the former, and accounts will call attention to the distribution of the sexes between torturers and their victims. Male torturers and some kind of ratioed distribution between male and female victims are likely to be the norm, but the historical record reveals that, in the case of the bloody countess, a female torturer and over six hundred female victims provided the basic statistics Pizarnik interprets. Rather, where sexuality enters explicitly—rhetorically—into the analysis of the confrontation between torturer and victim, it might well be because the author wishes to appeal to the sense of horror for the presumed reader associated with the violation of certain sexual taboos: torture as sex violates one taboo (grounded in the prohibition of necrophilia, but also because torture, like rape, involves unwilling participation by one of the partners in the act), and homosexuality sharpens the horror by underscoring the transgression of yet another taboo.

What serves as the central core of Pizarnik's narrative, as it does for the narrative of the historical record she is reproducing, is the series of oppositions of the powerful versus the unprotected, the authoritarian figure versus her protegées (in the case of the military dictatorship in Argentina, it is the government versus its citizens), absolute freedom versus historical necessity. The countess—like any one of the figures of the despotic she personifies—occupies a position from which she can dictate in an absolute manner the rules of society, and it is a dictatorship from which her victims can have no appeal or escape: they are absolutely circumscribed by the jail of the text she has forged. This relationship is cameoed in the vignette "La jaula mortal":

> Tapizada con cuchillos y adornada con filosas puntas de acero, su tamaño admite un cuerpo humano; se la iza mediante una polea. La ceremonia de la jaula se despliega así:
> La sirvienta Dorkó arrastra por los cabellos a una joven desnuda; la encierra en la jaula; alza la jaula. Aparece la "dama de estas ruinas," la sonámbula vestida de blanco. Lenta y silenciosa se sienta en un escabel situado debajo de la jaula.
> Rojo atizador en mano, Dorkó azuza a la prisionera quien, al retroceder —y he aquí la gracia de la jaula—, se clava por sí misma los filosos aceros mientras su sangre mana sobre la mujer pálida que la recibe impasible con los ojos puestos en ningún lado. Cuando se repone de su trance se aleja lentamente. Ha habido dos metamorfosis: su vestido blanco ahora es rojo y donde hubo una muchacha hay un cadáver (23–24).

> [Lined with knives and adorned by sharp steel spikes, it has the size of a human body; it can be drawn up by a pulley. The ceremony of the cages is as follows:
> Dorkó the servant drags a young naked girl by her hair; she locks her in the cage; she pulls the cage up. The "lady of these ruins" appears, a sleepwalker dressed in white. Slowly and silently she takes her seat on a stool located below the cage.
> Dorkó jabs the prisoner with a redhot poker, who—and this is the charm of the cage—impales herself on the sharp steel spikes, as her blood drips down on the pale woman who receives it impassively, a vacant look in her eyes. When she comes to from her trance, she walks slowly away. There have been two metamorphoses: her white dress is now red, and where there was a girl there is now a cadaver (my translation)].

The use of decorative words like *tapizado* and *gracia* contribute to the sense of aesthetic distancing, duplicated by the entranced detachment of the spectator countess, the "dama de estas ruinas." She contemplates the literal figure of her power, the cage in which the victim is imprisoned, just as the citizens of her realm are caged by the absolute power she wields over them. Caught between Dorkó's red-hot poker and the spikes of the cage, the victim "necessarily" dies by being driven against the hard-edged reality of her cage. The double transformation described at the end of the vignette is a process of confirmation of the countess's power: the transference to her of the blood of the girl nullifies the victim while invigorating the owner of the cage (the text speaks elsewhere of elements of witchcraft in Báthory's utilization of the blood of her victims to maintain her youth and beauty; one of the vignettes is entitled "Baños de sangre").

It is interesting to note that in these vignettes the narrator uses the present tense. Less than a remote historical event, what she is recounting is, to use a grammatical term, a durative present, an existing reality that is in a sense tenseless, much like the use of the present in mathematical formulas or scientific propositions. Báthory bespeaks the inherent coordinates of the exercise of violent power, a dynamic of horrifying oppression in which she is only a transitory agent but which she inherits and which will exist after her, as the Argentine *guerra sucia* and regrettably so many other historical circumstances have confirmed. Certainly, it is customary for poetry—and the texts of *La condesa sangrienta*, Pizarnik's only prose composition, are in reality prose poems—to be written in the durative present, to the extent that we associate with poetry the specification of "eternal truths" rather than the time-bound accounts of prose fiction. But the eternal truth of *La condesa sangrienta* is to be read as beyond all doubt sociohistorically grounded not because of the historical figure of Báthory, but because of the dynamic of power she exemplifies.

The irony of Pizarnik's sculptured prose, however, is that the beauty of the countess lies not in the images of her physical attributes, the ingeniousness of her handling of the landscape she controls, or the power of the symbols of her dramatic tableaux (e.g., the interplay between deathly white and enlivening blood red). Rather it lies in the economy of her horrible incarnation of the criminal whose acts are shown to lead us back into a historical materiality that imprisons us all. The lurid fascination of a narrative like *La condesa sangrienta* can only be the contemplation of a reality that, perhaps less vividly but at times in all of its literalness (e.g., the *guerra sucia*), we experience in our daily lives, confronted with the violent abusiveness of a sociopolitical system we have not yet been able to change, a murderous cage we have not yet been able to escape from. And the text's reference to how the girl is obliged to impale herself on the spikes of the cage, as though she were responsible for her own pain and death, is a token of how we are not just victims of a system that oppresses us but also its perpetuators and (re)inventors in the betrayal of the self: one understanding of oppression is the extreme coersion by which individuals collaborate in their own self-destruction, often without the victim's very awareness. A classic example of this is the suicide that lesbians and gays accept as the only choice open to them, thereby complying with the homophobic imperative that homosexuals "disappear." The passiveness of Báthory's victims, their inability to find a form of revolt, makes them accomplices in their own suffering until the threat of a peasant's revolt (the majority of Báthory's victims were peasant girls, although some noblewomen placed in her charge were involved) puts an end to the countess's highly efficient enactments of the larger structure of oppression.

Pizarnik's text turns on the motif of contemplation, of sexual voyeurism. Báthory contemplates the drama of suffering enacted for her by her servants and her victims (although she does, on occasion, handle the instruments of torture herself), and, of course, the reader contemplates Báthory's role as a spectator and, through her, the representation of absolute power. The vignette "La virgen de hierro" is only one of the texts that centers on voyeurism, and the reduplication of the countess in the object of the iron virgin serves to underscore the displacement between the countess and the instruments of her power she—and through her, the reader—contemplates:

> Había en Nuremberg un famoso autómata llamado "la Virgen de hierro." La condesa Báthory adquirió una réplica para la sala de torturas de su castillo de Csejthe. Esta dama metálica era del tamaño y del color de la criatura humana. Desnuda, maquillada, enjoyada, con rubios cabellos que llegaban al suelo, un mecanismo permitía que sus labios se abrieran en una sonrisa, que los ojos se movieran.
> La condesa, sentada en su trono, contempla.
> Para que la "Virgen" entre en acción es preciso tocar algunas piedras preciosas de su collar. Responde inmediatamente con horrible sonidos mecánicos y muy lentamente alza los blancos brazos para que se cierren en perfecto abrazo sobre lo que esté cerca de ella—en este caso una muchacha. La autómata la abraza y ya nadie podrá desanudar el cuerpo vivo del cuerpo de hierro, ambos iguales en belleza. De pronto se abren y aparecen cinco puñales que atraviesan a su viviente compañera de largos cabellos sueltos como los suyos.

Ya consumado el sacrificio, se toca otra piedra del collar: los brazos caen, la sonrisa se cierra así como los ojos, la asesina vuelve a ser la "Virgen" inmóvil en su féretro (15–16).

[In Nuremberg there was a famous automoton called "the Iron Virgin." Countess Báthory acquired a replica for the torture chamber of her castle in Csejthe. This metallic lady was the size and color of a human being. Naked, made up, bejewelled, with blond hair that reached the floor, she had a mechanism that made her lips smile and eyes that moved.

The Countess watched, seated on her throne.

In order for the "Virgin" to work, one presses certain precious stones in her necklace. She responds immediately with horrible mechanical sounds, slowly raising her white arms to totally embrace what is beside her—in this case, a girl. The automaton embraces her and it is impossible to separate the living body from the iron one, both of equal beauty. Suddenly five blades appear and stab the living companion, whose hair is as long as the automaton's.

When the sacrifice is complete, one touches another stone on the collar: the arms fall, the smile disappears and the eyes close, and the assassin becomes once again the still "Virgin" in her coffin (my translation)].

Voyeurism is also a sexual taboo, although perhaps not as strongly repudiated as necrophilia, rape, and homosexuality. One suspects we all allow ourselves an indulgence in voyeurism if we think we are not ourselves being watched engaged in the act of watching. Reading, which is above all a solitary vice, is a form of voyeurism—we contemplate a world that we are not likely otherwise have access to. Such voyeurism, with or without reference to sexuality, may be encoded metanarratively in the text or it may remain only a part of the reader's (un)conscious sense of invading the space of the Other being read about. An excellent example of this problematic is Julio Cortázar's short story "Las babas del diablo" ["Blow-up"] where the reader voyeuristically watches the agony of the photographer-voyeur as he contemplates, in the photograph he has taken and now away from a real-life situation in which he cannot intervene, the horror of a boy being doubly seduced by a man and his female accomplice. In Pizarnik's text, in addition to the explicit homosexuality of the act of voyeurism on the part of the countess, the text also incorporates a challenge to the gaze of the reader, who (through the eyes of the narrator, who is the mediating voyeur) watches the countess watch herself embracing her victim through the agency of the iron virgin: "Esta sombría ceremonia tiene una sola espectadora silenciosa" [This somber ceremony has a single spectator (my translation); (11)]. It is the horror of what the voyeur sees, compounded by the violation of the taboo of voyeurism that undoubtedly is the basis of repugnance many readers experience in the face of a text like *La condesa sangrienta*. Yet, it is this horror that must also be the basis of a reentry, through the literary text, into the reality of the social text and a perception of how the horror of the former, the product of the artful distillation of the resources of the artist's craft, is a figure of the horrors of the actual oppression of abusive power that permeates, albeit often in a diluted form, everyday historical reality. If voyeurs are often spellbound by what they see, it is because the scene evokes for them a logic of human relations they perceive to be expected, and if what is witnessed is felt to be horrible, that horror is not an independent aesthetic judgment but rather a reliable index of what we sense to be horrible in the world we are condemned inescapably to inhabit.

We need now to reconcile the figure of Báthory as a criminal both as she is constructed by her society and as she is a mirror of it. One of the vignettes entitled "El espejo de la melancolía" [the mirror of melancholy] adds a series of mirror metaphors to the subject of self-contemplation. Báthory, like every human being, is heir to the social code of her society. All individuals are instruments for the articulation of a social ideology, and the horizons of self-consciousness are basically defined by the code internalized as part of the process of socialization. For this reason, someone like Báthory cannot be conceived of as a "monster" that exists outside the structure of her society, and precisely the ideological slippage found in much literature of the horror and documentary reports on so-called monsters is to construe them as existing outside the structures of what is smugly called the "normal" world: the "abnormal" world of the pervert exists somewhere else, although its citizens will on occasion invade the world of the decent when the latter's defenses are carelessly lowered. But I have suggested that the sense of the Sartre quote is to view the criminal as the vivid encoding of the degrading principles of human commerce that circulate relatively unchecked in society: the criminal is the paradigm of all human beings and the persecution of the criminal derives from the threat of the eloquence with which he or she represents how the real world is. The bloody countess is, therefore, a circumstantial embodiment, but a very dramatic one, of the abusive power permitted to certain individuals in her age.

It is significant to note that, because of the loyalties sustaining the Hapsburg Empire, Erzébet Báthory was not executed for her amply documented crimes—just as the agents of the *guerra sucia* in Argentina and of similar operations in other Latin American countries went essentially unpunished for their crimes (some of the top military officials in Argentina were sentenced to prison by courts during the Alfonsín government, but they were all pardoned by Menem, his successor, in 1989). Báthory was immured in her castle, and her imprisonment, a replicated sign of the torture chamber of her victims, lasted three years until her death in 1614: "Nunca comprendió por qué la condenaron" [She never understood why they sentenced her (my translation); (76)]. Criminals often do not understand what their relationship is to the system that has engendered and then condemned them for what they embody, and Báthory (like the *generales* who to this day protest their innocence and insist that the country owes them a monument for their deeds on behalf of the fatherland) remained unaware of the system of power relations of her society that her sexual dramatics so efficiently enacted. Those power relations were to be given full representation on the broad stage of life during the Thirty Years War in which the Hapsburgs were to be involved between 1618 and 1648, one of the bloodiest conflicts of premodern European history, and one whose causes made the Hapsburg crown especially concerned about bonds of loyalty that involved Báthory's family.

One of the problems with a literature of the horrible is the chance that the horrors it portrays will become naturalized: motifs from *Halloween, Friday the Thirteenth, Carrie, The Exorcist, The Texas Chain-Saw Massacre* have become motifs in contemporary American pop culture to be repeated (the numerous sequels) and reelaborated (the numerous spinoffs). Naturalization here means that they become accepted as continuous with what is accepted unreflexively as natural in the cultural paradigm. As such they lose their shock value as being monstrous or horrible, perhaps retaining only the disembodied aesthetic thrill of the conventionally horrible mentioned at the outset of this discussion. There is an inherent contradiction here, of course. One does want to argue for the incorporation of the horrible within an understanding of what is possible in the dynamics of quotidian reality: torture, rape, and calculatedly sadistic murder are the consequence of the ideology that sustains known human experience, the historical materialism to which one constantly refers as the imperative grounding for cultural texts and the analyses made of them. But in the process of seeing someone like Báthory as the extreme embodiment of what we accept as the natural exercise of sociopolitical power, we cannot allow room for seeing her conduct as natural, as no longer inspiring horror or revulsion, in the realm of what we think our society to be or what we want it to be, which is the danger of seeing the bloody countess as beautiful in terms of the bourgeois concept of an ideal, other worldly beauty. Chávez Silverman goes more deeply into the questions that arise around Pizarnik's conjunction of Báthory's beauty and lesbian sadomasochism, chiding quite rightly critics' inability to come adequately to terms with this highly disturbing conjunction. The Sartre quote, it has been argued, separates itself from this notion of beauty, and Pizarnik is careful to enunciate at the end of her text a position that retains the bloody countess as a figure very much of this world, but precisely therefore not one deserving of either our sympathy or our emulation:

> Ella no sintió miedo, no tembló nunca. Entonces, ninguna compasión ni emoción ni admiración por ella. Sólo un quedar en suspenso en el exceso de horror, una fascinación por un vestido blanco que se vuelve rojo, por la idea de un absoluto desgarramiento, por la evocación de un silencio constelado de gritos en donde todo es la imagen de una belleza inaceptable. (76)

> [She felt no fear and never trembled. Thus, one need feel no compassion, no admiration for her. There is only, in the face of the excess of horror, a feeling of incompleteness, a fascination for a white dress that turns red, for the idea of an absolute rendering, for the conviction of a silence broken by screams in which everything is the image of an unacceptable beauty (my translation)].

As a consequence, our sense of the horror of the world as represented by *La condesa sangrienta* can only be a measure of our perception of the dynamics of abusive power that sustain the world we actually live in. This more than anything else explains the enormous importance Pizarnik's text—on a forgotten Hungarian countess of almost four hundred years ago, yet written at a dreadful time in recent Argentine history—has had among those struggling to understand the nature of their own immediate world.

Yet, there is an important distinction to be made between the image of the exercise of violence that Pizarnik portrays in terms of Erzébet Báthory and the human rights abuses documented for the military regimes under which many of the Argentine readers of *La condesa sangrienta* were formed. As dreadful as the use of torture and murder by the military was, it served a putatively practical purpose: the consolidation of political power whereby the use of violence would serve to stifle opposition to the dictatorship. By contrast, the already consolidated power that Báthory wielded from within absolutist confines of her castle could have had no other purpose than to allay the tedium of her melancholy. Although there are some references to blood rituals meant to preserve her youth and beauty, only some of the practices she engaged in were meant for that purpose. In the main, her activities had no more goal than the aesthetic display of the ingenuity of violence. While some of the agents of military repression may have been engaged in fulfilling personal needs akin to those of the countess, the apparatus as such served a very pragmatic function, absent in the universe Pizarnik describes.

Finally, we must return to the matter of Báthory as a figure of masculinist violence. It is cruelly ironic that *La condesa sangrienta* involves a woman exercising such power over other women, and she may be viewed as an example of what Mary Daly has called the female "token torturer," the woman who is an agent of the sado-rituals men practice on the bodies of women. But like Dante's Perillo (*Inferno* 27), Báthory becomes a victim of the masculinist power she embodies, as she is, in turn, sacrificed by the structure of oppression she has personified for her victims. Certainly, immurement hardly approximates the horror of the *jaula mortal*, but it does adequately figure how Báthory suffers also at the hands of a higher power—the society of men—from which there is no appeal. When it becomes politically expedient to punish her for her crimes, crimes made possible by the power invested in the criminal, she is condemned to immurement, which in its own way is a grim figure of "la jaula mortal."

Notes

1. Modified chapter from *Violence in Argentine Literature: Cultural Response to Tyranny* by David William Foster, by permission of the University of Missouri Press. Copyright © 1995 by the Curators of the University of Missouri.

2. The so-called "dirty war" against anything that could be accused of being leftist subversion was unleashed by the 1975 coup which was in turn prefigured by the dictatorships between 1966 and 1973, a period that saw a quantum jump in Argentina in the use of torture and political imprisonment and the invention of the transitive verb

desaparecer, as described in the report of the democratic government's commission on human rights abuse, *Nunca más* (see also Ortúzar; *Tortura en América;* and *Torture in the Eighties*). A brilliant investigation in the culture of torture is provided by Scarry, and Graziano has provided a highly suggestive reading of the set of cultural, religious, and social beliefs that underlay the dirty war.

Works Cited

Chávez Silverman, Suzanne. "The Look that Kills" The 'Unacceptable Beauty' of Alejandra Pizarnik's La condesa sangrienta." *Gay and Lesbian Issues in Hispanic Literature*. Emilie Bergmann and Paul Julian Smith, eds. Durham: Duke U P, forthcoming.

Daly, Mary. *Gyn/ecology; the Metaethics of Radical Feminism*. Boston: Beacon P, 1978.

Foster, David William. *Gay and Lesbian Themes in Latin American Literature*. Austin: U of Texas P, 1991.

Graziano, Frank. *Divine Violence: Spectacle, Psychosexuality, & Radical Christianity in the Argentine "Dirty War"*. Boulder: Westview P, 1992.

Nunca más: informe de la Comisión Nacional sobre la Desaparición de Personas. Buenos Aires: EUDEBA, 1984.

Ortúzar, Ximena. *Represión y tortura en el Cono Sur*. México, D.F.: Editorial Extemporáneos, 1977.

Pizarnik, Alejandra. *La condesa sangrienta*. Buenos Aires: López Creso Editor, 1976.

Partnoy, Alicia. *The Little School: Tales of Disappearance Survival in Argentina*. Trans. by Alicia Partnoy with Lois Athey and Sandra Braunstein. Pittsburgh: Cleis P, 1986.

Praz, Mario. *The Romantic Agony*. Trans. by Angus Davidson. 2nd ed. New York: Meridian Books, 1956.

Sartre, Jean-Paul. *Saint Genet: Actor and Martyr*. Trans. by Bernard Frechtman. New York: George Braziller, 1963.

Scarry, Elaine. *The Body in Pain, the Making and Unmaking of the World*. New York: Oxford U P, 1985.

La tortura en América latina. Buenos Aires: CODESEDH, 1987.

Torture in the Eighties; an Amnesty International Report. London: Amnesty International Publications, 1984.

Rosemary Geisdorfer Feal

THE POLITICS OF "WARGASM": SEXUALITY, DOMINATION AND FEMALE SUBVERSION IN LUISA VALENZUELA'S *CAMBIO DE ARMAS*

I take as the departure point for this essay a convergence of social and psychological issues in Luisa Valenzuela's collection of narrations, *Cambio de armas* (Other weapons)[1] (1982), which may be articulated through the following question: what is the relationship among power, male domination, violent political repression, feminine sexuality, and the social arrangements between men and women? In exploring such broad matters, I wish to construct a framework that is flexible enough to accommodate the individual protagonists in *Other Weapons* without denying the text its historical specificity. Nevertheless, I intend to show how Valenzuela's presentation of the politics of "wargasm" posits strategies for female subversion of dominant sexual, social, and political orders while simultaneously pointing out the wrinkles in those very sheets that women lie on as they pursue their self-determined forms of pleasure. If I take up some recent work drawn from diverse methodological camps dealing with feminism and psychoanalysis, terrorism and sexuality, pornography and female pleasure, or international politics and feminism, it is in an effort to elucidate Valenzuela's particular reconfigurations of the relation between sexuality and domination which, in my opinion, offer a highly sophisticated and disturbing picture of some very pressing realities of our times.[2]

Inasmuch as Valenzuela presents her female characters in various poses of complicity and rebellion vis-à-vis the dominant patriarchal economy that typifies the social settings in which they move about (or by which they are confined), it seems fitting that the critical postures deployed in this essay should be correspondingly mobile—even contradictory—in order to articulate some sets of meanings that come into play in *Other Weapons*. Thus we might begin with the approach to sexuality and terrorism put forth by Robin Morgan, a "feminist warrior" who has been at the forefront of the origins of the contemporary women's movement in the United States. In her book *The Demon Lover: On the Sexuality of Terrorism*, Morgan adopts the stance of a terrorist in her own right by employing a scare-tactic style through which she explores the spectrum of patriarchal violence that she calls "the politics of Thanatos" (16). By reducing the history of male-female relations to the stark claim that most women act peaceably and most men act belligerently (26), Morgan imputes all forms of violence across all periods of history, throughout all nations, among all peoples, to a story of patriarchy gone wild, unchecked by the kinder, gentler feminine forces which by nature would create a more harmonious outer world to reflect their peace-loving inner one. To her credit, Morgan also recognizes that women can be the agents of brutality and/or complicity in abuses such as clitoridectomy, incest, or child-battering, but she dismisses those acts as mechanisms of survival in a male-dominated world. Clearly, the kind of work carried out by Morgan and other feminists who engage in a monolithic critique of patriarchy may not offer much assistance in analyzing the work of Luisa Valenzuela, if for no other reason than the Argentine writer obviously does not share the ideological bases for these strains of feminism. Nevertheless, I have borrowed for the title of this essay Morgan's title for a chapter of her book, itself borrowed from the Weathermen's 1969 "We declare a wargasm in America!" (154), because the neologism linguistically fuses the discourses of war and sexuality into one explosive noun that, despite what Morgan claims, may be read on a masculine or feminine axis. In fact, Andrea Dworkin draws a similar image when she speaks of the "concentration camp orgasm" in discussing the masculine pornographic economy that depicts men as sadists, with women-victims in a maso-chistic position from which they falsely proclaim enjoyment of the brutalization to which they are subjected.

The politics of "wargasm" are directly related to Valenzuela's work, emerging as it does out of the context of repressive military regimes in which sexual violence achieves a highly ritualized role in the domination and oppression of both women and men. This topic has received wide treatment in recent Spanish American writing by women in works of fiction and in testimonial literature, owing to the political conditions in countries such as Chile, Argentina, Guatemala, El Salvador, and Uruguay.[3]

Valenzuela's innovations consist in her courageous examination not only of the "politics of Thanatos" but also of the "psychology of Eros," whereby domination, pleasure, and sexuality form part of the internal organizations of the feminine psyches as they interact with the social formations around them. Let us recontextualize the appropriated term "wargasm" to mean possible forms of feminine pleasure under repressive political systems of domination, be they subversive pleasures under bourgeois patriarchy, or co-opted experiences of pleasure under abusive sexual dominance, or sites of counter-pleasurable resistance under military rule, or the "revolutionary high" (Morgan's term) experienced by the partner of the "demon lover." I prefer the polysemous notion of "wargasm" thus redefined to, perhaps, a term like "sexploitation," which stresses the economic gains derived from the abuse/misuse, or Dworkin's "concentration camp orgasm," which forecloses on any renegotiation of female desire or agency. Note, though, that I am consciously distorting Morgan's use of "wargasm" by shifting my focus to the question of representations of feminine psychology and sexuality, an arena in which Morgan declines to tread, but in which Valenzuela breaks decidedly fresh ground.[4]

In the last narration of the collection, "Cambio de armas," whose title gives name and coherence to the book as a whole, the female protagonist is the "subversive" Laura, who, having survived detainment, torture, and loss of memory, finds herself married to the man she had attempted to kill, a military officer who keeps her under lock and key and sexually abuses her. This piece has evoked strong reactions from critics, and Valenzuela herself has said: "Para mí fue un texto muy difícil. Ese cuento quería trabajarlo, ampliarlo, pero es tan duro que no lo pude releer nunca más. El arma que se cambia es el sexo, se cambia el arma por el sexo. Es la dominación por el sexo" [For me it was a very difficult text. I wanted to work on that story, to expand it, but it is so hard that I never could reread it again. The weapon that is exchanged is sex, the weapon is exchanged for sex ("Máscaras," 517)]. Although the majority of critical commentaries react to the scenario of domination and repression from a variety of insightful perspectives, they also skirt the most disturbing questions of all: what possibilities for the emergence of feminine desire and sexual pleasure may be traced in the ritualized structure of domination contained in that simulacrum of a marriage; how do these relate to Laura's role as victim of political repression; and what links may be drawn between what María-Inés Lagos-Pope calls "the impression of a normal life"[5] and the normalcy of the confinement and abuse of some women in their domestic situations? While the woman called "Laura" evidences psychological reactions appropriate to her status as victim of military violence, she also assumes a coerced role as wife-victim, one against which she ultimately rebels, but only after having experienced both the terror—and the terrifying pleasures—available to her under those conditions. Yet Valenzuela does not limit her metaphoric exploration of domestic captivity to the psyche of Laura: she also encodes the psychology of male dominance, which, as we will see, manifests itself in ways that resemble the pornographic fantasies that Andrea Dworkin and others have condemned as degrading to all women. So Valenzuela creates a double-edged weapon indeed, since her "Other Weapons" centers on a drama of documentable abuse and violence, but it refuses to leave fantasy out of the hauntingly realistic portrait of a kind of marriage. This statement may be extended to the entire work. Valenzuela refrains from assigning knowable, stereotypical roles to her female protagonists and their male partners; rather, she suggests a series of gender-based positionings that may or may not open up avenues of resistance and subversion.

"Other Weapons" is the only narration in which the female protagonist lives in a domestic environment with a "husband" (or an unreasonable facsimile thereof, in this case). My contention is that Valenzuela has created a cruel parody of a male-dominated bourgeois marriage, not to nullify or diminish the serious nature of this unusual captive arrangement, a direct result of the political climate of the "dirty war" years of Argentina, but precisely to demonstrate the permeable borders between some forms of male dominance and other versions considered more "normal" (i.e., normalized, regularized, and institutionalized).[6] Here, then, is a (per)version of a marriage, but, as we know, perverse pleasures for some people require perverse realities. It is Roque, the dominator, who experiences the male "wargasm" in his staged scenes of cruelty, whereas Laura takes refuge in the dissociated and disembodied pleasures some women have known in captivities of a more conventional nature: oppositional pleasures gained through subversive powers of their own. Thus I must question Marta Morello-Frosch's statement that Laura exhibits "the absence of desire—if one omits the sexual encounters—of initiative, of dialogue, of will." Morello-Frosch omits the sexual encounters because she claims that "the narrative stresses that desire is involuntary, restricted to the only sexual outlet available to the prisoner" (86–87).[7] However, "desire" is not involuntary: while the wife-victim is stripped of her freedom, she is not an inflatable doll, and any pleasures she experiences in fact emerge from some form of agency or desire, even if we need to call them co-opted desires, compromised resistance, or masochism understood as "a devious act of defiance" of patriarchal law (Williams, 213).

This is not, however, a reductionist scenario in which Laura takes up a masochistic role or really enjoys pleasure through pain. As one of the (male) characters in *Novela negra con argentinos* [Black novel with Argentines] remarks when he visits a woman who specializes in sado-masochistic services in New York: "¿Cómo quiere que me guste la tortura sexual consentida cuando vengo de un país donde se torturaba dizque por razones políticas, por el puro horror, con víctimas desesperadas y para nada complacientes? ¿Cómo quiere que me guste o me interese, siquiera? Lo que necesito es saber por qué alguien se convierte en torturador, en asesino, saber por qué un ciudadano probo puede un día cualquiera y sin darse cuenta transformarse en un monstruo" ["How do you expect me to like consensual sexual torture when I come from a country where they torture supposedly for political reasons, for the pure horror of it, with desperate victims who are in no way complacent? How do you expect me to like it or even be interested in it? What I need to know is why someone can turn into a torturer, an assassin, to know why an upright citizen can be transformed into a monster one day and not even realize it" (134)]. In *Other Weapons*, Valenzuela in fact appears to be analyzing this very problem of understanding the mind of a torturer or assassin, as she has claimed elsewhere: "I want to decode the perverse discourse of those in power. Probably that is why I write fiction"("Five Days," 8), but here she does so under the guise of examining intimate and social relations among men and women. To repeat emphatically: Laura is not a partaker of "la tortura sexual consentida" ["consensual sexual torture"]. Rather, Valenzuela stages her female protagonist very much along the lines of the representational systems employed in violent pornographic film (those very ones that Andrea Dworkin deplores): Laura, the woman without memory of previous scripts; Laura, the creature to be molded, whipped into shape, dominated, and created ex nihilo by the man who forces her to perform as his wife. To claim that she is used as an actress in the narrative on two levels—through authorial voice and by the male protagonist—does not deprive her completely of agency, however, for it is in the ritual performance of certain aspects of her role that Laura discovers, much to the horror of some readers, her own stake in the matter, like a porno-graphic film character, like a sex worker, like a special kind of wife.

While fully acknowledging that Laura and Roque's marriage is a façade for a perverse scenario of sadistic domination, we might also entertain the notion that Valenzuela subversively stages or inserts an element of "play": the playing out of domestic roles, the sadomasochistic erotic play, the play of difference. She does so not to imply that there are pleasures to be found in bondage for women, but to highlight the distinctions between relationships of mutuality and freedom—including the freedom to perform master-slave roles. As Jessica Benjamin points out in *The Bonds of Love: Psychoanalysis, Feminism, and the Problem of Domination*, what "distinguishes Eros from perversion is not freedom from fantasies of power and surrender, for Eros does not purge sexual fantasy—it plays with it. The idea of destruction reminds us that the element of aggression is necessary in erotic life, it is the element of *survival*, the difference the other can make, which distinguishes erotic union, which plays with the fantasy of domination, from real domination" (74–75). In this case of real domination, then, where is Eros? From what position can Laura "desire" or even function as object of desire?

One notable aspect of this perverse scenario consists of Laura's unwitting acting out of some of the ritualized performances of her assigned role as "wife-prostitute," a role, some feminists tell us, that has been fully plotted by men in the name of "sexual liberation."[8] Take, for example, Laura's habit of calling Roque by a plethora of male names—names that mean as little, or as much, to her as his real name, since she has no memory of this Roque-husband: "—Daniel, Pedro, Ariel, Alberto, Alfonso—los llama con suavidad mientras lo acaricia.—Más—pide él y no se sabe si es por las caricias o por la sucesión de nombres. . . . Recitando nombres como ejercicio de la memoria y con cierto deleite. El de los infinitos nombres, el sin nombre duerme."(117–118) ["Daniel, Pedro, Ariel, Alberto, Alfonso, she calls him softly, caressing him. More, he asks, and it's not clear whether he's referring to the caresses or to the sequence of names . . . She recites names, exercising her memory with some delight. He of countless names, the nameless man, sleeps" (109)]. Not coincidentally, the names she recites "with some delight" include the names of some of the other "demon lovers" of earlier narrations in *Other Weapons*: Pedro, the ambassador of "Cuarta versión" [Fourth version]; and Alberto, which might correspond to the pseudonymous "Beto" of "De noche soy tu caballo" [I'm your horse in the night]. In this way, Valenzuela establishes generic intertextual connections between all the males who appear and disappear throughout these narrations: the men are ultimately interchangeable and even unnameable in the sense that they refuse to be known, possessed, or retained in intimate relation to the female characters. If woman's position in representational systems has been reduced to that of an object of exchange and exploitation among men, then here we witness a reversal of sorts, an objectification of those who seek to dominate. This strategy is subversive but yet it does not transform the hierarchies of power, or rather, it does so in name only. Laura does not consciously utter a string of names for "johns"; however, at the surface structure her subversive act achieves precisely this. Roque demands this objectification of himself from Laura, but she performs it at a level over which he ultimately has no control, because he cannot force his amnesiac wife to recognize his individual subjectivity. Thus the "erotic game" of prostitute and john becomes deconstructed by Valenzuela: it consists of a power play on Roque's part, one that is returned with a subversive word play that inscribes a site of powerful resistance of its own.[9]

Further evidence of Laura's subversive deconstructing of the role she has been assigned may be culled from her mental reaction to Roque's order: "Decime que sos una perra, una arrastrada. Decime cómo te cogen los otros, ¿así te cogen?" (125) ["Tell me you're a bitch, a whore. Tell me how the others fuck you. Do they fuck you like this?" (117)]. She almost answers: "probá, hacé entrar a los dos tipos que tenés afuera" ["try it, call in those guys who are waiting outside the door"] because then at least she would know "que existen otros hombres, otros cogibles. Pero ésta es la clase de pensamientos que prefiere callar" (126) ["other men exist, other [fuckable] ones. But she prefers to keep thoughts such as those to herself" (117)]. Inasmuch as the narrative reproduces Laura's utterances and penetrates her silences, the reader may construct a resisting wife-victim whereas Roque fails to perceive, much less comprehend, the signs of her rebellion, her play-acting, and her own "wargasms" (Valenzuela: "The weapon that is exchanged is sex, the weapon is exchanged for sex" ["Máscaras," 517]). On the one hand, then, Laura appears to be the complicit amnesiac who has been disarmed; on the other hand, she subverts the structures of dominance through strategies drawn from a traditional feminine arsenal so that she may partially liberate those confining positions to which she is relegated. If she will not profess the love of bonds, she can remake the bonds of love in preparation for her final move of casting them off.

Another mechanism of Laura's (unconscious) resistance may be detected in her reactions to Roque's sexual "performances," those sadistic staged sex acts in which he forces her to observe herself in a mirror while calling her a whore or violates her in view of the two guards, "One" and "Two," who observe at the peephole of the locked door for which only Roque holds the correct key. When Roque orders her "—Abrí los ojos y mirá bien lo que te voy a hacer porque es algo que merece ser visto" (122) ["Open your eyes and [watch what I'm going to do to you because] it's going to be well worth seeing" (114)] in a sense he assigns to himself the role of actor in a pornographic scenario. He demands attention as performer, and he disengages himself from the real subject with whom he has sexual relations in favor of a depersonalized spectacle. The narrative voice, however, is aligned with Laura's reaction, which, upon close examination, reveals both a corresponding disembodied or depersonalized performance and a recuperation of desire under those terms that she does not control:

> y resulta doloroso el seguir mirando, y la lengua sube y él la va cubriendo, tratando eso sí de no cubrirla demasiado, dejándola verse en el espejo del techo, y ella va descubriendo el despertar de sus propios pezones, ve su boca que se abre como si no le perteneciera pero sí, le pertenece, siente esa boca . . . y más abajo también los nervios se estremecen y la lengua está por llegar y ella abre bien las piernas, del todo separadas y son de ella las piernas aunque respondan a un impulso que ella no ordenó pero que partió de ella, todo un estremecimiento deleitoso, tan al borde del dolor justo cuando la lengua de él alcanza el centro del placer, un estremecimiento que ella quisiera hacer durar apretando bien los párpados y entonces él grita
>
> ¡Abrí los ojos, puta!
>
> y es como si la destrozara, como si la mordiera por dentro . . . (124)

> [and it's painful to keep on looking, and his tongue creeps up and he covers her, but tries not to cover her too much; he lets her see herself in the mirror on the ceiling, and she discovers her own nipples as they awaken, she sees her mouth open as if it didn't belong to her, but it does, it does belong to her, she feels that mouth . . . and further down the nerves quiver, and the tongue's about to get there and she spreads her legs wide, as wide as she can and they're her legs although they're responding to an impulse she didn't order but that came out of her anyway, a deep shudder of delight, right at the edge of pain just when his tongue reaches the center of pleasure, a shudder she would want to prolong shutting her eyes tight and then he shouts
>
> "Open your eyes, you [whore]!"
>
> and it [is] as if he shattered her, as if he bit her inside . . . (114–115).]

In his staged drama, Roque attempts to force her to confess, as if this were a torture session designed to extract information from a detainee: she shouts "un *no* que parece hacer estallar el espejo del techo, que multiplica y mutila y destroza la imagen de él, casi como un balazo aunque él no lo perciba . . . y ella al exhalar el aire retenido sople Roque, por primera vez el verdadero nombre de él, pero tampoco eso oye él, ajeno como está a tanto desgarramiento interno" (125) [*"no* that seems to shatter the mirror on the ceiling, that multiplies and maims and destroys his image, almost like a bullet shot although he doesn't perceive it . . . and she exhaling the air she'd kept in, whispers Roque, his real name, for the first time. But he doesn't hear that either, as distant as he is from so much [inner tearing]" (115)]. Valenzuela negotiates the narrative and specular levels here with remarkable mobility. By narrating lucidly from within the consciousness of a drugged woman with no memory, the text posits a woman who both "knows" and "does not know," a psychological state highly typical of a coerced participant in the "bonds of love," which is in reality a sadistic domination. And by staging the sexual scene as she does, Valenzuela forces the reader/viewer to look in the textual mirror along with Laura, or to peep through the keyhole along with "One" and "Two." But because the narration focuses on Laura's internal experience, one that Roque ignores as he seeks his "wargasm," the sadistic perverse pleasures of Roque are shattered and mutilated much like the mirror above him. More specifically, Roque himself is shown to be a shattered, mutilated and destroyed image whose humanity and individuality has been extinguished: even his real name fails to reach him, pronounced as it is by someone unwilling and incapable of recognizing him.[10]

In her study of power, pleasure, and perversion, Linda Williams examines sadomasochistic film pornography, carefully distinguishing male dominance and violence in the world from constructions and representations of fantasy. Thus concerning the "concentration camp orgasm," she remarks that it "*is* a troubling concept, certainly if we think of it as belonging to the sadist who destroys, but perhaps even more so if we take it to include the victim. The idea of this latter pleasure is what most troubles feminism, for it represents the possibility of an absolute loss of humanity and intersubjectivity in sexual relations, the total abandonment of the self to the will of the other." She goes on to discuss the masochism of a woman viewer identifying with her annihilated surrogate: "If 'concentration camp orgasm' means the pure pleasure of victimization, then such pleasure cannot exist. For . . . without a modicum of power, without some leeway for play within assigned sexual roles, and without the possibility of some intersubjective give-and-take, there can be no pleasure for either the victim or the totally identified viewer. There can be no pleasure, in other words, without some power" (227). Laura's pleasures, thus understood, must be attributed to the power of depersonalization: she disappears from Roque in a mental escape that permits her a completely self-enclosed space of resistance. It is provisional, partial, and apart, but we must integrate it into the story, for without it, no female subversion could take place at all.

The psychology of domination has particular nuances in regard to the political situation of which Valenzuela writes. Sexual torture was an integral part of the repressive regimes of the mid 1970s through early 1980s in Argentina: both men and women received electroshock to the genitals; women were raped and verbally humiliated in the same manner as Roque treats Laura.[11] In fact, it may be argued that the association of "female subversive" and "prostitute" is a psychologically explicable formation of male political dominance: "good" women submit to male rule and thus conform to patriarchal (per)versions of sexuality and social order. "Good" women perform their assigned roles as "pure" and submissive mothers, wives, daughters; when they acquire agency, when they rebel, they become "subversives" in the larger sense. In a classic operation of splitting, the male will cast out the "female subversive" as the binary opposite of the subduable woman: the "puta" is the necessary counterpart to the "pura."[12] Roque's compromise formation takes the form of a stunning synthesis of "wife-prostitute" whom he both controls and dominates, but who also casts him in the role of objectified "john" from whom she attains some physical pleasure "que ella no ordenó *pero que partió de ella*" ["she didn't order *but that came out of her anyway*" (emphasis mine)].

Valenzuela has made this link between sexual violence and domestic control in other texts, notably the short story "Unlimited Rapes United, Argentina" from *Aquí pasan cosas raras* [*Strange Things Happen Here*]. In this story, the male protagonist complains that the "Violadores de Frente" ["Frontal Rapists"] division of the URU is failing to carry out its civic duty of producing the minimum number of rapes to ensure that social and domestic order remain intact. The voice on the other end of the phone justifies the situation: "Pero debe comprender que los tiempos están difíciles y las mujeres ya no se nos resisten como antes. No podemos obrar con el mismo ímpetu" (56) ["But you must understand that times are hard and women don't offer us resistance like before. We can't work with the same impetus."] The complainant responds: "Cuentos. Todavía no se ha perdido el pudor, mujeres serias hay a montones . . . . Crónicas de violaciones—no violaciones a escondidas—eso es lo que exigimos los ciudadanos probos para sentir que todo sigue su curso normal y podemos quedarnos en paz en nuestros sillones leyendo el diario" (56). ["That's a lie. Modesty hasn't been completely lost, there are still plenty of serious women. Reports of rapes—not rapes committed in secrecy—that's what we upright citizens want so we can feel as if everything were on its normal course and we can stay at home peacefully seated in our armchairs reading the paper."] The other party alleges that Argentine women no longer exhibit fear, that they laugh at men's attempts to assault them and even "criticize their instruments," and then return home without contacting the police after being raped. To the comment "ya no quedan damas" ["there are no ladies left,"] the complainant offers "Sí que quedan. Mi esposa, sin ir más lejos. Una verdadera dama. Es por ella que me suscribí a la Vedeefe, por ella pago la elevadísima cuota mensual y por ella—porque es una dama—es que ahora presento esta queja que espero sea tenida muy en cuenta" ["Of course there are. My wife, in the first place. A real lady. It's for her sake that I became a member of the Frontal Rapists, it's for her sake that I pay the outrageous monthly fees, and it's for her sake—because she is a lady—that I now make this complaint that I expect to be taken very seriously" (56–57)]. Valenzuela, with typical irony, establishes the link between respectable domesticity, sexual terrorism, and economics when she conflates the husband with his surrogate rapists in the URU. In a society in which men view themselves as buyers of women's sexual services, a purchase of this sort seems logical: the members of the Vedeefe objectify their spouses by contracting rape services in an attempt to keep these women in their place as "good wives" who will fearfully depend on their husbands' protection from outside menace. The beloved wife is thus a kept woman in all senses, but Valenzuela sketches a subversive scenario whereby women rebel against their oppression by taking to the streets, though they may risk their lives in the process. The "street-walker" or "mujer pública" in Valenzuela's version is a radicalized woman who remakes the meaning of those words by refusing to carry out their sexist orders.

Even though Laura embodies the "subversive woman" in a variety of senses, she also incarnates the submissive one—and it is here that

"Cambio de armas" deeply disturbs us. Critics are absolutely correct to insist on Laura's lack of choice or free will in her captivity, but Valenzuela operates at a subversive level in making of Laura a wholly involuntary masochistic partner in a parody of a violent, male-dominated bourgeois marriage. Laura learns lessons of love through domination in her amnesiac state, and psychologically, her experiences ring true. Thus at times she suspects "que podría tratarse del llamado amor" (125) ["it could be what they call love" (116)]. She seeks physical protection from Roque much like a helpless child: "lo llama de vuelta a su lado, para que la cubra con su cuerpo, no para que la satisfaga. Cubrirse con el cuerpo de él como una funda" (136) ["she calls him back to her side, for him to cover her with his body, not for him to satisfy her. Cover herself with his body like a [sheath]" (127)]. Laura's dependency is predicated on her being, literally, a "desaparecida" ["disappeared one"], a victim of military repression. But she also occupies the position of a psychologically "disappeared one" who seeks signs of her identity through the male other; she aspires to disappear beneath his body because facing herself, recovering her identity, is a process that ushers in unendurable pain. Jessica Benjamin remarks that in "erotic submission, fear of the master's power takes the place of a deeper fear—of the separation that feels like death. . . . His assertion of subjectivity and difference is like a breath of the inaccessible outdoors. He embodies activity and difference for her" (79). Laura is medicinally numbed, surgically rendered without memory, physically tortured. But psychologically, she occupies a position that has been fully accounted for in Benjamin's and Williams's analyses of the slave-master relationship, a role that has a direct translation in certain social arrangements of domesticity and marriage. As Roque's wife-victim, Laura feels as if she were made of moldable clay, of wet sand from which the childlike husband can construct his castles and his illusions.

Thus when Roque finally forces Laura to learn the truth of her situation at the exact moment when he must flee because his regime is threatened, Laura begs him not to abandon her and to return to their bed. As he heads for the door, she lifts and points the gun he has shown to her—the gun with which she had attempted to kill him when she was not his Laura.[13] Her final assertion of her subjectivity coincides with his inability to occupy the master's position: the equilibrium is ruptured, and she emerges alone, having broken the bonds of what she might have called "love" at one point. We may even argue that Roque, operating in the psychological economy of the sadist, masochistically sets up his own punishment by arming Laura in what becomes a symbolic transference of a stereotypic phallic symbol: his castration thus corresponds to her empowerment. While this ending looks like a triumph of memory, of will, of feminine agency and even of political change, it is far too neat. Laura's previous subversions of the scenarios of domination, fraught as they are with structural masochistic complicity, seem to me to be far more suggestive of the possibilities and obstacles for feminine liberation under the specific social and psychological conditions that enslave many women.

If Laura plays out dramas of subversion and rebellion, if the narrative focuses both on her inner reality and her external circumstances, then what of Martina, the maid, the other woman in the household who carries out Roque's orders, who attends Laura's petitions after clearing them with the Colonel, and who even goes so far as to spread a blanket over the naked partners after their sexual display before "One" and "Two"? Morello-Frosch remarks that Martina functions as an extension of Roque's presence, and "does not provide any possibility of differentiation, of otherness from him, and difference that may help Laura define herself" (83). Further, she claims that "the bonding of the maid with the master is a gender bonding type in which the female accepts and upholds the terms of the opposite sex. It is not sex-determined" (87). Not sex-determined per se, but de facto: Martina takes up a typical female role in a middle-class Argentine marriage in that she is the wife's servant but she acts under the master's rules. While Martina often "disappears" seamlessly from the narrative, her function is more significant than Morello-Frosch allows. Because this political tragedy plays out in terms of a domestic parody, Martina is the necessary other to the objectified wife-victim. Although she depends economically on "the master," she ultimately has the freedom to leave. After Roque fails to return to the household, Martina "no sabe si dejar a la pobre loca sola o esperar un día más o irse para siempre. El señor le ha dejado dinero suficiente como para que se sienta libre, y quizá ahora él esté aburrido de este juego y a ella le corresponda retirarse a tiempo y olvidarse de todo" (141) ["doesn't know whether she should leave the poor crazy lady alone or wait one more day or leave forever. The master has left her enough money for her to feel free, and he may have gotten tired of the game; she should take off before it's too late and forget about it all" (131)]. Unlike the captive Laura, Martina consciously assumes a role and accepts a job, one that she can abandon with relative freedom (although her ultimate freedom in the larger patriarchal economy certainly should be cast into doubt).[14] Laura would have chosen a different type of maid: "a Martina sí que la eligió él, la deben de haber fabricado a medida para él, porque de haber sido por ella tendría a su lado una mujer con vida, de esas que cantan mientras barren el piso" (120). ["He did choose Martina. She was probably custom-made for him, because if it had been up to her she would probably have chosen someone full of life, one of those women who sing while they sweep the floor" (112)]. Could not we read into Laura's specifications for a carefree, happy servant some of the implied critiques that Valenzuela makes of bourgeois domesticity, where one woman sings while she sweeps, and the other sweeps her subjectivity under the sheets of her dominated condition? Is the phone call to "Unlimited Rapes United" ever far removed when one lives inside the pink walls of female oppression? "Other Weapons" dramatically stages military violence and male domination; it subtly encodes an equally institutionalized form of captivity, one that is not blown away with "wargasms" or even gunfire, for that matter.

Space permits only a brief sketch of what is a fascinating literary parallel with this story: Margaret Atwood's dystopian novel, *The Handmaid's Tale*. Valenzuela writes about an occurrence with frightening real political bases; Atwood takes many contemporary situations and extends them to chilling futuristic conclusions. The handmaid is known by the patronymic "Offred," which erases her given name and identity; she exists as a reproductive vessel in service to class hierarchies in a male-dominated world. Like Laura, she undergoes forced sexual relations within the context of an oppressive socio-sexual-political setting, and she struggles to retain her memories of life as it used to be when she had the freedom to choose a mate, to earn a living, to go out alone. Under the new order, the handmaids are indoctrinated to profess, for example, that rape is always a woman's fault and is a punishment from God. Like Laura, Offred is a coerced participant in a system that totally subjugates her: she uses the "weapons"of her sex—the weapons men force women to be—in subversive fashion when she has the opportunity. The handmaid splits her consciousness from her body much like the split ceremonial procreation process involving one man and two women: she lies between the legs of the barren wife such that the Commander "is fucking the lower part of [her] body" (121). Like "Cambio de armas," this novel is open-ended: we never learn Offred's final fate, but of course this device centers attention on the larger political questions incarnated in individual women characters.

In the collection *Other Weapons*, Laura, the actress who rediscovers her role in her lost script, has as her counterpart the other actress, Bella, who in "Fourth Version" dies from a gunshot aimed at her lover, the ambassador Pedro.[15] The passive Laura takes action and resumes her oppositional labors, whereas the politically active Bella, who works on the margins from her unofficial role as lover, perishes in a passive manner by receiving the bullet intended for the one with authority to act. Naturally, Valenzuela suggests throughout "Fourth Version" that Bella is the real subversive {Pedro remarks "la subversión es ella misma," (50) ["she's the embodiment of subversion," (48)]}, precisely because she performs in self-made roles upon which there are conferred no social, cultural, or political authorizations. As she has done with her character Laura, Valenzuela positions Bella in the context of an intense personal relationship that serves to detract attention from the larger political structures that eventually erupt violently , thus overtaking and extinguishing the intimate spheres where desire finds immediate expression. In a parallel to the domestic parody Valenzuela stages in "Other Weapons," Bella plays a part in a subversive parody of diplomatic relations: she disrupts the smooth efficacy of the system by occupying a position outside the law (of the military regime and of social order).

In *Bananas, Beaches and Bases*, Cynthia Enloe sketches a wide context for the feminist analysis of international politics as she shows how certain constructions of masculinity and notions of nationalism have had an impact on everything from sex tourism to the consumption of bananas. Of interest to our present concerns are the remarks on "Diplomatic Wives" as an essential component of conventional political systems: "Government men depend on women's unpaid labor to carry on relations with their political counterparts. . . . They could use marriage both to grease the wheels of man-to-man negotiations and to ensure that no women reached positions of influence" (123). The diplomatic wife would tend to the "home," a site that contains not only the private quarters of domesticity, but also serves as the official residence, "the place where this trust between men can best be cultivated" (97). In "Fourth Version," however, the diplomatic wife is depicted by her own husband as "mi mujercita rubia" (15) ["My little blond wife" (14)] who eventually returns to her country to flee the tensions of living in a nation where cadavers appear floating in the Río de la Plata, and where the ambassador's residence itself serves as a place of refuge for those seeking asylum. The ambassador's wife, then, fails to carry out the duties expected of her by the larger political system, thus creating a lacuna that Bella fills. Rather, Bella's ancillary position constitutes an upheaval of domestic, diplomatic, and political orders: her death may be an indication of the untenable roles that Bella, the actress, has tried to perform. In a system that demands "official" roles for women, a subversive like Bella finds herself written out of the script. Like Laura, she is "disappeared" as a result of her political activities *and* as a consequence of the gendered bases on which the system stands.

The parallels between Laura and Bella find correspondence in the bonds that join the "demon lovers," the rock-solid Roque and Pedro. Take, for example, this early exchange from "Fourth Version":

—No entiendo por qué anda suelta una mujer tan encantadora.
—Por que soy una bestia solitaria y voraz. Arff. Devoradora, depredadora. ¿Acaso no te diste cuenta? ¿No te da miedo?
—¿Cómo no me va a dar miedo? (15)

["I don't understand how such a charming woman can be roaming on her own."
"Because I'm a solitary, voracious beast. Grrr. A devouring predator. Haven't you noticed? Aren't you frightened?"
"How could I not be frightened?" (14)]

Under the apparent guise of flirtatious banter, Pedro has articulated the classic line of male dominance, even though it is Bella who equates herself with a devouring beast. A woman who "runs around loose" presents both an attraction and a threat to the man who enjoys a sense of security with his "little blond wife"; Bella must be tamed, dominated and claimed so that male psychological fears may be appeased. Note, though, that Bella "the witch" is the necessary counterpart to "the good little woman" in a split psychological and social economy such as this: her attractiveness lies in the pleasures *and* dangers she radiates, as demonstrated by this metaphoric telephone play:

—Hola. Aquí la luciérnaga.
—Aquí el sapo.
—¿Por qué me pisas, Pedro?
—Y, tú, ¿por qué reluces? (44)

["Hello. This is the glow-worm."
"This is the toad."
"Why are you stepping on me Pedro?"
"Why are you glowing?" (42)]

For Bella as well as for Pedro, theirs is a dream "con ensoñaciones en las que imágenes del amor podían ser intercambiadas por imágenes del miedo" (10) ["with fantasies in which images of love could be interchanged with images of fear" (9)], except that Pedro conquers his fears through attempts at imposing forms of dominance and measures of distance, whereas Bella's fear of separation from her *homme fatal* causes her to be extirpated from his side.

Valenzuela's innovation in this ancient story of love and death centers on the larger political situation that constitutes the frame for *Other Weapons*. Thus the narrator of Bella's story tries to make sense of the relationship: "Bella ya convertida para Pedro es la encarnación de ese país al que necesitaba aferrarse, con el que no quería romper relaciones diplomáticas si le llegaba la orden telefónica. Pedro reteniendo a Bella, mágicamente conquistándola para que en otro plano no se plantee el fracaso de sus gestiones oficiales" (26) ["For Pedro, Bella already embodied the country he had to hold on to, with which he didn't want to sever diplomatic relations if he received the order on the phone. Pedro was holding Bella back, magically conquering her so that an another level he wouldn't have to question the failure of his official endeavors" (25)]. Bella may be read as a sign: she symbolizes the political tensions of her country, she signals "gender trouble" for Pedro with his codes of masculinity, and she metaphorically becomes a type of lightening rod or diffusional device to which the stonelike Pedro can take hold [*aferrarse*, from *ferro*, *iron*]. Bella's subversive role, which reaches its height when she stars in a farewell party attended by masses of "friends" seeking political asylum, thus hinges on her status as outlaw to the diplomatic system and to the sociosexual economy surrounding it. Only in this triply subversive position could Bella function optimally as sign, and only in the absence of an accommodating signifying system must the sign be eradicated. As a woman with desires of her own and with individual agency, Bella is doomed to extinction under this regime. Although Robin Morgan's analysis of the "demon lover's woman" is highly flawed, the following points seem particularly applicable to Bella and the ambassador:

The woman who lies in terror's arms is clasped in an intricate emotional bondage. One cord, coiled around her brain, is her own justifiable human indignation at the suffering of her people, her country, or her planet . . . another bond slips into place—her rage at being a woman in what appears to be a male universe of perception, thought, and action. . . . So she who lies in terror's arms clutches for another bond or reassurance, and it is waiting to curl and knot around her loins: charisma. . . . And the final bond, pure satin steel the color of blood ruby, is knotted tight around her heart: it is, in almost every case, her own personal passion for an individual man (215–216).

According to the "bonds of love" as formulated by Morgan, the romantic passion of an individual woman toward a charismatic "demon lover" is destined to meet with emotional and political disaster. Valenzuela grapples with this issue in *Other Weapons* in highly complex terms: perhaps we should read Bella's death not as triumph of male dominance or of political repression, but as symptom of the resistance to change inherent in the structures that Bella attempts to subvert from her position as outlawed lover. We might turn to another scene of feminine agency so poignantly described by Valenzuela as a different model for political and social reconstruction. Here Valenzuela recounts her activities on December 6, 1990: "This paper has to be written, it is already written, practically. Renée Epelbaum [head of the Línea Fundadora of the Mothers of the Plaza de Mayo] calls on the phone to ask if I'm going to the closing of the march. I can't, I have to write on value: where is it now? Renée tells me that when the Mothers of the Plaza de Mayo first started to get together, in 1977, they felt absolutely powerless against the almighty military. Now the military are still almighty, but the Mothers feel powerful, they have the moral power, the strength of legitimacy" ("Five Days," 9). The Mothers of the Plaza, also called "las locas" ["the crazy women"], are individuals primarily of humble origins whose family members had been "disappeared"; they came together to risk their lives in public, collective demonstrations of opposition in the seventies, and, on the date of which Valenzuela speaks, they were protesting the amnesty granted to most of the officers who had carried out the "dirty war." When Valenzuela tells how she feels compelled to write while other women march, she self-consciously acknowledges the different forms of resistance and subversion available to women. There is courage (*valor*) in recognizing those differences; there is *valor* or value in taking up word-weapons in the way that Valenzuela does. Her Bella incarnates this very struggle between individual agency and collective action, between sexual desire and social order, between economic privilege and political power. Valenzuela's most subversive textual act may be to kill off her actresses when they fall short as actors.

Thus far I have focused on those sites of resistance occupied by a wife-victim and an outlaw lover: the remaining three short stories in *Other Weapons* present other models for female subversion that merit brief analysis here. In "La palabra asesino" ["The word killer"], the nameless female protagonist is involved with a twenty-six-year-old "killer," called simply "he," who descends from a Cherokee grand-mother, a Latina mother, and a "padre como él de cobre oscuro" (71) ["father like himself, dark copper" (67)]. This narration explores the question of feminine sexual desire as an autonomous, separate aspect of the self, and here Valenzuela interrogates the conventional notions that would depict women as naturally capable and desirous of love, mutuality, or integration of sexuality, emotions, and intimacy. Rather, Valenzuela demonstrates the degree to which feminine desire has been produced by culture: she tries to free up erotic strivings from the bonds of what has been constructed on the one hand as female instinct or nature (passivity in sexual relations; protective, nurturing behavior toward others), and, on the other hand, what has been socialized into compulsory gender norms for women (adherence to a monogamous, reproductive hetero-sexual coupling).[16] Valenzuela does so through a character who, in con-trast to her lover, works desire through the intellect. By depicting this character in a state of intense inner reflection, Valenzuela uncovers a fundamental ambivalence with regard to a resolution of these matters of mind and body, nature and culture. If the female protagonist eventually comes into consciousness of the disparity between instinct and intellect, it is a triumph of the word and of the self-recovery made possible through the act of naming.

The male lover assumes the form of an "animal de la noche" (69) ["night-animal" (65)] a street-wise youth who has had to live by his instincts. She conquers her fear of him by taming her animal-lover so as to overcome her impulse to "empujar al hombre a que la mate" (70) ["push the man to kill her" (66)]. Like Bella, this character recognizes the images of love and fear as they converge in the figure of a "demon lover," and it is through her sexual union with him that she faces the same well of fear and desire in herself, "tragando mi horror, mi espanto" (71–72) ["swallowing the horror, the shock" (67)]. She thus vacillates between fearful self-protection ("ese hombre me va a golpear" 78, ["[that man is] going to beat me" (74)] and reckless surrender to her own inner demons ["No darle la espalda a la asesina en ella, que lo ama" 79, ["She can't turn her back on the killer in her who loves him," 74)]. As she contemplates the lines she thought were scars on his back, she thinks: "Esas marcas quizá hubiera querido hacerlas ella en la espalda de ese hombre que más que un hombre era la personificación de su deseo" (80) "[Maybe she would] have wanted to make those marks herself on the back of a man who, [more than a man, was the personification] of her desire" (75)]. In "Other Weapons," Laura bore a long scar on her back, which symbolizes her condition of having been dominated by a masculinist, military sociosexual (dis)order; in this story, Valenzuela executes a reversal of sorts, since this female character thinks herself capable of leaving the marks of objectified desire on her lover's back, a desire whose paths lead to a mutual tearing apart. This male lover has little recourse to words or signs with which to identify himself: the female character possesses an excess of words, symbols, and even of consciousness, which drives her to install the abyss that can separate her from her lover : "La intolerable tentación del salto y de golpe ASESINO grita. Y la voz consigue por fin escapar con fuerza de su ser y podría tratarse de una acusación o de un llamado pero se trata en realidad de un parto" (83) ["The unbearable urge to jump [and all of a sudden] KILLER she shouts. And the voice finally manages to bolt out of her and [it could be an accusation or a call but in reality it's an act of] birth" (78)].[17]

Psychologically, this final movement {"¿Cuál será el movimiento que libera?" (82) ["Which is the movement that sets you free?" (77)]} points to the recognition of the other's subjectivity, with its corresponding demand for the self's being recognized in like terms. This is not at all to say that sexuality freed up from this mutual recognition is impossible or even undesirable: in fact, this may be Valenzuela's main point. As the female character experiences ecstasy with her lover, she thinks, "Puta, qué desgarramiento, quisiera gritar, qué desgarramiento necesario, qué euforia, reconoce en nuevos gritos sordos mientras, cara al techo, siente que estalla en mil pedazos" (82) ["[Whore], I'm being ripped apart, she wanted to shout, [what necessary tearing], it's bliss, she acknowledges in new, muffled cries and, facing the ceiling, she [feels herself explode] in a thousand pieces" (77)]. The parallels are striking between this scene and the one cited earlier from "Other Weapons," where Laura, having been called "puta" "whore" by Roque, is forced to watch herself in an overhead mirror as he performs sexually, impervious to her "desgarramiento interno" ["internal tearing"]. Roque's image shatters in a thousand pieces as Laura retreats to the inner spaces from which she can undergo some degree of physical arousal, but she can never completely surrender herself since she is controlled by Roque, and since she has not yet recovered a self to lose—or reclaim. The female protagonist in "The Word 'Killer'" effectuates a split between her sexual self and her introspective self: her ecstasy depends on the smooth functioning of this split. What disrupts its efficacy is language: "Puede decir experiencia, puede decir intensidad pero esas palabras a la vez la traicionan, se marchitan. Abandonada está hasta por su propio reino, el del lenguaje" (82) ["She can say experience, she can say intense, but those words betray her, [and wilt away]. She's been banished from her own kingdom, language" (77)]. If we accept Lacan's premise that fragmentation is an irreducible human condition covered over by a simulacrum of ego integrity and language, then it makes sense that "la palabra asesina," ["the word kills"]. As language erupts, it kills off the possibility for recreating the imaginary blissful ecstasy of primary union, and it kills off the suspension of consciousness, the "animal" state. Valenzuela's female protagonist liberates instinct and desire long enough to enjoy ecstatic visits to the "negro profundo pozo" ["deep black well"] (this is Laura's metaphor), where abandonment seems possible and desirable. That is, until words catch up with her: yet although they overtake her and compel her in new directions, they do not negate her pleasures nor take away her agency to pursue them.

How do female characters in *Other Weapons* rid themselves of the demon lover when and if they deem it desirable to do so? In "Ceremonias de rechazo" ["Rituals of rejection"] and "De noche soy tu caballo" ["I'm your horse in the night"], the protagonists find themselves involved with revolutionary activists who appear and reappear according to the demands of their political clandestine activities. In these stories, the women occupy the traditional role of waiting for their men, and any involvement they maintain with subversive movements is linked to their sexual liaisons with the more visible, active partner. Dorothy Mull views Amanda in "Rituals of Rejection" as one who is transformed from "a cowed, obsessed woman to a free, self-sufficient one—a symbolic death and rebirth, complete with aspects of purification. . . . Through her own initiative, Amanda has carried out a series of acts that transform her from the meek person whom el Coyote addresses as 'mamacita' to a god-desslike state approaching that of the archetypal Mother Earth" (92–93).

Mull concludes that the rites Amanda performs (cosmetic masks, hair removal, a scented bath) are "a defense and an assertion of self, not a beautification ritual designed to please someone else" (94–95). If her body and what she does with it constitute a change of weapons for Mull, what exactly is the significance of the narcissistic gratifications from which Amanda derives the *jouissance* of the self-sufficient goddess? While I would like to agree completely with Mull's lucid analysis, my thinking on *Other Weapons* as a whole leads me to suspect a more subversive scenario that falls short of an unambivalent feminine triumph. Amanda does not merely fabricate and eradicate masks: she partakes of the psychological masquerade of femininity in that she has internalized herself as spectacle and as object of desire. Her pleasures before the mirror that "paso a paso le devuelve las formas" (101) ["step by step . . . gives back her shape" (94)] seem to be inexplicable if they emerge from some mythical, inner core of femininity exempt from cultural constructs or extricable from male desire. Amanda has cast off one mask as she celebrates her rituals of rejection, but what she has rejected is one man, not the larger system that produces him or that inscribes desire into its economy. Her retreat into narcissistic self-enclosure may be viewed as a ritual of healing, but let us be clear about the multisymptomatic nature of her stinging pain: "Y hela aquí con el pellejo dolorido y ardiente. Estos ritos caseros habría que emprenderlos con menos fanatismo y más ternura. No tan al pie de la letra esto de querer borrarse la cara" (96) ["And there she is, her skin smarting and burning. These domestic rites should be enacted with less fanaticism and more tenderness. One shouldn't erase one's face quite so literally" (89)]. Amanda strenuously scrubs her own face in such a way that she inflicts the pain of self-revelation from within to mask that of degradation from without.

The role of masks in the works of Valenzuela may provide additional clues to Amanda's psychic "makeup." The following citation is taken from an essay by Valenzuela, "Las malas palabras" ["Dirty Words"]:

> ¿Por qué tanto miedo a las lágrimas? Porque las máscaras que usamos son de sal. Una sal roja, ardiente, que nos devuelve hieráticas y bellas, pero nos devora la piel.
>
> Bajo las rojas máscaras tenemos el rostro en carne viva y las lágrimas bien podrían disolver la sal y dejar al descubierto nuestras llagas. . . . .
>
> Con máscara de sal nos acoplamos y a veces los sedientos vienen a lamernos. Es un placer perverso: ellos quedan con más sed que nunca

y a nosotras nos duele y nos aterra la disolución de la máscara. Ellos lamen más y más, ellos gimen de desesperación, nosotras de dolor y de miedo. ¿Qué será de nosotras cuando afloren nuestros rostros ardidos? ¿Quién nos querrá sin máscara, quién en carne viva?

Ellos no. Ellos nos odiarán por eso, por habernos lamido, por habernos expuesto.

[Why so afraid of tears? Because the masks that we wear are made of salt. Red salt, burning, that turn us hieratic and beautiful, but that devour our skin.

Beneath the red masks our face is raw flesh and tears could well dissolve the salt and leave our wounds uncovered. . . .

With our salt masks in place we mate and sometimes the thirsty ones come to lick us. It is a perverse pleasure: they are left thirstier than ever and the dissolution of our masks pains us and terrifies us. They lick more and more, they moan with desperation, we moan with pain and fear. What will happen to us when our burning faces appear? Who will love us without the mask, who, in the raw flesh?

Not them. They will hate us for it, because they licked us, because they exposed us (490–491)].

Even though it is Amanda herself who harshly scrubs her face until it turns into reddened skin, and not el Coyote who licks it raw, Valenzuela undoubtedly confers on the "demon lover" the powers and perverse pleasures in performing the operation. Like the "nosotras" ["we"] in the above citation, Amanda represses her tears, and joyfully contemplates her "rostro en carne viva" ["face of raw flesh"]. But the "raw flesh" stings because women still wonder who will love them if they shed the mask of femininity, that defensive barrier between self and other. "Nuestra máscara es ahora el texto" ["Our mask is now the text" (491)], Valenzuela affirms: the battle between masculine and feminine desire, the fight for mutual recognition and equilibrium of power, is never definitively won, but merely reconfigured. Thus Amanda has achieved self-dominance only to a degree, since the structures of gender relations have been altered at a level that is only skin-deep. Bella, who puts on makeup to meet the ambassador, thinks of a bumper sticker that says *"La mujer es como el indio, se pinta cuando quiere guerra"* [*"Women are like indians, they paint themselves up for war"* (7)]. If Amanda has cast off her weapons to take up a "change of weapons," can we say for sure that she has come home from the war once and for all? Or will she seek "wargasms" anew?[18]

The ambivalent response to these questions, I believe, is contained in "I'm Your Horse in the Night," where the female protagonist offers to be her "disappeared" lover's horse in the night in fantasy and in reality: "Beto, si es cierto que te han matado o donde andes, de noche soy tu caballo y podés venir a habitarme cuando quieras aunque yo estoy entre rejas" (109) ["if it's true that they killed you, or wherever you may be, Beto, I'm your horse in the night and you can inhabit me whenever you wish, even if I'm behind bars" (101)]. The desires expressed by this female character and those voiced by her lover exist in disharmonious tension: she mystically relates spirit and flesh to the words of the Gal Costa song, "A noite eu so teu cavallo," whereas Beto interprets the words on a carnal level only {"si de noche sos mi caballo es porque te monto, así" 107, ["If you're my horse in the night it's because I ride you, like this" (99)]}. Although the female character assumes what looks like a masochistic role—she wants love, she waits, she makes herself available to this man at any time, she suffers physical torture on his account—she finds enough satisfactions in her passion for Beto to justify them to herself (until that choice is taken from her by external political forces).

The routes through which feminine desires travel, as Valenzuela shows through a multiplicity of scenarios, may be compatible at times with masculine desires, or they may stand in fundamental opposition to the desire of the other. Women's willingness to derive pleasures of their own requires of them a series of compromises: rituals of rejection, scenes of complicity, reversal of roles, acts of rebellion and subversion, taking up roles, donning masks. It is clear by now that none of these positionings can be performed in a political vacuum; rather, the success of the female characters in installing their desires must be measured against the larger framework in which those desires are regulated or accommodated. Magnarelli claims: "Valenzuela seems to warn us that political oppression will have no remedy until interpersonal relationships are modified" (192), but my current reading would allow for the complementary opposite of this thesis precisely because the political is personal. Cynthia Enloe has placed this very inversion at the core of her analysis: "Every time a woman explains how her government is trying to control her fears, her hopes and her labor"—and her desires, we may add—she is making feminist sense of international politics and dismantling the wall that often separates theory from practice (201). Valenzuela's versions and perversions of feminine and masculine sexuality as manifested in *Other Weapons* reveal with courageous authenticity what those inner desires look like when played out in a world where women try "to become the weapon he desires, the weapon he is," as Morgan puts it. But Valenzuela provides suggestive answers to an even more perplexing problem: "If one is a weapon, how can power not mean dominance?" (Morgan, 177-179) or, more exactly, a struggle for dominance? Valenzuela's *Other Weapons* thus marks a new level of sophistication in literary texts that focus on politics, pleasure, and power, and her *sub*versions hold the potential to contest, albeit provisionally, the "wargasms" propagated by means of other ideologies and representations.

Notes

1. Translations from *Cambio de armas* are taken from the published English version *Other Weapons*, with some modifications as indicated by brackets. All other translations in this essay are mine.

2. I should make it clear that in this essay I am taking a social construction approach to sexuality which, as Carol Vance puts it, would seek to "examine the range of behavior, ideology, and subjective meaning among and within human groups, and would view the body, its functions, and sensations as potentials (and limits) which are incorporated and mediated by culture" (879). However, I also put great stock in some psychoanalytic and linguistic models that may seem more impervious to cultural mediations. These divergent models are not incompatible if we remind ourselves that psychoanalytic theories also construct versions of human sexualities as they explicate them through their particular discourses and structures, as many revisionists in social history and feminism have demonstrated with respect to the ideas of Freud.

3. Valenzuela's writing does not function generically as *testimonio* of the horrors of sexual torture committed during the "dirty war" in Argentina, and my analytical methods do not approach her work primarily for its potential as sociopsychological documentation. This route of analysis certainly is plausible, however, and it could be fully supported by studies such as Judith Herman's *Trauma and Recovery* or Elaine Scarry's *The Body in Pain*. For specific sources related to women and Latin America, see the excellent bibliographic article by M. Brinton Lykes and colleagues. They note, for example, the following: "Exposure of the gendered nature of public violence in Latin America . . . suggests a more comprehensive model that integrates the multiple expressions of structural violence and personal dynamics of patriarchal power" (530).

4. Kathy Myers's words summarize some of my basic assumptions along these lines: "One of the oppressions of patriarchy is to constrain female sexuality through a system of binary oppositions: e.g. masculine as opposed to feminine, passive versus active . . . . feminist sexual practice cannot simply position itself in opposition to dominant ideology. The kind of questions which it must ask have implications not only for what is meant by a representational system (and the part it plays in structuring fantasy and the imagination) but also what is meant by power, sexuality and pleasure" (200). Judith Butler's notions of "gender trouble" also inform my analysis: "If sexuality is

culturally constructed within existing power relations, then the postulation of a normative sexuality that is 'before,' 'outside,' or "beyond' power is a cultural impossibility and a politically impracticable dream, one that postpones the contemporary task of rethinking subversive possibilities for sexuality and identity within the terms of power itself" (30).

5. She defines "normal life" as "una mujer que vive en su casa con una criada que se encarga de todos los quehaceres y necesidades de la mujer, y el coronel actúa como si fuera el marido" ["a woman who lives in her home with a maid who takes care of all the chores and needs of the woman, and the coronel acts as if he were the husband" (78)].

6. Debra Castillo states that "one of the terrifying implications of 'Other Weapons' lies in its highlighting of the darker side of traditional domestic arrangements, where ties of tenderness or comfort or custom show their hidden affinity with manacles and violent repression and prisons and where the torture chamber mimics the home so as to enhance the charge of horror" (113–114). Her insightful analysis of *Other Weapons*, which appeared after I had written this study, contains many observations that work along lines I also take here. I thank Debra Castillo for reading my essay and offering me helpful comments.

7. Sharon Magnarelli says something similar: the protagonist has been reduced to "a nonbeing, mere reflection of masculinist desire . . . without any needs or desires of her own" (189).

8. Sheila Jeffries, for example, analyzes Alex Comfort's *The Joy of Sex* as a call for women to act like professional sex workers: "It is because men have such difficulty in imagining a kind of sex not organised around dominance and submission that they can confuse what a prostitute does with what they want their girlfriends to do so disastrously" (122). (I'm not sure whether men's confusion or women's performance is perceived as disastrous here). In a similar vein Margaret Jackson in "'Facts of Life' or the Eroticization of Women's Oppression" takes a historical survey of "hetero-relations" to show how feminine sexuality has been subordinated to naturalized forms of masculine sexual dominance, also to the detriment of liberation for women. For a wholly different point of view, we may turn to *Re-Making Love: The Feminization of Sex* by Ehrenreich, Hess, and Jacobs, where the authors claim: "But to imagine that there was only 'the' sexual revolution and that it was a victory for men and a joke on women, to see women as victims even of their self-chosen ventures, is not only to falsify the past but to foreclose the future" (192–193).

9. Laura García-Moreno observes: "multiple naming allows the protagonist to distance herself from pain and to appropriate a sense of power otherwise denied to her. By rendering his identity unprecise and unstable, Laura can limit the power he has over her." She further suggests that "the relation of repression is not limited to a specific man named Roque but to a broader social situation of male domination" (14–15).

10. In her comments on *Story of O*, Jessica Benjamin says: "Since a slave who is completely dominated loses the quality of being able to give recognition, the struggle to possess her must be prolonged. . . . The narrative moves through these ever deeper levels of submission, tracing the impact of each fresh negation of her will, each new defeat of her resistance" (58).

11. Cristina Peri Rossi refers to a work by Argentine Arturo Bonasso, *Recuerdo de la muerte* [Reminder of death] in which he discusses the tortures he underwent as a political prisoner: "El libro, desgarrado documento personal, narra las demoníacas y demenciales

sesiones de sexo y tortura que ocurrieron en ese país, hipérbole de la psicosis perversa al servicio de la política y del orgasmo" (110) ["The book, an anguished personal document, narrates the demonic and demential sessions of sex and torture that occurred in that country, hyperbole of the perverse psychosis at the service of politics and orgasm"]. She also notes how military personnel in the Persian Gulf War were exposed to violent pornography before they went on bomb raids, further proof of the link between political and sexual violence. For specific data on the "dirty wars" in Argentina, see Bennett and Simpson's *The Disappeared*. The book also comments on the film *La historia oficial* [The Official Story], which intersects on deep levels with "Other Weapons": Alicia's "awakening" in "el país de no me acuerdo" ["the land of I don't remember"]; her military husband's domestic violence; the moment when he tries to exit, like Roque, as "todo . . . viene abajo" ["everything . . . is falling down"]. Joanne Saltz makes particular connections between Argentine history and *Cambio de armas*, but believes that individual, social, and "political components in the public sphere are treated from a marginalized, feminine position" (66).

12. Ximena Bunster remarks that state violence toward women in Argentina seeks to teach them that they must retreat into the home and fulfill traditional gender roles (307), and further notes that "violent sexual treatment administered by the state becomes most cruelly doubly disorienting; it exacerbates and magnifies the woman's already subservient, prescribed, passive, secondary position in Latin American society and culture" (298).

13. Helena Araújo views the ending of this story as follows: "Liberty or death. The moment arrives along with this resplendent revelation: the wife-whore-slave glimpses how to cease being so. And she risks a change of weapons" (80–81). Magnarelli says that Laura utilizes "his own instruments against him in order to avenge herself, assert herself, and dominate as he has" (189).

14. Valenzuela's recent novel, *Realidad nacional desde la cama*, [National reality viewed from bed] further develops the maid-mistress relationship with respect to power and politics: the exchanges between María and the "señora" dramatically reveal how the chambermaid serves other interests than those of her bed-bound lady.

15. Sharon Magnarelli has offered an unsurpassable analysis of narrative structure, language, silence, writing and reading with regard to this story (and Valenzuela's works in general, for that matter).

16. García-Moreno notes that not even "a repressive system is simply prohibitive; it can generate certain desires, pass them in the form of natural drives, and thus create compulsory subjugation as the law of a woman body's desire" (19).

17. Barbara Fulks views this shout as the moment in which "she is born into the Symbolic Order, the Law of the Fathers [sic]" (187). Using a Lacanian and Kristevian paradigm, Fulks thus posits that the female character triumphantly emerges from the space of the Imaginary (read: feminine psychosis) through access to language. While this analysis is suggestive, it claims that feminine desire becomes unspeakable, even unimaginable or unsustainable, except through the Symbolic Order, here conflated with the language of patriarchy. Recent critiques of the Kristevian take on Lacan have problematized this leap (see, for example, Chapter 4 of Kaja Silverman's *The Acoustic Mirror*).

18. Lagos-Pope affirms that the female characters "son mujeres que se sienten fuertemente atraídas a los hombres y que desean una comunicación no sólo sexual sino

también afectiva y espiritual con ellos, pero éstos, machos redomados, no se dan enteros, sino sólo por fragmentos, lo cual produce una gran frustración en las mujeres" ["are women who feel strongly attracted to men and who desire communication with them not only of a sexual nature but also emotional and spiritual, yet these utter machos do not give themselves completely but only in fragments, which causes great frustration in the women" (80)]. She finds it curious that these characters seek such men as objects of pleasure and do not feel attracted toward "un tipo más sensible" ["a more sensitive type" (81)]. I would say that the female characters have psychological motives for also giving themselves in fragments and for seeking a split between "appropriate love objects" and suitable "objects of pleasure."

Works Cited

Araújo, Helena. "Valenzuela's *Other Weapons.*" *Review of Contemporary Fiction* 6:3 (1986): 78–81.

Atwood, Margaret. *The Handmaid's Tale.* 1985. New York: Fawcett Crest-Ballantine, 1987.

Benjamin, Jessica. *The Bonds of Love: Psychoanalysis, Feminism, and the Problem of Domination.* New York: Pantheon, 1988.

Bennett, Jana, and John Simpson. *The Disappeared and the Mothers of the Plaza de Mayo.* New York: St. Martin Press, 1985.

Bunster, Ximena. "Surviving Beyond Fear: Women and Torture in Latin America." *Women and Change in Latin America.* Ed. June Nash and Helen Safa. South Hadley, MA: Bergin and Garvey, 1986. 297–325.

Butler, Judith. *Gender Trouble: Feminism and the Subversion of Identity.* New York: Routledge, 1990.

Castillo, Debra A. *Talking Back: Toward a Latin American Feminist Literary Criticism.* Ithaca: Cornell U P, 1992.

Dworkin, Andrea. *Pornography: Men Possessing Women.* New York: Perigee, 1979.

Ehrenreich, Barbara, Elizabeth Hess, and Gloria Jacobs. *Re-Making Love: The Feminization of Sex.* New York: Anchor-Doubleday, 1986.

Enloe, Cynthia. *Bananas, Beaches and Bases: Making Feminist Sense of International Politics.* Berkeley: University of California Press, 1989.

Fulks, Barbara Pauler. "A Reading of Luisa Valenzuela's Short Story, 'La palabra asesino.'" *Monographic Review/Revista Monográfica* 4 (1988): 179–188.

García-Moreno, Laura. "Other Weapons, Other Words: Literary and Political Reconsiderations in Luisa Valenzuela's Other Weapons." *Latin American Literary Review* 19:38 (1991): 7–22.

Herman, Judith. *Trauma and Recovery*. New York: Basic Books, 1992.

Jackson, Margaret. "'Facts of Life' or the Eroticization of Women's Oppression? Sexology and the Social Construction of Heterosexuality." *The Cultural Construction of Sexuality*. Ed. Pat Caplan. London: Tavistock, 1987. 52–81.

Jeffries, Sheila. *Anticlimax: A Feminist Perspective on the Sexual Revolution*. New York: New York U P, 1990.

Lagos-Pope, María-Inés. "Mujer y política en *Cambio de armas*." *Hispamérica* 16:46-47 (1987): 71–83.

Lykes, M. Brinton, Mary M. Brabeck, Theresa Ferns, and Angela Radan. "Human Rights and Mental Health Among Latin American Women in Situations of State-Sponsored Violence." *Psychology of Women Quarterly* 17 (1993): 525–544.

Magnarelli, Sharon. *Reflections/Refractions: Reading Luisa Valenzuela*. New York: Peter Lang, 1988.

Morello-Frosch, Marta. "'Other Weapons': When Metaphors Become Real." *Review of Contemporary Fiction* 6:3 (1986): 82–87.

Morgan, Robin. *The Demon Lover: On the Sexuality of Terrorism*. New York: Norton, 1989.

Mull, Dorothy S. "Ritual Transformation in Luisa Valenzuela's 'Rituals of Rejection.'" *Review of Contemporary Fiction* 6:3 (1986): 88–96.

Myers, Kathy. "Towards a Feminist Erotica." *Camerawork* 24 (1982): 189–202.

Peri Rossi, Cristina. *Fantasías eróticas*. Colección Biblioteca Erótica. Madrid: Ediciones Temas de Hoy, 1991.

Saltz, Joanne. "Luisa Valenzuela's *Cambio de armas*: Rhetoric of Politics." *Confluencia* 3 (1987): 61–66.

Scarry, Elaine. *The Body in Pain: The Making and Unmaking of the World*. New York: Oxford U P, 1985.

Silverman, Kaja. *The Acoustic Mirror: The Female Voice in Psychoanalysis and Cinema*. Theories of Representation and Difference. Bloomington: Indiana U P, 1988.

Valenzuela, Luisa. *Aquí pasan cosas raras*. Buenos Aires: Ediciones de la Flor, 1975.

Valenzuela, Luisa. *Cambio de armas*. Hanover, N.H.: Ediciones del Norte, 1982.

Valenzuela, Luisa. "The Five Days That Changed My Paper." *Profession* (1991): 6–9.

Valenzuela, Luisa. "La mala palabra." *Revista Iberoamericana* 51: 132–133 (1985): 489–491.

Valenzuela, Luisa. "Máscaras de espejos, un juego especular. Entrevista-asociaciones con la escritora argentina Luisa Valenzuela." With Montserrat Ordóñez. *Revista Iberoamericana* 51: 132–133 (1985): 511–519.

Valenzuela, Luisa. *Novela negra con argentinos.* Barcelona: Plaza y Janés, 1990.

Valenzuela, Luisa. *Other Weapons.* Trans. Deborah Bonner. Hanover, N.H.: Ediciones del Norte, 1985.

Valenzuela, Luisa. *Realidad nacional desde la cama.* Buenos Aires: Grupo Editor Latinoamericano, 1990.

Vance, Carol S. "Anthropology Rediscovers Sexuality: A Theoretical Comment." *Social Science and Medicine* 33:8 (1991): 875–884.

Williams, Linda. *Hard Core: Power, Pleasure, and the "Frenzy of the Visible."* Berkeley: U of California P, 1989.

INDEX